Malevolent Managers

First published 2016 by Gower Publishing

2 Park Square, Milton Park, Abingdon, Oxfordshire OX14 4RN
52 Vanderbilt Avenue, New York, NY 10017

Routledge is an imprint of the Taylor & Francis Group, an informa business

First issued in paperback 2020

Copyright © 2016 Terry A. Sheridan

Terry A. Sheridan has asserted her moral right under the Copyright, Designs and Patents Act, 1988, to be identified as the author of this work.

All rights reserved. No part of this book may be reprinted or reproduced or utilised in any form or by any electronic, mechanical, or other means, now known or hereafter invented, including photocopying and recording, or in any information storage or retrieval system, without permission in writing from the publishers.

Notice:
Product or corporate names may be trademarks or registered trademarks, and are used only for identification and explanation without intent to infringe.

British Library Cataloguing in Publication Data
A catalogue record for this book is available from the British Library

Library of Congress Cataloging-in-Publication Data
Sheridan, Terry A., author.
Malevolent managers : insights using executive impression management / by Terry A. Sheridan.
pages cm
Includes bibliographical references and index.
ISBN 978-1-4724-1601-8 (hardback)
1. Executives--Selection and appointment. 2. Executives--Psychology. 3. Executives--Rating of. 4. Problem employees. 5. Personnel management. I. Title.
HF5549.5.S38S535 2016
658.4'07--dc23

2015028548

ISBN 978-1-4724-1601-8 (hbk)
ISBN 978-0-367-60605-3 (pbk)

Contents

List of Figures

List of Tables

Acknowledgements

I would like to thank my family who have carried the brunt of my disappearances up to Bali where I write, and I owe them much for their patience. My husband John has carried the burden of tolerating my absence which he has done with good humour and understanding. Paradise is a beautiful place to write in, but I could not have done so without my friends Made, Jimmy and Jacky. Each of you has made my life comfortable by reducing stress and inviting me into your families.

I am eternally grateful that I did not have to write this in a shed at the bottom of the garden!

Having had an ongoing health problem during the writing of this book leaves me to thank my medical and health practitioners, particularly Adam and Eddie. This has led me to delay deadlines for my manuscript and I must thank Kristina Abbotts and Donna Shanks at Gower Publishing for their patience and understanding.

I would also like to thank all the malevolent managers whom I have worked with during my career; without that experience I would not have been so able to understand the core process of Executive Impression Management. The stress and the tears were worth it, as I can come from a place of knowledge and experience to write this book.

Despite all the checking and rechecking there may still be errors. These I remain responsible for and I would like to apologise in advance should this disturb your reading.

Bali

Foreword

Everyone Deserves Respect in the Workplace

Executive Impression Management is a simple way of sorting out malevolent managers who pretend that they are effective and decent. It means that we can see our managers for who they really are, deal with them and allow us to have peace and harmony in every workplace.

First Aid

If you find yourself in an untenable situation at work, ask for a transfer to another department. If the organisation is too small, then look for another job. DO NOT leave your employment until another job offer (in writing) is given. If the stress is unbearable, then seek stress or sickness leave. DO all job searching in another location, not your workplace. It is far better to seek work elsewhere than be bullied; this will ultimately affect your health, sanity and family. Use meditation and or strenuous physical activity to reduce your stress immediately. Keep doing this daily until you reach a state of calm.

Chapter 1

A New Typology of Discerning Management Behaviour

This book was born out of the findings that inadvertently emerged out of a qualitative study of managerial fraudsters. In this book there are the previously missing pieces to the management jigsaw: the 'whys' and 'hows' of bad management are presented for the first time. Executive Impression Management typology gives an understanding how bad management works and therefore how to find good managers to give you the respect that we all deserve in the workplace.

The doctoral research that I undertook was centred on the problem of how to identify managers who will defraud an organisation. The question came about through my work with managers as I had set up a locum management service for small business owners. Being a previous business owner myself for many years I knew how hard it was to find someone trustworthy.

It seemed to me to be a sensible proposition that an unemployed manager could be placed for a short time in a business to perform the stewardship function. After all there were many small business owners and unfortunately many unemployed managers at the time. Having had a stint as a locum manager I realised that indeed it was feasible. What was important was quick learning, shadowing the business owner before his absence and documenting all procedures. This was based on a foundation of trust between the business owner and the locum. In fact what happened was even a better outcome than just business-sitting, the small businesses were improved with the locum manager's knowledge of systems and business efficiencies. However, it founded on being able to trust the locum I was sending in, particularly as I knew that many small business owners tended to be conservative in their outlook and suspicious of everyone. One failure meant the demise of the venture. There is no such thing in the locum business of a D grade; it is all or nothing. Not only that, having a small business usually entailed tying up the family home and other assets, so the ramifications of allowing in a fraudster in their absence were extremely high.

As I interviewed many managers I became anxious on not knowing if I could really trust the person sitting in front of me. The desperation at that time with relatively high unemployment rate of managers was palpable, and having had a taste of it myself I knew how important a job, even a short-term assignment, made all the difference to a tired résumé. The competition was fierce and the demand to be placed was high.

I knew that people could easily lie through many of the psychological tests, which are based on self-reporting. If a person was honest the test had a better chance of reflecting what was within a person's character, but I also knew that people had a good chance of being self-delusional – myself included, which led me to think that I was a better manager than I actually was. Sometimes we are blind to our faults and we cannot see them. A beautifully written résumé and a presentable candidate could be very persuasive, but a liar could easily provide that presentation even with a slick interview.

My experience taught me that the current selection and recruitment process was inherently flawed. Superficiality blossomed on cronyism and connections rather than intelligence, qualifications and life experience. This was my observation gathered from my UK, Canadian as well as Australian experience, and I learnt that merit was a good thing to have, but will not necessarily lead to success. My career spanned academia, non-profit management, small business and later large organisations, so I knew what I was talking about, being on either side as a candidate or as an employer.

Knowing this 'fact of life' which was not particularly fair but it was either join them or not work at all, eventually led me to hold psychological testing, the testers and the recruiters at some distance. There was obviously no holy grail of finding out if the candidate was a good one or not, it was based on other irrelevant factors. Being a female manager was one count against me and coming from England – being a 'Pom' was the second black mark when I arrived in Australia. I must say that I had some fun with my first name being Terry and spelt with a 'y' not an 'i': most Australian recruiters and employers thought I was a male. I would get the look of total desperation by the receptionist up to the chief honcho who clearly did not know what to say. One employer admitted that they were only looking at males for the position despite the fact of equal opportunity legislation. I got in the front door with my résumé and career experience but I was shown the back door through other factors, other than what was required for the management position.

Apart from not choosing me, I wondered what was going on in the selection process. I followed the careers of the successful candidates of the positions that I competed for, in the newspapers and media. Before long I saw a pattern of revolving doors and put it down to toxic organisations and was thankful that I did not receive the poisoned chalice. But over time there were a minority who seemed to be toxic themselves. Whichever position they achieved somehow the implicit knowledge in managerial circles opined that it would not work out, and the result was exactly as predicted. The problem I faced with wanting to hire a candidate for a locum position was: whom could I trust? I could probably have selected someone that had a good probability to being successful, but the probability and possibility of that risk management decision was too high, I needed a nil result. I was therefore in a hazardous situation and I needed to manage it, otherwise I would lose everything.

This challenge was easily overcome by existing executive recruiters who offered a second candidate if the original placement 'did not work' out in the first six months. This is all well and good, but what happens if the agency places another dud, or worse, a corporate psychopath who wrecks the organisation? I took the responsibility heavily regarding the selection process and I felt driven to ensure that I had the right person to place as a locum.

This personal history was the reason that led me into framing the research question of which manager could I trust. I was beginning to develop my own theoretical model, which will be discussed later, but while it was effective, it did not show up potential fraudsters. At the beginning I only had the Myers-Briggs Type Inventory (MBTI),[1] a world-renowned and accepted test in personality traits, and my own intuition, which was normally good but could be completely wrong in some instances. The MBTI is a brilliant way of sorting out people's choices for careers. It also gives insight into the stress response of an individual when the type 'inverted'. Jung[2] regarded this as the Shadow coming out, but it only happens when we are under continual stress.

Being an avid researcher I was always looking up studies about people and had developed quite an inventory of knowledge of various aspects and the

1 Briggs Myers, I. and P.B. Myers (1995). *Gifts Differing: Understanding Personality Type*. Mountain View, CA, Davies-Black Publishing.

2 Jung, C.G. (1971). *Psychological Types*. London, Routledge & Kegan Paul.

resulting tests. Nothing seemed apparent to tell me about whom I could trust, and absolutely nothing about if someone would defraud a business either. So I set up the study looking at a group of convicted fraudulent managers and explored another group of non-fraudster managers. As I knew that the fraudsters would most likely tell me that they were innocent or some other rationale for their imprisonment, I felt that I should talk to the co-workers of these managers rather than waste time on fabricated stories. The fraudster group of co-workers was fascinating and I believe that I have found a way of identifying the possibility of a manager becoming a fraudster. What I was not expecting was that the new bit of theory that I discovered would give insight to the managers who were not fraudsters but neither were they good for the organisation. The co-workers described an underlying malevolence to these managers and now totally accidentally, we have a way of identifying these toxic managers, despite their protests to otherwise.

The inadvertent discovery of different types of impression management that co-workers perceive has led me to write about the findings and their implications for organisations. From an extensive literature review I learnt that this was the first time that co-workers were studied and that it was also the first time that managerial fraudsters of any type were investigated through the perspective of their co-workers.

Using impression management theory as a framework I found five different types of impression management given off to the co-workers. Because there is confusion naming this phenomenon as Managerial Impression Management, I named it Executive Impression Management. It exists in the workplace, and it was different from 'normal' impression management. With this new piece of theory we can now identify two types of interaction that fraudster managers exude, plus a further three types that non-fraudster managers give off. The two fraudster types of Executive Impression Management have been dealt with in *Managerial Fraud*.[3] This book will concentrate on the latter three non-fraudster types, namely the Tyrant Executive Impression Management, the Mediocre Executive Impression Management and the Respectful Executive Impression Management, how they were discovered, what are their characteristics and an evaluation of their usefulness. Executive Impression Management gives us the answer to the 'whys' and 'hows' of bad management. No one wants it in their organisation, but I dare say that most organisations have it whether they like it or not.

3 Sheridan, T.A. (2014). *Managerial Fraud: Executive Impression Management, Beyond Red Flags*. Farnham, Gower.

The benefit for us to understand these different types of Executive Impression Management is that decisions can be made with far more insight at hiring or at internal promotion so that the best manager may be selected. Another area of usefulness is when there are investigations into behaviour that are a matter of complaint and grievance, a logical typology can be used to understand what is underlying the aggrieved performance. This can be used by senior managers or other employees as the typology is simple to understand and this book will act as a reference to the overt managerial behaviour as to what is going on underneath.

In matters of bullying for instance, often the target is unaware of what is happening, apart from having conflict with a particular manager. Once the behaviour is put into the Executive Impression Management framework, the type of impression management can be identified and the ensuing complaint about the bullying has a point of reference and therefore legitimacy. The latter criterion is particularly beneficial as frequently the target of bullying is confused and is unable to identify the true cause; Human Resource managers sometimes have loyalties elsewhere in the organisation and other staff can unwittingly add to the pressure on the recipient. Often a target will blame himself and there are known cases of suicide after a bullying episode by malevolent managers.[4]

The typology is also very powerful in giving the bullying target the means to understand the violence perpetrated towards him particularly as performance issues are often used as a cover for bullying behaviour. Furthermore, other managers can easily be hoodwinked into the debate when the perpetrator states that it is a lack of performance as the central issue. Whenever performance is a problem, look to the person labelling it as such, together with, one hopes, the self-evident data that are used for the indictment. Without proof and understanding of what really is happening, these two factors muddle any review of what is identified as a performance problem. Furthermore, using the typology will give a clearer understanding of violence in the workplace, the means to how it is conducted and who is likely to be a perpetrator.

On the other hand, a workplace that is dominated by Respectful Executive Impression Management will be successful not only due to harmony with employees, but they will be productive, which in turn will realise in greater

4 Read, L. (2013). 'BBC criticised over workplace bullying after death of Russell Joslin'. *Coventry Telegraph*. Coventry, Trinity Mirror Midlands.

profit as there is far less energy spent on negativity. As simplistic as this may be, a company that is bringing in good returns may not necessarily be one whose managers are respectful. Other factors can interfere, such as monopolies, dirty tactics, over-charging customers, government interference, and so on, that disturb the equilibrium of the market place. However, a company based on respect for each other and demonstrates it clearly in its management, will inevitably be profitable.

Some people ask how many organisations are negative versus those entities that are managed with the positive energy of respect. My guess is that malevolent management administers about 80 per cent of organisations and that is why so many employees are suffering from work stress, become disaffected and are not inclined to give their all in their work performance. Tell-tale signs are poor customer or supplier relations, high employee turnover, strikes, abuse of privilege in travel arrangements and receipts, taking longer to do what another can do in far less time. This describes of course, most workplaces. Those run by respectful management are rare to come by and are strikingly different, completely opposite to malevolent managed workplaces.

To me this is an inevitable sign of negativity of the management. It is absolutely pointless to declare 'Do what I say, not what I do.' It is also ridiculous to put up cute statements of values and/or ethics in the reception area, when back-office behaviour is a daily contradiction. Employees are not stupid; they quickly learn the modus operandi via tacit knowledge in the organisation on what to do or what not to do.[5] The new employee's learning curve is quickly ascertained via what the management say and do. This informal line of information to the new employee also demonstrates the subtlety of power in organisations. But no one notices the informal induction method as it is as much to us as eating breakfast in the morning. It is part of our humanity, our everyday social interaction.

This book will outline why and how the study was implemented as it gives the reader considerations of data never before collected. The focus of the study and the methodology used meant that the results would be more likely exploratory in account rather than hypothesis testing. The theory behind the new Executive Impression Management types will be discussed. The types will be described in some detail using the respondents' words to comprehend the nature of these managers. The managers who use particular types of Executive

5 Smith, E.A. (2001). 'The role of tacit and explicit knowledge in the workplace'. *Journal of Knowledge Management* 5(4): 311–21.

Impression Management determine the type of violence in the workplace will also be addressed. Finally, a forward move into non-violent workplaces as expressed by managers who use Respectful Executive Impression Management will be discussed.

Chapter 2

Theoretical Underpinnings to the Research

This chapter addresses some of the theoretical underpinnings to the interplay between managers and those people around them in the workplace. First there is some discussion about consensus and conflict based social theories, then into economic and business theory to achieve theoretical underpinnings to the virtues of morality and honesty. This discussion represents an attempt to understand the complexity of human interaction in the workplace.

Nature of Social Interaction

This type of interaction is seen as an ever-changing succession of social actions between individuals, who adapt their reactions with each other. It is a dynamic process of social interchange, not 'one-off' individual and/or independent actions. To do this, both sides must understand and share the meaning of what is going on between them. A traditional explanation of interaction is the consensual approach espoused by social interactionist writers led by Mead,[1] Simmel[2] and Blau.[3] This theory held sway over many decades and still holds credibility.[4] The theory assumes that society is composed of self-interested individuals who seek assistance from others to achieve individual goals that they cannot achieve on their own. Two or more people, who have something of value to each other, conduct a transaction. The application to business owners is immediately appealing. For instance, an owner of a manufacturing concern needs labour to produce products. Men and women need to have food and shelter to survive. The decision is made by the two parties to exchange

1 Mead, G.H. (1963). *Mind, Self and Society from the Stand-point of a Social Behaviorist*. Chicago, IL, University of Chicago.

2 Simmel, G. (1904). 'The sociology of conflict'. *The American Journal of Sociology* 9(4): 490–525.

3 Blau, P.M. (1964). *Exchange and Power in Social Life*. New York, John Wiley and Sons Inc.

4 Kollock, P. (1994). 'The emergence of exchange structures: An experimental study of uncertainty, commitment, and trust'. *The American Journal of Sociology* 100(2): 313–45.

labour for wages, and vice versa, and there is agreement to what amount. The exchange is made on a rational basis, and relies on self-interest and mutual interdependence between quite separate individuals.[5] Similarly, management serves a stewardship function, and a manager is paid for his services by the business owner to ensure all within the business is functioning as it should. Stewardship theory basically says that managers will act as responsible stewards of an organisation.[6] This is opposed to Agency theory that there is an inequality in information between shareholders and management and the manager will always act in his own self-interest.[7]

Social Exchange

Social exchange, say Shore, Bommer and Shore[8] is unlike economic exchange and state that social interaction is distinguished by an 'anticipated reciprocity' based on two premises: that if an individual receives a benefit from another then he or she has to give in return, and secondly, and that no harm should be undertaken against those who have helped that individual. By giving their loyalty to a manager, social exchange theory would predict that co-workers would expect that the manager would therefore look after their interests.

Another salient point of exchange theory is that power is accumulated by winning 'brownie points' with others. To use Blau's words:

> *An apparent 'altruism' pervades social life; people are anxious to benefit one another and to reciprocate for the benefits they receive. But beneath this seeming selflessness an underlying 'egoism' can be discovered; the tendency to help others is frequently motivated by the expectation that doing so will bring social rewards.*[9]

Accordingly, an individual may only be given power if he has earned it. To extend this line of thinking to managerial behaviour, employees will 'grant'

5 Lawler, E.J. and S.R. Thye (1999). 'Bringing emotions into social exchange theory'. *Annual Review of Sociology* 25: 217–44.

6 Davis, J.H., F.D. Schoorman and L. Donaldson (1997). 'Towards a stewardship theory of management'. *Academy of Management* 22(1): 20–47.

7 Eisenhart, K.M. (1989). 'Agency theory: An assessment and review'. *Academy of Management* 14(1): 57–74.

8 Shore, T.H., W.H. Bommer and L.M. Shore (2008). 'An integrative model of managerial perceptions of employee commitment: Antecedents and influences on employee treatment'. *Journal of Organizational Behaviour* 29(5): 635–55.

9 Ibid., 17.

power once the manager has earned it. Gabarro[10] found support for this in his longitudinal study about senior managers parachuted in to new units. He found it took senior managers much longer than expected to successfully take charge of their new units or divisions, as much as two to three years. Gabarro assigned this slow process to one of massive learning and integration. However, Gabarro found that the most important factor for predicting success of the new manager was making relationships with key people within the new section in the first year.

The Growth and Dominance of Free Market Ideology

Social exchange theory is a sociological projection (despite Shore Bommer and Shore's[11] objections,) developed from the concept of self-interest in an economic market place, which in itself comes from a long tradition of the philosophy of economic activity. It was Adam Smith's *An Inquiry into the Nature and Causes of Wealth of Nations* in 1776,[12] which is often regarded as the beginning of modern capitalism. He thought that a commercial society was a natural result of unfettered human civilisation.[13] He wrote three major premises that form the foundation of free market economics: the division of labour, the pursuit of self-interest and freedom of trade. If these premises were upheld then the market would be regulated through an 'invisible hand' which would produce the right amount of supply of products and services, at the most competitive price to suit all customers of the marketplace. The market mechanism would therefore keep prices low and interestingly, offset human nature of greed and avarice by the promotion of frugality and savings.[14] The division of labour, by breaking down tasks into menial streamlined functions, was advocated because it increased output per worker. However, this new system required supervisors and managers, replacing guilds and communities as work supervisors and thus production-oriented hierarchies emerged.[15] Smith also realised that there would be wage inequalities according to specialised knowledge and the length

10 Gabarro, J.J. (2007). 'When a new manager takes charge'. *Harvard Business Review* 85(1): 104–17.
11 Ibid.
12 For a modern treatment of Smith's work see M. Fry, ed. (1992). *Adam Smith's Legacy: His Place in the Development of Modern Economics*. London, Routledge.
13 Prieto, J.H. (2004). 'Bernard Mandeville's heir: Adam Smith or Jean Jacques Rousseau on the possibility of economic analysis'. *European Journal of the History of Economic Thought* 11(1): 1–32.
14 Ibid.
15 Thompson, E.P. (1968). *The Making of the English Working Class*. Harmondsworth, Penguin Books.

of time to acquire this knowledge, thus managers would be paid more than workers depending on how much knowledge was required together with carrying the responsibility of the operation, and those without the work ethic, that is the lazy and indigent should be kept poor.[16]

Further developers of this economic model were John Stuart Mill and Jeremy Bentham who later developed the ideas of utilitarianism and the concept of the public good. Mill considered that what was best for society as a whole was a preferred outcome even if it disadvantaged a few, while Bentham promoted this further and spurred government intervention to provide public amenities such as public sanitation to offset disease and disability caused by dense industrialised urban areas.[17] This idea of government intervention was revised somewhat by John Maynard Keynes, in the first half of the twentieth century,[18] who thought that at times that the free market needed intervention especially in the light of long recessions and world wars that impoverished millions of people.[19] However, Keynes was essentially a free market thinker and upheld the basic premises of Adam Smith. Milton Friedman[20] became the face of the free market in the latter half of the twentieth century, fiercely defending businesses against any interference (especially by governments) of the free market. This protectionism has long dominated American business thinking. Western industrialised democracies have variations on the Keynesian free market theme but with more government intervention allowed than the United States. For example, Great Britain,[21] Australia,[22] New Zealand,[23] France, Germany and Italy[24] have a long tradition of government intervention. All developed welfare states with varying degree of government control. The growth of welfare states were in reality, temporary interventions to assist those who were left out of the economic revival after the world wars,

16 Mathias, P. (1979). *The Transformation of England*. London, Methuen.

17 Lee, D. and H. Newby (1983). Sociology and the growth of industrial society. *The Problem of Sociology: An Introduction to the Discipline*. London, Unwin Hyman: 26–39.

18 Originally written in 1936. Keynes, J.M. (2007). *General Theory of Employment, Interest and Money*. New Delhi, Atlantic Publishers and Distributors.

19 Harris, S.E., ed. (1960). *The New Economics: Keynes' Influence on Theory and Public Policy*. London, Dennis Dobson.

20 Friedman, M. (1963). *Capitalism and Freedom*. Chicago, IL, The University of Chicago Press.

21 Titmuss, R.M. (1976). *Essays on the Welfare State*. London, Allen & Unwin.

22 Jones, M.A. (1983). *The Australian Welfare State: The Growth, Crisis and Change*. Sydney, Allen & Unwin.

23 Easton, B.H. (1980). *Social Policy and the Welfare State in New Zealand*. Auckland, Allen & Unwin.

24 Hage, J., R. Hanneman and E.T. Gargan (1989). *State Responsiveness and State Activism: An Examination of the Social Forces and State Strategies that Explain the Rise in Social Expenditures in Britain, France, Germany, and Italy, 1870–1968*. London, Unwin Hyman.

particularly the Second World War.[25] By the end of the twentieth century a variety of mixed economies prevailed in the industrialised and post-industrialised countries, with the USA as leader of capitalism.[26]

The Growth of Understanding Conflict in the Free Market

America's and Britain's freedom of restraint in their growing industrialisation which grew prolifically, had huge social costs.[27] Consequently the theory of capitalism was seriously challenged in the nineteenth century by Karl Marx.[28] Marx realised that whoever owned the means of production would have the dominant economic power. He advocated that to have the wealth of the country in only a few hands was morally wrong and exploitative of millions of people who were forced to work in factories for the lowest wages possible. And importantly in a theoretical context for this discussion on managers, social interaction was far from consensual and marked by conflict. Managers were viewed as the stewards of the powerful elite and despised for their co-optation into the elite's way of thinking and doing the dirty work for their masters.[29] Consensus in society, in Marx's view, would only happen when the owners of the means of production were overthrown thereby allowing workers to willingly cooperate with each other.[30] But this philosophy, although sparking off socialism and communism, which has had a profound effect on the world, was developed on a critique of the British and the US economies, which were transitioning from feudal into industrial mode.[31]

Currently, with widespread development and industrialisation Marxism has generally become outdated within post-industrial societies, and the inherent determinism of Marx's theory – that ultimately capitalism would collapse – has not happened.[32] Although there have been some near misses from time to time –

25 Little, A. (1998). *Post-Industrial Socialism: Towards a New Politics of Welfare*. London and New York, Routledge. And Titmuss (1976).
26 Slater, D. (1995). Trajectories of development theory: Capitalism, socialism and beyond. *Geographies of Global Change*, ed. R.J. Johnston, P.J. Taylor and M. Watts. Oxford, Blackwell.
27 Thompson (1968).
28 Worsley, P. (1982). *Marx and Marxism*. Chichester, Ellis Horwood.
29 Ibid.
30 Marx, K. (1976). Cooperation. *Capital: A Critique of Political Economy*. London, Harmondsworth, 439–54.
31 Morrison, K.L. (2006). *Marx, Durkheim, Weber: Formations of Modern Social Thought*. Thousand Oaks, CA, Sage.
32 Ganguly-Scrase, R. (2003). The Search for change: Karl Marx. *Sociology: Australian Connections*, ed. R. Jureidini and M. Poole. Crows Nest, NSW, Allen & Unwin.

for example, the Great Depression of the 1930s[33] – the capitalist view of social order has been maintained.[34] In fact quite the contrary occurred at the end of the twentieth century, which saw the collapse of socialist and communist states and their assumption of the capitalist model.[35] Capitalism with its inherent free market and freedom from government interference has lasted longer than its competing alternative social systems.[36]

However, Marx's legacy is seen in the growth of radical and socialist literatures, with conflict theories developing rapidly to explain such problems as subjugation of women,[37] racism and colonialism,[38] the influence of the state,[39] the structure of society[40] and the power of discourse[41] to cover a few topics. In Australia, examples are seen in writings by Connell[42] about class and social structure, and Caine and Pringle's work on Australian feminist issues.[43] Many conflict theories offer an alternative to the consensual free market model, but the consensus view of society still rules.

Morality

With Adam Smith's free enterprise model, everyone is in agreement that business and entrepreneurship is traditionally seen as purely an extrapolation of activity in an unrestrained free market, with money-making left to the individual.[44] By doing so, the pursuit of self-interest would produce the greatest good for society. Recent writers reaffirm this proposition Anderson, Park, and

33 Kuhn, R. (1995). 'Capitalism's collapse: Henryk Grossmann's Marxism'. *Science and Society* 59(2): 174–91.

34 Miliband, R. (1973). *The State in Capitalist Society*. London, Quartet Books.

35 Kerlin, M. (1998). 'The end of history, specters of Marx and business ethics'. *Journal of Business Ethics* 17(15): 1717–26.

36 Wenger, M.G. (1994). 'Idealism redux: The class-historical truth of postmodernism'. *Critical Sociology* 20(1): 53–78.

37 Rowbottom, S. (1975). *Hidden from History*. London, Pluto Press.

38 Sartre, J.P. (1991). Critique of Dialectical Reason. London, Verso, 2.

39 Miliband (1973).

40 Giddens, A. (1973). *The Class Structure of the Advanced Societies*. London, Hutchinson and Co.

41 Foucault, M. (1972). *The Archaeology of Knowledge and the Discourse on Language*. New York, Panteon Books.

42 Connell, R.W. (1977). *Ruling Class Ruling Structure*. Cambridge, Cambridge University Press.

43 Ang, I. (1995). I'm a feminist but ... 'Other' women and postnational feminism. *Transitions: New Australian Feminisms*, ed. B. Caine and R. Pringle. St Leonards, NSW, Allen & Unwin, 57–73.

44 Fry (1992).

Jack;[45] Coleman[46] with Newbert[47] arguing that in pursuing profit, there are many benefits that are bestowed upon society, with the resultant increase of employment, consumption and enjoyment of the goods and services provided. Entrepreneurs need not be seen as selfish and solely creating disbenefits for the community – for example, pollution and poverty line wages. Because companies in the USA particularly take on a philanthropic mantle with their success, this is seen as part of the redistribution of wealth[48] by sharing corporate profits, and their encouragement of others to form their own businesses for example in the release of venture capital for small business.[49]

Newbert states that:

> *Interestingly, Smith argued that the rational pursuit of self-interest was ethical to some extent. Like all Calvinists, as well as many Protestants of his time, Smith believed that any success in any venture, including business activity, was evidence that one had been chosen by God. And, since one's vocation was determined by God, failure to engage in it passionately would call one's faith into question.*[50]

Hence, the pursuit of profit was seen as a 'ticket to heaven'. Ethics and morality was inferred from the noble quest of a state of goodness as outlined in Smith's earlier work *The Theory of Moral Sentiments*.[51] Smith never envisaged that businesses would harm society due to this philosophical grounding, furthermore by participating in the free market people would integrate morality through tacit rules of behaviour and that these rules 'become part of self'.[52] However, because the traditional interpretation of Adam Smith's work revolves around the unfettered market with little government intervention concentrating entirely on self-gain (for example, Milton Friedman's work) it

45 Anderson, A., J. Park and S. Jack (2007). 'Entrepreneurial social capital'. *International Small Business Journal* 25(3): 245–72.

46 Coleman, J.S. (1990). Social Capital. *Foundations of Social Theory*. Cambridge, MA, Harvard University Press, 300–12.

47 Newbert, S.L. (2003). 'Realizing the spirit and impact of Adam Smith's capitalism through entrepreneurship'. *Journal of Business Ethics* 46(3): 251–61.

48 Love, T. and C. Higgins (2007). 'Do we know enough about corporate philanthropy?' *The Journal of Corporate Citizenship* (27): 18–22.

49 Johns, B.L., W.C. Dunlop and W.J. Sheehan (1989). *Small Business in Australia*. Sydney, Allen & Unwin. And Wetzel Jr, W.E. (1987). 'The informal venture capital market: Aspects of scale and market efficiency'. *Journal of Business Venturing* 2(4): 299–314.

50 Newbert, S.L. (2003). 'Realizing the spirit and impact of Adam Smith's capitalism through entrepreneurship'. *Journal of Business Ethics* 46(3): 251–61, at 255.

51 Ibid.

52 Prieto (2004: 18).

omits implicit rules of behaviour. Newbert concludes with an explanation that the USA business schools' adoption of the traditional view of the unfettered market and people's selfish motivation and not for reasons of altruism and philanthropy, may well be instituting a regime of greed and immorality in business students.[53] Some writers including Ghoshal and Huehn are extremely concerned by amoral 'economism' which has permeated management practice by putting aside responsibility and use 'quasi mathematical models' to justify their irrational and selfish actions.[54]

Newbert and Huehn are not alone; another critic of the traditional interpretations of self-interest of companies is Frey[55] who argues that when the Puritan ethic is studied there is actually a moral tension with self-interest and the good of the community, for it was recognised long ago that pure self-interest can harm society severely. The assumption being that the common good must be held central to offset any harm of the selfish pursuit of money. Thus the progenitors of the free market system realised that selfishness and greed alone would be harmful to society. Unlike the later exponents of capitalism who espoused that to pursue profit was in itself the only motivation, and that morality and ethics were up to the individual and not really a matter of public discussion as it is taken as a given.[56] For instance on an ideological capitalism website there is an explanation about capitalism is singled out on being the only honest structure: *Capitalism is the only moral social system because it is the only system that respects the freedom of the producers to think and the right of the individual to set his own goals and pursue his own happiness.*[57]

On a more theoretical level, Ayn Rand states: 'Capitalism and altruism are incompatible; they are philosophical opposites; they cannot coexist in the same man or in the same society.'[58] Here Rand is referring to altruism as the self-sacrifice component of Christian ethics, as she saw it as being a negative action

53 Newbert (2003).

54 Ghoshal, S. (2005). 'Bad management theories are destroying good management practices'. *Academy of Management Learning and Education* 4(1): 75–91. And Huehn, M.P. (2008). 'Unenlighteded economism: The antecedents of bad corporate governance and ethical decline'. *Journal of Business Ethics* 81(4): 823–36.

55 Frey, D.E. (1998). 'Individualist economic values and self-interest: The problem of the Puritan ethic'. *Academy of Management* 17(14): 1573–80.

56 George, R.J. (1987). 'Teaching business ethics: Is there a gap between rhetoric and reality?'. *Journal of Business Ethics* 6(7): 513–19.

57 Tracinski, R.W. (2015). 'The Moral Basis of Capitalism'. Retrieved 15 March 2015, from http://www.capitalismcenter.org/Philosophy/Essays/The_Moral_Basis_of_Capitalism.htm./

58 Rand, A. (1967). *Capitalism: The Unknown Ideal.* New York, New American Library, 194.

against life itself.[59] However, she points out that man needs ethical guidance as he is a rational being and ethics are not instinctual to humans.[60] She stated that one of the six virtues to be developed in mankind was honesty. With these virtues, social action will be guided and dishonest actions will not happen, as dishonesty is self-negating, which goes against the life force of a rational human being, as does altruism.

Dishonesty as an Illusion

Honesty has been seen as a virtue of social consequences, it is about reality and telling it as it is, despite the pain that truthfulness may cause to the listener. Those who tell lies are weaving an illusion[61] and as others do not know what the reality is, they take in the illusion and it proves harmful to them. However, Smith[62] argues that creating illusions is very self-destructive as ultimately success in life actually depends on reality. Moreover, there is a twist in who can be honest and who cannot in the face of a liar:

> *The dishonest man is secretly counting on a double standard: dishonesty for himself and honesty for everyone else. At the deepest level he is counting on everyone else not to fake reality so that he can get away with faking it in other words, he wants other people make his unreality real.*[63]

To use Rand's words 'Honesty is not a social duty, not a sacrifice for the sake of others, but the most profoundly selfish virtue man can practice: his refusal to sacrifice the reality of his own existence to the deluded consciousness of others.'[64] Smith is in agreement when she argues that dishonesty is the worst sin of all as it prevents rational thinking and stops a person from achieving their life goals.[65] Dishonesty exploits others and finally does not change the facts – reality. A liar cannot fool reality she asserts. In conclusion she says: 'The need for honesty stems from our self-interested need to respect the law

59 Burns, J. (2004). 'Godless capitalism: Ayn Rand and the Conservative movement'. *Modern Intellectual History* 1(3): 359–85.
60 Rand, A. (1957). *Atlas Shrugged*. New York, Random House.
61 Broughton, T.A. (1995). Some notes on the art of lying. *The Best Writing on Writing*, ed. J. Heffron. New York, Story Press, 1–14.
62 Smith, T. (2003). 'The metaphysical case for honesty'. *Journal of Value Inquiry* 37(4): 517–31.
63 Locke, E.A. and J. Woiceshyn (1995). 'Why businessmen should be honest: The argument from rational egoism'. *Journal of Organizational Behavior* 16(5): 405–14.
64 Rand (1957: 945).
65 Smith (2003).

of identity ... Since the reason to be honest is self-interested and the facts necessitating honesty are inescapable, we have a compelling motivation for honesty'.[66] That being the case, it would be expected that honesty would be the best policy in all managerial social interaction.

Deception

Despite all good and noble intentions, deception, however, has been seen as a necessary part of business and that managers have to have a 'special ethical outlook'.[67]

Carr explained that:

> *Most executives from time to time are almost compelled, in the interests of their companies or themselves, to practice some form of deception when negotiating with customers, dealers, government officials, labor unions, or even other departments of their companies. By conscious misstatements, concealment of pertinent facts, or exaggeration – in short, by bluffing – they seek to persuade others to agree with them.*[68]

The potential of today's management practice can therefore encompass a degree of cunning, lying, deceit and acts of omission to gain power over competitors.[69] An explanation from Livingstone Smith[70] gave reasons for how lying and deception became part of the human psyche, evolving for millennia to assist in everyday living. Essentially lies are not tolerated within the tribe but are used outside the tribe. This explanation would cover lying to outsiders, presumably for strategic reasons, however, as Tara Smith[71] argued there are no differences in lying (apart from severity, she claimed) as all lies are dishonest, disregard reality and harm the listeners in the short run, and the perpetrators in the long run.

66 Smith (2003: 531).

67 Carr, A.Z. (1968). 'Is business bluffing unethical?' *Harvard Business Review* 46(1): 143–53, at 153.

68 Ibid., 144.

69 Takala, T. and J. Urpilainen (1999). 'Managerial work and lying: A conceptual framework and an explorative case study'. *Journal of Business Ethics* 20(3): 181–95.

70 Livingstone Smith, D. (2007). *Why We Lie: The Evolutionary Roots of Deception and the Unconscious Mind*. New York, St Martin's Griffin.

71 Smith (2003).

The prevailing theory of consensus based free markets based on self-interest, has become a theatre for some business owners and managers to create fraudulent activities for their own gain outside as well as inside their organisations. These people do not play by the rules. Social exchange theory does not explain such conflict as enduring, it is seen as merely a temporary imbalance in social relationships. This does not fit well with executive fraudulent behaviour that carries over years, sometimes 10 or more in some cases that have been established as part of this investigation. Conflict based theories offer explanations of greed and exploitation on the nature of those who hold power; the adage that 'power corrupts' is often quoted in the political sphere, but it is also very applicable in businesses and its management.[72]

For example, the collapse of the US sub-prime mortgage market, circa 2008 threatened global economic stability. The accounting and management professions (and many other interested parties including governments and national banks) failed to notice warning signs and act upon the incredible risks being taken. In the period of 2005–2007, investment banks were accessing a ready supply of new assets for securitisation, that is, sub-prime mortgages. Securitising meant turning these high-risk loans into assets and the investment banks were able to pass the credit risk along to investors and in turn earn fees from arranging the securitisation transactions.[73] This dangerous new business practice raised two red flags of business fraud notably: (1) unethical management taking advantage of gullible investors and (2) excessive trust in key executives who convinced an otherwise conservative industry to take such a enormous risk with disastrous consequences.[74] As would be expected by not playing by the rules, there is an increase of 31 per cent in mortgage fraud in the first half of the fiscal year of 2008, with a concomitant increase in corporations committing fraud as linked to the sub-prime crisis reported by the FBI.[75] Such reckless corporate behaviour led to a recession, for which many people suffered job loss, poverty and family break-up.

72 Ashforth, B.E. and V. Anand (2003). 'The normalization of corruption in organizations'. *Research in Organizational Behavior* 25: 1–52.

73 Wood, D. (2006). 'Sub-prime time'. *Risk Management* 19(2): 36–6.

74 Ip, G. (2008). World news: OECD speaks up on subprime's heavy toll. *Wall Street Journal*, A.11.

75 *Boston Globe* (2008). 'FBI reports rise in mortgage fraud'. *Boston Globe*, C.4.

Business Ethics

Business ethics as a subject on its own was developed in the 1970s.[76] There was particular concern with the overt lack of morality in business, in the pursuit of profits. There were many scandals including the production of Ford's Pinto car with known faults with the fuel tank but were not fixed by the production managers, resulting in 27 deaths.[77] The debate heightened with Mintzberg[78] and Drucker,[79] two leading management academics of the latter half of the last century, who were equally concerned about general management practice being unethical and immoral and sought to raise management's game in their books.

Business ethics can be classified in several ways. Zimmerli and Asslander[80] chose to divide it into the personal, institutional and the macro level. It is a discipline that is largely normative in approach aimed at improving management practice.[81] However, there is a growing body of empirical work to explain that unethical managers produce unethical work practices and infect other workers in the organisation. Similarly, there is the development of a growing literature on the lack of business ethics but as Weymes noted:

> *Despite the plethora of articles and books that have appeared over 25 years to support this 'new' approach to management, organisations and CEOs are still bound by return on investment and shareholder value. Hard numbers and stock market performance continue to dictate and define performance, while an organisation's impact on society and the environment receives only passing comment.*[82]

76 Brinkmann, J. (2001). 'On business ethics and moralism'. *Business Ethics: A European Review* 10(4): 311–19.

77 Gioia, D.A. (1992). 'Pinto Fires and Personal Ethics: A Script Analysis of Missed Opportunities'. *Journal of Business Ethics* 11(5/6): 379–89.

78 Mintzberg, H. (2004). *Managers not MBAs: A Hard Look at the Soft Practice of Managing and Management Development*. San Francisco, Berrett-Koehler.

79 Drucker, P.F. (1999). *Management challenges for the 21st Century*. Oxford, Butterworth-Heinemann.

80 Zimmerli, W.C. and M.S. Asslander (2007). Business ethics as applied ethics. *Corporate Ethics and Corporate Governance*, ed. W.C. Zimmerli, K. Richter and M. Holzinger. Berlin and New York, Springer: 37–54.

81 Price, T.L. (2003). 'The ethics of authentic transformational leadership'. *Leadership Quarterly* 14(1): 67–82; Fleming, P. and S. Zyglidopoulos (2008). 'The escalation of deception in organizations'. *Journal of Business Ethics* 81(4): 837–50; Moore, G. (2008). 'Re-imagining the morality of management: A modern virtue ethics approach'. *Business Ethics Quarterly* 18(4): 483–511.

82 Weymes, E. (2004). 'Management theory: Balancing individual freedom with organisational needs'. *The Journal of Corporate Citizenship* Winter 2004(16): 85–99, at 88.

Modern management has its critics who describe despotic coercive management practices that are incompetent and inefficient as well as highly destructive to workers.[83] Theoretically there has been a development of the construct of transformational leaders, this is seen as the emergence of a new style manager, who is empathetic, visionary[84] as opposed to transactional leaders. This is obviously based on social exchange theory, with transactions taking place between worker and manager to be effective. However, these 'exchanges' are predicated on power and are coercive.[85] For example, an employee puts in time and effort at the workplace to complete his duties, the manager can theoretically withhold wages if he feels that the work is not up to standard.

The new style transformational management is seen as having an ethical approach to practice and has been empirically tested.[86] Despite the plethora of studies that prove transactional management does not work, criticism of managerial morality continues unabated. Management is in a sad state of affairs in the free market system, and immorality is seen at the top of business organisations, with dishonesty and lying appearing to be rife inside and outside organisations.[87] What is needed now is a theory that can explain the normative plus the reality of social interaction; the observed against the implied, even if tiny social actions have to be analysed.

When reviewing theories of managerial behaviour, they tend to view society as either consensus or conflict based. At first glance, there seems to be very few concepts that can explain the contradictory viewpoints. However, one such theory stands out that contends with both views and has been embraced by the consensus based empirical researchers as well as, somewhat surprisingly, the conflict theorists, and that is the theory of impression management.

83 For instance: Konovsky, M.A. and F. Jaster (1989). '"Blaming the victim" and other ways business men and women account for questionable behaviour'. *Journal of Business Ethics* 8(5): 391–8; Conger, J.A. (1990). 'The dark side of leadership'. *Organizational Dynamics* 19(2): 44–56; Hogan, R. and J. Hogan (2001). 'Assessing leadership: A view from the dark side'. *International Journal of Selection and Assessment* 9(1–2): 40–51.

84 Tucker, S., N. Turner, J. Barling, E.M. Reid and C. Elving (2006). 'Apologies and transformational leadership'. *Journal of Business Ethics* 63(2): 195–207.

85 McCarthy, D., S.M. Puffer, R.C. May, D.E. Ledgerwood and W.H. Stewart (2008). 'Overcoming resistance to change in Russian organizations: The legacy of transactional leadership'. *Organizational Dynamics* 37(3): 221–35.

86 Turner, N., J. Barling, O. Epitropaki, V. Butcher and C. Milner (2002). 'Transformational leadership and moral reasoning'. *Journal of Applied Psychology* 87(2): 304–11.

87 Avolio, B.J. and B.M. Bass (1999). 'Re-examining the components of transformational and transactional leadership using the Multifactor Leadership Questionnaire'. *Journal of Occupational* and *Organizational Psychology* 72(4): 441–62.

Impression Management Theory

Impression Management was the theory used in my research because it gave a framework in which to investigate and make sense of what the co-workers' saw. Impression Management is a theory devised by Erving Goffman.[88] It may be seen as naïve but in fact it is highly complex and elegant in its way of explaining social interaction. Basically Goffman saw social action as having an initiator referred to as the actor – the person playing out a role, and an audience – that is, whoever is listening or seeing what is happening with the actor. Impression Management does not exist when a person is without an audience, it is solely a social phenomenon.

A good example is when a person goes to see a doctor. The scene is set with a receptionist in the outer office with other people waiting for their appointments. There are the obligatory out-of-date magazines provided to relieve the tedium of having to wait for the doctor. Almost always people have to wait, no matter how junior or senior their social rank may be. This is part of the theatre adding to the drama of the doctor's status and industriousness. Eventually the person is called into the doctor's office, and from thereon in is referred to as a patient. Here the room is decorated with medical certificates to build confidence with the patient that the doctor is a practicing within his area of expertise. If the practice is very busy and located near a hospital the doctor will be wearing a white coat with stethoscope around his neck. If not, dress is slightly more casual. Finer dressing with suits and bow ties are the prerogative of the higher echelons of specialists and consultants, a clearly delineated role to treat more complicated patients.

The doctor, after the normal pleasantries will initiate the process of a consultation with a 'How are you today?' type of introduction. The patient then recites the list of things that are upsetting him. There is no questioning of the doctor's skill, and neither is there any questioning if the patient can afford the doctor's fees. The fact of being in a doctor's office implies many things. We accept that a doctor's visit is fairly routine and therefore, accept it willingly. The audience in this scenario is the patient. The role of the audience in impression management is to act as a check or balance to the situation. The patient waits for the doctor to give a diagnosis and treatment and leaves the office comfortably that the doctor has completed his task satisfactorily.

88 Goffman, E. (1959). *The Presentation of Self in Everyday Life*. New York, Anchor Books, Doubleday.

However, if the doctor were sitting at his desk in a full wet suit with scuba gear, the patient would be so surprised that he would most likely leave the office immediately. The shock experienced by the patient is the necessary check that is required in our social interactions. The doctor is not playing his role correctly, and therefore the routine impression management is broken. Along with that, the underlying trust is broken with the doctor, and the patient will not return again.

As you are reading this right now, you may be thinking that the situation is ludicrous and would never happen. You are right. We expect every role-play to be exactly what we anticipate and when it fails to confirm this expectation we regard the person as a charlatan or perhaps insane. As we check and recheck constantly we are unaware of it happening until pressure is upon us to perform. A good example of this is going to a job interview. Every candidate will ensure his clothes are appropriate to the task at hand. He wants the job and he will do everything in his power to make sure he makes the right impression. The interviewer will also do the same. The list of questions will be ready, pencils will be sharpened and so on. When both parties are ready the interplay of impression management will commence.[89]

Erving Goffman was not the first to consider social action as a form of theatre. Others before him had referred to it. But what is interesting is that Goffman is the only theorist to add the audience's role of counterbalance. In a real theatre the audience can boo and hiss if they do not like what it happening onstage. Perhaps some audience members will walk out. It was Goffman's insight that the audience plays a far more reaching role and it is only the audience's belief in the actor that enables the impression management to exist in the first place. There may be no hissing and booing in the doctor's office but the audience ultimately calls the shots and either believes or disbelieves the performance given by the medic. This social interaction is regardless of what the performance is about or the outcome. To sue a doctor for malpractice does not negate the belief that he is a medical doctor. Malpractice is (unfortunately) part of his role – medical errors are made. The fundamental premise that he is a doctor remains no matter what. Impersonating doctors, police officers, fire service workers is dealt with severely by the courts as the offenders trespass our social law of impression management: you must be who you say you are. Legitimacy therefore is paramount.

89 Gilmore, D.C. and G.R. Ferris (1989). 'The effects of applicant impression management tactics on interviewer judgments'. *Journal of Management* 15(4): 557–64.

Because of the normality of impression management it is hard to see it in action. Goffman himself recognised that problem, but what he did was deconstruct normal social performance and synthesised the underlying interplay between actor and audience. He tested this with his doctoral research in the Shetland Isles. As a Canadian he was not familiar with the Shetland culture having never been there before and could more easily observe the social phenomena being an outsider. He would observe keenly like an anthropologist the micro-elements to the social interaction that ensued with the islanders.

Later he developed his theory by looking at exceptions to the rule, as he found it easier to highlight and extend the theory to cover more complicated of cases. He wrote a book called *Asylums*,[90] and uncovered the interplay that went on between doctors, nurses and patients. He saw patients quite deliberately con the psychiatrists by acting as mad, that they were merely playing a role that was foisted upon them, whether they were mad or not. Goffman lived in the wards for several months collecting his data and was able to observe considerable complex interplays.

It is in this fashion that I devised the study of looking at the exceptions to managers, the apparent faithful stewards[91] of organisations. The interview respondents were the co-workers of convicted fraudster managers who transgressed the social rules and were in fact stealing millions of dollars from the business, right under their very noses. In all of the fraud cases that I looked at, the fraud went on for some period of time. In one case for eight years and in another for an amount nearly $20 million over five years. My question was how could the co-workers miss the fraud and all of its complicated deceit for so long? Then I compared this group of co-workers to another group of co-workers of non-fraudulent managers to explore any differences. It was the findings about this latter group that are the subject of this book.

I used the qualitative methodologies of grounded theory and constant comparison on two sets of data that came out at interview of each respondent. One set was in response to: Tell me your story; and the other was yes/no answers to questions relevant to areas that the literature described as factors for fraud.

90 Goffman, E. (1962). *Asylums: Essays on the Social Situation of Mental Patients and Other Inmates*. Chicago, IL, Aldine.

91 Davis (1997).

These factors were drawn from a 'theoretical hodgepodge'[92] of literature on what causes white collar crime. Many theories emerged. There are several that do require some attention as various academics and practitioners have made them popular. Cressey[93] offered an interesting Fraud Triangle with its opportunity, unsharable problem that could only be resolved through money, and rationalisation, for instance 'borrowing from the company to pay back later'. Also the Red Flags phenomenon that auditors use to see if there are any fraudulent actions and some of the Red Flags referred to personal characteristics, which were added in.

Of the latter theories, the co-workers were asked if they saw indicators which would apply to impression management theory itself, psychopathic personality, narcissism, Machiavellianism and so on. This was done in the question section of the interview.

In total there were 17 interviews that gave immense amount of information. The value of qualitative methodology is that the researcher continues to test the constructs until added information informs no more. And that was done in this study. There was a total of 16 hours, 20 minutes of recorded interviews. Out of this data, coding was generated into 3,859 separate references, which were aggregated into 2,029 nodes units of meaning. This is not an inconsiderable amount of data and the steps taken to coalesce the data into categories are long and arduous.

This approach and reliance on data in this manner causes many quantitative academics problems. Their approach is to test a rational hypothesis. This must be derived from existing theory to give it gravitas and several hypotheses are generated. Then the study designs its collection methods, the most familiar of course is a questionnaire. My study is equivalent to a qualitative questionnaire of 20 questions that are answered by 192 people – if we could ever compare such studies! It will end up with the same number of data points. If a business management study gets over say 190 responses, from a send out rate of 50 per cent, then this is considered to be good research and likely to be published. If the interviewees are 'randomly selected' quantitative methodologists will take one stage further and infer from the data to the general population. This last step is at risk due to the impossibility of randomness in social sciences, but that is another argument, which will not be dealt with here.

92 Shover, N. and F.T. Cullen (2008). 'Studying and teaching white collar crime: Populist and patrician perspectives'. *Journal of Criminal Justice Education* 19(2): 155–74.

93 Cressey, D. (1973). *Other People's Money: A Study in the Social Psychology of Embezzlement*. Montclair, NJ, Patterson-Smith.

The Findings

The main finding of my study was that there emerged five themes of Executive Impression Management based on two underlying core concepts of consistency of impression management and the power relationship 'given off' with the impression management as perceived by the recipients. Table 2.1 below lists the five types and their main impression management characteristics.

Table 2.1 Types and characteristics of Executive Impression Management

Type of Executive Impression Management	Characteristics
The Arrogant Fraudster	Disguised as benign.
	Inconsistent, Malevolent and Superior.
The Likeable Fraudster	Disguised as benign.
	Inconsistent, Malevolent and Inferior.
The Respectful Manager	Benign and Consistent.
The Tyrant Manager	Inconsistent, Malevolent and Superior.
The Mediocre Manager	Inconsistent, Malevolent and Inferior.

It is the last three types that are the subject of this book and are described in detail in the following two chapters.

Chapter 3

The Findings Regarding the Respectful Executive Impression Management

There is a clear emergence from the non-fraudster manager group of three types of Executive Impression Management: The Tyrant, the Mediocre and the Respectful. Each impression management style is given off from the type of manager the co-workers worked with. First I will describe the manager who gives off Respectful Executive Impression Management, as this type forms the foundation of comparison with the other two malevolent but non-fraudulent types of managers.

The co-workers who were working with what turned out to be the Respectful type of impression management used consistent words to describe their manager. These were grouped into three areas: 'good management practice', 'good manager' and 'good to work with'. It is important to elucidate more, so that the type can be understood directly from the co-workers' voices.

Good Management Practice

The co-workers perceived the manager working hard for the organisation. These managers ensured that there was a standardised hiring and intake process for new employees. The manager concerned used competitive hiring practices to get the best staff that was available, even resorting to advertising on Internet sites if necessary. Australia has strict rules regarding foreign workers, so the competition is therefore restricted to Australian permanent residents and citizens, but nevertheless for all positions that the co-workers saw that were being filled used an open advertised and competitive selection process. This type of recruitment practice was at odds with those co-workers who had fraudster managers. Almost all of these entered the organisation through irregular hiring, for instance being installed by a director of a company so no one could question that decision, let alone apply for the position.

It was also perceived that the Respectful managers had good employment procedures, having human resource policies that if not written down in small companies were normalised and not deviated from during their employment. Policies about their job, duty statements and other practices were noted. Administrative duties were viewed as necessary and one newly expanding company realised that they needed to have someone dedicated to this role. Often the administrative duties fall upon the shoulders of a business owner, or unfortunately their spouse who may not be conversant with all of the protocols in a small start-up business and it stays that way until the business owner or spouse is over-worked with the administrative load and needs assistance.

Leaving the organisation was also standardised. A written resignation had to be given. Almost always the business owners or directors would be involved in losing an employee. They took the attitude that something may be wrong with the job and that this must be fixed. However, personal reasons were accepted gracefully and the door was left open if the employee wished to return. The Exit Interview is an important strategy to find out if there is anything wrong at that employee level or department and it would be seen as a time to fix it. Respectful managers realised that not everything is perfect that sometimes changes should be made but employees are reluctant to talk about it. Taking a resignation from a valued employee was difficult for the Respectful manager, but they take it kindly wishing the employee future success. A good example of saying goodbye to an organisation I witnessed when I was shopping in an Apple Store in Australia. Despite the busy store, with every employee dealing with hordes of customers, co-workers started to applaud the leaving individual. He was carrying flowers and balloons and his co-workers shouted good luck to him. Everyone contributed to the sending off, time stood still but it was only a matter of seconds when he left the store and we returned to our activities.

Another characteristic of good management practice that was noted by the co-workers was the system of checks and balances on every financial transaction. Even small travel expenses were checked against original receipts. These sorts of actions may be criticised by others as too much attention to detail. However, they send a solid message to all employees that any fraud has a good chance to be discovered no matter how small. One fraudster manager in the study went out to buy himself a chair that was four times more expensive than expected, but administration allowed the expense to be granted. If a lower echelon staff person did the same it would have been refused. Therefore having a system in place that checks all the expenditures and has policies in place, this sort of abuse will not happen in the Respectful manager's remit.

Systematic workplace practices put in place a normative consensual view of what it happening. There is no uncertainty to the rules and there is common consensus of what is fair and what is not. Everyone knows what is standard practice and there is no deviation. As the rules are at a high standard of expectation it falls on everyone to follow. To use the instance of the expensive chair, in a Respectful workplace, administration would have set out guidelines to what is acceptable and what is not. In a large organisation a simple telephone call would produce the standard chair from the internal supply store. A requisition form is filled out and the older chair is reviewed for further use or to discarded through the proper channels. Because there is no deviation it certainly prevents any manager from purchasing a chair that is four times beyond the anticipated expenditure. The ruling gives everyone the same option and everyone knows it. The only exception to the rule may be for health reasons – for instance having a bad back. Even here it would be down to occupational health staff to assess and then purchase the correct chair. So having a systematic way of using resources yet being able to cater for individual health needs, if required, give the co-workers a sense of fairness and equality within the workplace. One chair may seem petty, but it makes sense in any organisation no matter the size or profitability.

I have worked in a large organisation where managers had 'status' chairs and that the other staff did not. It is a bit like walking through Business Class on airplanes. It must be obvious that business managers are very overweight and have extra-long legs to need such large seats. My own chair in that organisation was precisely that, large and tall in height. As I am a standard height for a woman, my feet dangled in the breeze when I sat down. I managed to get a more sensible option within a couple of weeks.

One of the co-workers picked up on the reverse of this idea that all should be treated equally. She felt that there was no need for a manager in her organisation to be fraudulent as the higher up the echelons of power the more status symbols were bestowed. She felt that this prevented anyone being more greedy, with the proviso that the organisation was so standardised that it would be impossible to work a fraud and get away with it through the rigid controls in place. Also that such an avaricious manager would receive the better benefits bestowed upon managers of the workplace, so why steal in the first place? However, it is clear from this study that greedy managers do exist and the status symbol of a chair and overseas conference expenses and aircraft seating preferences did not satisfy their need for money, power and control.

Having strong controls in place demonstrates to all that stealing is not approved of, so that if anyone steals they will forfeit their job. Anyone having a teenager on their hands will know this very well. More structure makes better behaviour. This gives the young person a sense of security by knowing where the boundaries are. Beyond the boundaries the world is not safe any more and anything can happen. Similarly an organisation must have set rules and regulations and expectations on staff behaviour, directors have their rules as does the office cleaner. This is for their safety and security. Beyond that lies unemployment and all of its attendant misery.

Humans need to know where the boundaries are. It could be surmised that this is a latent safety mechanism for survival from time immemorial. It would have been perilous to stray far from the home cave. Spatial boundaries were one of the first priorities of the individualised treatment programmes that I was involved with many years ago in Ontario, Canada. Where was the highly dangerous adolescent going to be housed was the first question that had to be answered. After spatial boundaries there had to be temporal ones put in place. Time is valued in our society and wasting it is seen as almost a sin. Again, this could well come from times past, where being out after dark was fraught with danger.

In today's world, time is measured accurately and being punctual is valued; time-wasting is not. Surfing the Internet during work time is often seen by employers as unproductive, emails are restricted and certain websites are prohibited. The temporal boundaries are firmly in place in a workplace run by a Respectful manager. Expectations are laid down of workplace behaviour too, despite the fact that the manager may and usually does work longer hours. This all makes for good working practices that the co-workers expressed in their interviews.

Good to Work With

It is no wonder that those co-workers felt lucky to be working for Respectful managers. They felt much trust with their manager who was 'good to work with'. They were content with just saying that. A few words speaks volumes for them. Going to work is not a chore, it is a pleasant duty to perform. Getting up at 7 a.m. is not a burden, co-workers love their work. Enough said in a short phrase. The respondents could not elucidate further, despite my open-ended questioning. I would ask 'In what way?' and no matter what I tried it was almost a shrug of the shoulders, as if, isn't the rest of the world like this? The co-workers, however, do not take the Respectful manager for granted; the dynamic is more of 'That's what happens.'

Good Manager

Similarly with the Respectful being described as 'Good'. The most I could squeeze out was Good or Great! This came to be my burden as I investigated further with different co-workers and different managers. 'Good' and 'Great' was all I could obtain to describe their manager. At one point this became somewhat frustrating as the one thing you need in qualitative research is information. Receiving such short epithets became the norm for the data that later turned out to be the Respectful Executive Impression Management. I even tried triangulating the data with others in the organisation about the same manager, and the same reply came back: Good or Great! So it can be surmised that these single words convey all that is within and all the behaviour and impression management that exudes. It is good and great to work with a Respectful manager. No more needs to be said. An 'A' grade is an 'A' grade. The grading gives us much information about the student. Good and Great do the same for a manager without the accompanying proof of examination results. But the co-workers have their proof in their years of working with the Respectful manager and enjoying it.

Underlying themes mentioned in the Good manager construct were that Respectful managers 'grow' their subordinates. They trained and developed workers' skills and even groomed some to greater roles than they held themselves in the organisation. Their interest in doing so was to assist the individual – not to develop a power base of cronies or other nefarious needs. The co-workers knew that the Respectful manager wanted them to be their best and therefore resources were given to them for training. A Respectful manager supervises new tasks as a mentor rather than as an 'inspector'. The co-workers concerned would respond with supplying work that was to the best of their ability, this in turn reduced the workload for many a CEO in informing the board with precise activity summaries and so on. Some of the co-workers were in organisations that had to report to statutory bodies and even government departments. The Respectful manager was able to develop a trusting relationship so that details of such reporting were accurate and the manager could do no more than overview the given product.

With the toll of pure supervision less on the Respectful manager's time, it allowed the manager to use their time more effectively. For instance, developing the company, cleaning up problem areas, dealing with customers and suppliers and idea creation and so on. This did not mean that their life became a bed of roses, rather it was just as hard work with noted long hours. However, it was a different workload as the co-workers were able to complete their duties without having to have a manager breathing down their neck. Trust reigns in such an organisation. Not only is there trust between the individual and their manager but with colleagues and subordinates. Trust becomes the glue that holds the organisation together. Some co-workers mentioned bad times in the past for the organisation, but in doing so they gave a picture of a collective effort to overcome obstacles. These organisations are marked with the same 'hard work ethic' that their manager demonstrated. Everyone was doing their best including the manager.

Naturally, mistakes will occur in even the best of organisations. One noticeable characteristic with the Respectful manager was that he did his best to clean up the mistake; this was without making a fuss and making the co-worker concerned feeling bad. In fact, if the manager made the mistake he would admit it straight away and sometimes laugh at himself for making such a silly or stupid error.

Being able to laugh at mistakes is one of the signs of a good manager, as it shows that the manager is being self-aware. This is demonstrating acceptance of the manager's faults with the good. 'Knowing thyself' is the way for the self to be individuated, using Jungian psychology. The phrase stems from what was allegedly the Delphic Oracles, knowing yourself prevents conceit and makes the person pay no attention to others who may say otherwise. Self-awareness makes the individual strong in purpose and in attitude. It takes away the delusion of perfection that we cling to in our unwise choices. If this quality is received from the manager to the co-worker, it supplies positive emotional energy to the recipient, making fear disappear that it is allowed to make mistakes and that there ways for them to be rectified. The rectification has to be followed and therefore the organisation learns how to deal with this problem.

The fear of making mistakes is like a plague in the workplace. I had a boss once who stayed until the early hours of the morning to double check financial reports down to every single expenditure. Whereas this activity is welcomed in an auditor it is not a requirement for the CEO's job. Equally I have seen people go over and over work that has been handed in by a subordinate or colleague, in order to find a mistake so that they could crow about it to themselves and others. I have never seen in a duty statement that it is essential to prove others wrong. Of course there is exactness in our work, there has to be, but to waste time trawling through others' work to find the mistake is a useless exercise at best and abusive at worst.

I am not sure when it will be appreciated that to make mistakes is beneficial and part of our learning process. Watching an infant taking his first steps is a wonderful lesson that mistakes are an absolute part of our learning. A baby naturally wants to be on his feet, and there is much standing and holding on to things. Finally when the standing feels steady to the baby, the first tentative step is made without holding onto anything. This voyage into space is part of our humanness, and has to be learnt to be like other children and adults, which act as role models to the baby. However, it is not a straightforward first step to go onto taking many steps. The baby falls over many times, but it must be noticed that the young child does not give up. He stands up and tries again, repeating the pattern until he can walk fall-free.

Similarly, managers learn by making mistakes. By owning up to errors demonstrates trust with other employees, just as the baby does with his caregivers. Laughing is another mechanism to unite with the dark side. Self-awareness is paramount and managers who do this retain respect from their employees. Co-workers talked about trusting relationships and these behaviours demonstrate their trust with their manager. Co-workers say that there is a lot of trust between Respectful managers and themselves. Being able to carry on with their work without constant supervision is another aspect of this relationship.

Co-workers also mention the positive characteristics of their managers. Intelligence and being smart were noted as very positive attributes about their manager. They also mentioned kindness and of course the trust that was shown from this type of manager.

Consistency

Another critical attribute was that their managers were consistent. This was about everything, including:

> *didn't change a lot, good balance about things, open, treats everyone equally.*

Consistency was positive, never seen as a negative quality. Another note to the consistency was that it produced lower or no fear in what the manager would do or say. If the manager was always the same this makes the fence building on boundaries. Take away fear and (using the CAT model) then people have courage about their manager and also receive encouragement. The dynamic is again being able to trust.

What You See Is What You Get

The most beautiful construct that came out of the Respectful Executive Impression Management was *'what you see is what you get'*. The elegance of this is built upon the openness and trustworthiness of the manager concerned. Co-workers were impressed that there was no hidden negativity that could spring out of the manager. No matter how much stress, no matter what the situation was they could rely upon him to be the same as he always was. If this is considered at length, as does one sitting and watching a beautiful natural scene, the majesty of this construct is seen in all of its dimensions. 'What you see is what you get' means total trust can occur therefore dependability and reliability. It makes the perfect co-worker go into battle with in the maelstrom of commerce and trade. There is nothing higher or better that could be asked for out of a manager. He will be looking out for his co-workers as much as the co-workers will be looking out for him. The free flowing positive energy between them is a wonderful sight to behold.

Confident

In the interviews I noticed the co-workers faces lit up, the relaxed state when they talked the Respectful manager. It was like they were recounting the antics of an old friend. One co-worker mentioned that her manager was prone to losing things. She recounted that one day he came in to her office and asked what had happened to a particular client file. She smiled as she told me that she walked him straight back to his office, and there it was on his desk. This was not a description of a case of early dementia, just human foibles at their best. And recalling her smile now even brings joy to me to write this down. He was hard-working, intelligent, worked many hours even on weekends, looked after his staff and yet could not find a simple file. File location was his downfall that is all. As she summed up:

I don't think a day goes by without us having to search his office for something. If you can't find something - it's in his office!

To return to the subject of perfection, this manager was not perfect. In fact if he was given the job of filing, it would seem that all hell would be let loose. He was not perfect but totally transparent, warts and all. In order for the manager to do this he must have the awareness of his weaker areas and asks others to pitch in where he would likely to make errors, so that means others do the filing. It was not a status action linked with power and control, it is purely a failing and he knew that he was not good at retrieving files. Another co-worker mentioned that her finance manager had a sense of humour as well:

No we can give her some jokes like that and she will laugh them off too. So she's good ... But no ... she's not traditionally like that I think which is good. It's nice to have a bit of fun - in an accounting way.

Over time the workplace becomes a tapestry of threads weaving in and out and bringing colours where they should be; an interweaving of action and positive energy of workplace duties, behaviour and expectations. This makes the organisation strong yet flexible, as manager and co-workers work together swapping roles and duties as the environment demands. As one co-worker remarked:

... I think now that we both have, I guess what I would characterise as mutual respect if you like, of each other's knowledge or what have you it's settled into a really easy working relationship.

'What you see is what you get' is the perfect reference for anyone applying for a job. Couple that with consistency then the rest falls into place of a Respectful manager. Upline management will know this about their manager as much as subordinates, as the impression management is uniform and consistent. In the study, due to a set of circumstances, the co-workers happened to include upline managers, for example board directors and CEOs. This meant a check could be made about the impression management upwards and downwards. For the manager giving off Respectful Executive Impression Management the story is the same no matter who he interacts with. He is transparent, consistent, 'good' and 'great'.

Hard-Working

This construct emerged from the three categories of keeping their personal activities apart from work, striving to better oneself and hard-working.

Keeps *personal life apart* was mentioned by a couple of recipients:

> *He doesn't often speak of his personal life, when he does, you know how some people can make derogatory comments about their wives, he never does that.*

This is far from the fraudster managers divisive attempts of keeping their spouse away from all work-based get-togethers, for instance Christmas parties and so on. I was quite surprised to hear about all the excuses that fraudster managers gave to not have their partner or spouse present. It may be that they do not want their partner to say anything that gave the game away. However, further into the study I found that spouses were kept in the dark about the clandestine activities and divorce was very likely to follow conviction. The fraudster managers did not and probably could not trust the person closest to them. Again it demonstrates how deep down Executive Impression Management is firmly entrenched. In contrast, they notice that the manager who gives off Respectful Executive Impression Management is respectful to their spouses, a good sign of consistency in all their Executive Impression Management.

An interesting subtext to 'strives to better herself or himself' was that it was seen as a very positive attribute similar to continuous learning:

> *always always strives to better herself but not in a you know climbing, greedy, nasty way.*

Another characteristic, hard-working, was also discussed by recipients in a positive manner, although several acknowledged that it had some disadvantages such as encouraging 'tunnel vision' and adverse effects on leisure:

> *I think sometimes he's a bit oblivious to what's going on around him but I don't think that comes out of lack of care, I think it's just his tunnel vision.*

Nonetheless, even this trait was seen as positive and did not express to the co-worker notions of being heartless.

Moral Character

Moral character is an important construct to the Respectful manager and refers to categories of data where co-workers discussed particular moral characteristics that they assigned to their non-fraudster executive. In these discussions, recipients referred to a range of issues such as ethical behaviour, participation in community work and having good values. Some co-workers aligned business ethics with evidence of moral character:

> *In terms of this context and business ethics and that sort of stuff certainly I've seen evidence that she is a person of moral character.*

One senior manager was noted for her community *work*:

> *I guess, but I guess I know that she puts in a lot of her time for things like her club and causes like that, so I know she's a person that gives up some of her time for no money and in fact she keeps some of her time free and won't commit to more hours because she wants to keep time available to do these things that she doesn't get paid for so I guess there's an indication that she's somebody who's willing to put into the community.*

Another manager was noted for her *country values,* which were seen as positive and also restrained from over-doing things. Referring to one non-fraudster manager an upline manager noted:

> *I think it's strong and she chairs our environmental committee so she's generally got a broader society community balance of that stuff. So again a country girl, simple wants and standards of living and interested in those sorts of things environmental, not to the extreme, just interested in driving those things.*

Referring to cutting down hours, one recipient agreed that her executive was very generous. In the question data I could drill deeper to assign if there was greed present with the manager.

> *But rather than reduce ours [hours], he reduces his. And he gives us bonuses and things like that. No, not at all. (greedy)*
>
> *Researcher: So he's very generous, the opposite of greedy in fact.*

I would say yes.

Honesty is another category of the **Moral character** construct, and it was noticeable to the co-worker that honesty was part of his Respectful manager.

... she's quite open and honest more than in general people are. She just puts it out there rather than being requested too, she's quite open about a lot of stuff she will share with us which is good.

One recipient noted that his manager would have been a failure of trying to be 'false'. Therefore honesty is integral to the personality of the Respectful manager.

I don't see him as ever presenting a false person. Yeah and I don't know that he'd do that very well.

Respectful

The final construct for the Respectful Executive theme is being **Respectful**. This comprises categories of data where recipients described behaviour as *caring, good to work with, recognised potential, having sensible limits, treats people with respect* and *tries to keep everyone happy.*

Caring is a one-off reference that refers to the executive's broken marriage:

Did he care about the marriage breakup?

I think he still was worried about how it was affecting the other party. I think he really did care especially about his kids and how this was affecting them and everything.

Data within the 'good to work' with category were very similar to the category with the same name that was discussed in the Respectful Executive Their Stories data. It contained data about good working relationships, sociable managers and collegial work practices, for instance:

I hope we have a good working relationship. I think we have after working so long.

He's just a really good boss.

Recognising potential in an employee included a range of behaviours including the provision of training programmes, providing support and mentorship to facilitate employee development:

> *We also have training programs obviously within business leadership development programs, executive development programs and a couple of other more broader we call them leadership programs but they're broader than that.*

And on a more personal level:

> *I think she taught me very ethically ... her work ethic as far as doing things the way they should and you know when we talked about cutting corners before I would never every cut a corner and neither would [the executive] if we felt that it would compromise the result. Yeah I think she really taught me well.*

One upline manager talked about the high career potential of his executive:

> *She's good, we've got a few that we think are capable of doing other things. That's what you try and make sure you provide them as a business, as a manager but as a business, they have to develop over time otherwise they are no value to the organisation or to themselves. No no. She's a very capable girl, [sic] which is good.*

'Sensible limits' is a category that contained data describing actions as being sensibly guarded and withdrawn when under stress:

> *I think he strikes me as a sort of person who [is] sensibly guarded as far as trusting people particularly in the business world. But then he takes people as they come so if they prove a good honest person then that's how he takes them.*

Several recipients discussed the extent to which their non-fraudster manager treats people with respect and this category comprised a variety data indicating the ways in which this was demonstrated. Examples included treating people in 'a nice way' that was consistent with maintaining dignity and not belittling employees. The following data provide some examples of the range of behaviour described by recipients:

Like if a job has to be done and its urgent, you can always tell the way he comes in …

And there was no fear in pointing out mistakes either:

I said [to the executive] I don't think this is right, something that he has done. He'll say sure, I mean he'll listen to me and if he's wrong he'll say fine.

As noted previously, I faced some challenges drawing co-workers out their initial brief answers. A possible conclusion from the brevity of the unstructured part of the interview is that this aspect is, in the recipient's minds, a given fact. The construct of Consistent behaviour came out in some detail in the Question data, possibly due to the questions about differences in performance in impression management. However many of the references are from other questions as well, and therefore unprompted. Finally, there was no distinction made for a Superior (arrogant) or Inferior (manipulative) type of Executive Impression Management. Recipients saw these managers as their equals – and that was from co-workers who may have been their upline manager as well as a subordinate. In addition, there is no reference to a disguise, difference in impression management to clients for instance, or a mask, or putting on a front. The co-workers did, however, refer to their managers as being open and not closed personalities.

Respectful Executive Impression Management Equals Transformational Management?

This type of Executive Impression Management is consistent and benign. It appears to represent the good side of management with its traits of honesty, trustworthiness and authenticity. This is reflected in the literature as mentioned before particularly with the notion of transformational leadership.

There have been empirical studies that show that transformational leaders demonstrate moral reasoning, ethics and trust,[1] all aspects of authenticity.

1 Podsakoff, P.M., S.B. MacKenzie, R.H. Moorman and R. Fetter (1990). 'Transformational leader behaviors and their effects on followers' trust in leader, satisfaction, and organizational citizenship behaviors'. *The Leadership Quarterly* 1(2): 107–42; Bass, B.M. and P. Steidmeier (1999). 'Ethics, character, and authentic transformational leadership behaviour'. 10: 181–217; Kanungo, R.N. (2001). 'Ethical values of transactional and transformational leaders'. *Canadian Journal of Administrative Sciences* 18(4): 257–65; Connell, J., N. Ferres and T. Travaglione (2003).

Therefore it can be assumed that it would be impossible for a Respectful manager to be a transactional manager, that is, relying solely on coercive authority in the organisation to get things done.

What we have to be careful here though is that a manager who is a fraudster, having disguised Executive Impression Management can and will push the buttons of authenticity. This means that they can delude their co-workers easily into thinking that they are indeed authentic, and therefore having a moral character.

One interesting characteristic of being able to apologise appears to be a predictor of morality in the Respectful Executive Impression Management, as no fraudster executives were noted as apologetic before discovery of their fraud.[2] Tucker et al. found that far from being perceived as a weakness, being able to apologise is regarded as an enhanced quality of leadership as it engenders long lasting and trusting relationships and this was the case with the Respectful executive impression management from the semi-structured interview guide. Trust, is therefore is a key factor in the relationship with recipients and their managers and is discussed later.

'Engendering trust in manager-subordinate relationships: Predictors and outcomes'. *Personnel Review* 32(5): 569–87; Price, T.L. (2003). 'The ethics of authentic transformational leadership'. *Leadership Quarterly* 14(1): 67–82.

2 Tucker, S., N. Turner, J. Barling, E.M. Reid and C. Elving (2006). 'Apologies and transformational leadership'. *Journal of Business Ethics* 63(2): 195–207.

Chapter 4

The Tyrant and Mediocre Executive Impression Management

Those managers giving off the Tyrant and Mediocre forms of Executive Impression Management were exceedingly different than the Respectful type. The Tyrants are like slave-drivers and expect everything yesterday, without any mistakes. The name Tyrant was gained from the co-workers who were unfortunate enough to have worked with such a manager. They offered this name freely when asked how to categorise this type of manager in one word. This follows the name given to the other malevolent Executive Impression Management type. Mediocre was the name assigned. The managers who gave off Mediocre type of Executive Impression Management behaved very differently, being devious and manipulative, yet outwardly everybody's friend or colleague.

These two types are malevolent and use people and organisations for their own purposes to ultimately achieve power and control. They shared many similarities which are presented now, and their differences are explored later in this chapter.

Inconsistency

Both types were inconsistent. This construct comprised three categories: differential behaviour, risky behaviour and remarks made about their spouses who were deliberately separated from work.

Differential behaviour – that is, favouritism – is an interesting category as it was also noted within the fraudster impression management themes. The category arose in this context in discussions about how the impression management differentiated in regard for others:

You know, she had her favourites, she was allowed to have her favourites.

Favouritism is found with the malevolent and never with the Respectful Executive Impression Management. This needs some discussion as it has ramifications to management practice. Among the first works on favouritism was by Prendergast[1] who found that there was a trade-off from allowing favouritism to exist versus inefficiencies in production and outcomes. Fisher[2] found that favouritism existed in organisations that were dominated by authoritarian management.

I was once asked by a manager if because she liked some of their employees more than others was that favouritism? I happened to be observing her unit in a large institution and the various employees coming and going. Some were clearly working hard and one or two others were obviously marking time and chatting on phones and so on. If I were in her shoes as I don't tolerate substandard work, no matter how funny, easy-going or nasty it can be, after a period of observation I would pull them aside and talk about increasing productivity. If that failed I would suggest perusal of other career options as the organisation was not serving their needs. It would be on my say so if an employee was to be fired and I never took that function lightly. Usually this process would take several weeks of my mentoring the individual personally and I would give resources, including time out for job interviews if that individual so desired. But in large institutions, particularly with governmental and quasi-governmental organisations a manager had no power to hire or fire, unions often stepped in and the Human Resources department never wanted to go through the difficulties of dismissal, as it would get too political for them.

So basically she had to put up with whoever was assigned to her unit. In this situation I recognised that she could do nothing about recalcitrant employees on her unit and apart from performance evaluations, which were almost non-existent, she had no way to legitimately ask for improvement. With this situation in mind she was asking is it right of her to like staff that she preferred.

This dilemma is solved through the trust that she gave in her impression management. She was clearly a manager who gave off Respectful Executive Impression Management and her co-workers felt that she treated everyone like an equal. And that is where she learnt that through this equality she gave out

1 Prendergast, C. and R.H. Topel (1996). 'Favoritism in organizations'. *Journal of Political Economy* 104(5): 958–78.

2 Fisher, J.E. (1977). 'Playing favorites in large organizations'. *Business Horizons* 20(3): 68–74.

and her own sense of fairness she would have exuded trust and respect to all regardless. Husted[3] concludes similarly that trust is not just simply that, there has to be a component of fairness in trusting. His point was that a manager cannot trust everyone – there have to be limits – but fairness in trust is the way out of not allowing himself or his organisation to be exposed to harm due to runaway trusting behaviour. This fairness, or lack of it, is explained by one co-worker:

> *... Yeah, so to me she wasn't the fairest of people, it was just people she was close to that she was fair to. If she wasn't that close to you, you know then you didn't matter too much.*

Several co-workers referred to the difficulties of working in an environment in with cliques exhibited in the organisation:

> *I had known him in a corporate conduct kind of situation the same as the rest of his staff and it was only when I was invited into the inner sanctum so to speak, where we had this informal thing and then this other language appeared that was far more basic and [had] inappropriate references. So I tolerated it for a little while, I couldn't join in because it was below standard, my standard, so then of course that would cause me to not be part of the group, I was different and that in itself had it's own ramifications on a daily basis.*

And of course non-favourites were left out in the cold, as one co-worker puts it.

> *She would have believed in the worst of me because I was with the other person (and she would have thought she doesn't care for me so she's going to be telling her things) and therefore I was sort of left out in the cold really.*

And interestingly, a recipient can be a non-favourite, no matter what he or she did:

> *I was in a bad position right from the word go, but it was the arrogance that came through that you know, if you're not on my side, then you don't get entertained really.*

3 Husted, B.W. (1998). 'The ethical limits of trust in business relations'. *Business Ethics Quarterly* 8(2).

The differential behaviour observed by fraudster manager co-workers and malevolent non-fraudster co-workers is that the non-fraudster behaviours were not associated with concealment. These behaviours were openly apparent. Tyrant and the Mediocre managers did not appear to bother to disguise, in fact they were described as open in the different aspects of their behaviour for example:

> *You know if you were on the bad end of her you saw the real her, you saw the her that wasn't this nice old lady, that was pretty bitter and nasty and had the right words for you too, could cut you right down. Other people would say what a lovely lady she was and there were people in the office who thought she was wonderful, but she was wonderful to them.*

It must have been heart breaking to be on the receiving end of this type of exclusionary behaviour. It actually is a facet of bullying, which I will come to later. Some other open behaviours were noticed as well

Addictions

On a different note the co-workers of non-fraudster managers were also asked if they saw any addictions. For example drinking:

> *I used to think to myself when he came back in the afternoon his behaviour in the afternoon after he'd been out for lunch was different. And that would be because he'd been drinking in the afternoon, so I would say he'd have had a drink every day, so I'm sure that that probably amounts to an addiction, wouldn't it?*

What is interesting is that not one manager exuding the Respectful Executive Impression Management had any addictions noted by their co-workers.

Absence of Spouses at Work Events

Strikingly similar to the fraudster Executive Impression Management, there appeared data for malevolent non-fraudster managers that their *spouses* rarely appeared at work functions as well. A co-worker remarks:

> *I can't remember any function when he's brought his wife or any other outside friend or associate.*
>
> *Researcher: He didn't bring his wife?*
>
> *Not to any of the functions. He has brought his children but not his wife.*

Needless to say it is odd that the wife never came. In fact the same co-worker recalled later that the wife did not even come to the celebration when he was made CEO of his organisation after 10 years of service.

Inconsistency is Open

The characteristic that was quite striking out of all the data that were collected was that this Executive Impression Management type was that it was openly inconsistent. There was no fear of being seen as inconsistent. These managers would use all the devices that people use to cover deceit. This could be in a number of ways: lies were told that later were found out, treating staff in different ways, enormous pressure to produce work, and after the honeymoon period wore off the real tyrant came through. Also, another telling characteristic is that 'What they said is *not* what you got', quite the opposite of what the Respectful Executive Impression Management gives off, that is 'What you see is what you get'.

Lying

There were many instances of lying; this co-worker explains one situation:

> *They started putting the pressure on me and I think what was the worst thing they did, was to actually tell me that I was doing things in the office that I knew that I couldn't be doing but I was being blamed for.*

This co-worker identifies that telling untruths was the worst thing possible, and points to how damaging deceit is to the listener. Having an experience similar to this, I know how 'crazy making' this can be. The target knows the truth, but being told otherwise begins a process of denying one's own reality, which is highly abusive. When a target is forced to question his memory that in itself is an insult to an individual's humanity. After all, it is our cognitive ability that separates us from our cousins the primates, take away our memories then we are left being automatons. Unfortunately there is no means to measure the damage of lies. This measurement seems to have eluded scholars, as Tyler found that there were no studies before 2006 that empirically investigated the effects of lying.[4]

As mentioned earlier, to try and delude someone by telling a lie is quite ridiculous, as the truth will often come out sooner or later. Most people tell lies, and we know this to be divisive, emotionally abusive and against the Golden Rule of doing unto others as they would do to you. If we do not have truth in our lives then we have malevolent anarchy and madness. 'Truthfulness', says Frank Cioffi, along with every other moral rule, is capable of conflicting with the obligation to benevolence.'[5] Therefore truth is an important foundation for benevolent interaction, that is, respect for others.

Inconsistent behaviour was also associated with the placing of undue pressure on other staff:

> *... and anyway they first of all started on the other girl, started putting pressure on her and her work and finding fault with things and this sort of thing. It was really nasty stuff and she would be taken into the office; she would come out she would be crying...*

This is a typical example of how open the Tyrants are with their malevolent behaviour. They do not care if other co-workers see them 'being nasty'.

Being nice at first but 'hard nosed' later is an inconsistency through time:

> *... although I thought initially that he had regard for my ability and I thought on that basis that I would get his respect ... he accused me [later] of not having done something right ... if he hadn't been such a hard nosed person, it probably could have worked.*

This co-worker has no idea that her boss was truly like. He wooed her into the job with his overt appreciation of her ability, but it was only a ploy to get her in. And to comment on the fact that underneath he was 'hard nosed' something he did not wish to show her at the beginning demonstrates the hidden agenda he had for her employment.

4 Tyler, J.M., R.S. Feldman and A. Reichert (2006). 'The price of deceptive behavior: Disliking and lying to people who lie to us'. *Journal of Experimental Social Psychology* 42(1): 69–77.

5 Cioffi, F. (1994). 'Porky-Talky. Review of *A Pack of Lies: Towards a Sociology of Lying*'. *London Review of Books* 16(18): 16.

This hidden agenda comes out with this comment:

Like he had a bit of personality but I didn't realise that that's probably, not a front, it like's what you see is not what you get.

Personality Clashes

In my experience working with unemployed mature aged managers I have heard this time and time again as they explained why they left jobs that outwardly looked promising. A quick turnover in employers is often an indicator of the employee having a 'personality'. This is an euphemism in the recruitment game that means that the individual concerned is unemployable. As this is a death sentence to any job seeker's activities I need to develop this theme further and go into some detail about what personality is seen to be.

It is often said that there were a clash of personalities for a person to leave or be fired. Again the underlying comment is that if an individual is a 'good' worker there would be an accommodation for differences with other co-workers idiosyncrasies. Usually when a difference occurs and one co-worker makes that comment then he is talking about things far deeper than having a difficulty in working with each other. Using the CAT model, it is a clash of emotional energy of positive versus negative, benign work as opposed to malevolence. This is not personalities at all. It is blaming the victim, that somehow the target has an unemployable personality therefore it is a sign of abuse.

The personality literature by psychologists refers specifically to certain traits. To me the Myers Briggs Type Indicator[6] is the gold standard. It is based on theoretical grounds rather than picking out at random almost personality traits that appear to indicate subliminal traits that are seen as good or bad for the individual. With the MBTI, there is only appreciation of the different gifts that are bestowed upon us genetically. Each 'factor' has its positive connotation. It is only in stress that 'bad' features are found. Again, as we all have these configurations of personality there are features to our stressed behaviour. It is beautifully appreciative of the individual. For every client whom I have met, when they find out their type they are amazed at the accuracy of the information about themselves. As indeed myself when I first took the test.

6 Briggs Myers and Myers (1995).

And when faced with the information that when I am stressed that I could show 'nit-picking' behaviour – that is, over-attention to detail, as my sensory function (for details) is the least preferred in my type. I realised that I did do this, and when it appears I feel negative to the whole world. Others, however, will see me as overly strict, like a school teacher gone mad. We never want to hear that we can be less than well-behaved, but in times of stress we all are! This opens doors for the individual to accept how they present in relationships to others. The wonderful thing about this typing is that once a person starts reading about the bad news of how we operate when stressed, awareness dawns and with that, understanding and acceptance. No other personality test can give this to an individual. Let me elaborate.

On a personality test I may score high on being narcissistic but so what? I will think I am the best because I know that I am the best, and others should know it too! It does not offer the person a pathway to acceptance or reigning in their narcissism; the test only demonstrates that I have a high opinion of myself. It may very well be that I use narcissism to hide a deep-seated fear of being rejected, but the test result does not and cannot offer that. The opposite of the coin is not shown. Thus if a high narcissism score is revealed in a job recruitment situation, employers may want a 'confident' individual, to save their company from liquidation for instance, whereas when things are going well, there would be less need for a self-opinionated manager. Therefore, the MBTI comes from a theoretical standpoint, the personality tests were created from a pathological point of view, that is, does this person suffer from a mental disease? Studying pathology has its home in the natural sciences with understanding physical disease. Psychology stems from the same scientific origin; however, its focus is on mental illness or characteristics thereof. Hence the generation of diagnostic manuals[7]with carefully constructed criteria for producing a diagnosis.

Social psychologists took a step further in the last century to investigate social pathology, that is, the study of the problems of social interaction including the origins of the pathology and its effect on people. This is based on 'scientific' evidence, which in my view is hazardous to draw inferences to larger populations from the sample group under investigation. Since the Second World War there has developed a whole industry of social psychology with the corresponding growth in academic literature.

---

7 American Psychiatric Association (1994). *Diagnostic and Statistical Manual of Mental Disorders*. Washington DC, American Psychiatric Association; American Psychiatric Association (2013). *Diagnostic and Statistical Manual of Mental Disorders*. Arlington, VA, American Psychiatric Association.

This means that today there are a host of other tests that measure various things. One that is often used nowadays in recruitment is the 'Big 5'. This is based on the Five Factor Inventory; the traits measured are: openness, conscientiousness, extraversion, agreeableness and neuroticism.[8] Obviously to be the ideal manager, the traits to have in abundance would be all except the neuroticism, which points to, in many an employer's mind, as an unhealthy attitude to work. The Big 5 factors are widely held to be the foundation of all personality traits. Despite the fact that people can fake their responses.[9] These factors are questionable in my mind. Openness is the heart of extraversion; introverts are maltreated as being closed personalities because they are quiet – as compared to an extravert. Also agreeableness will also be correlated with extraversion. Introverts have, according to the MBTI team, a world of internal imagination and they will think things through before then speak.[10] If it turns out that what they pronounce to their co-workers' statements that are contrary to the extraverted consensus then they will be labelled as having a lack of agreeableness and even a tendency to dominance when in a group setting, as they are not timid.[11]

Again the Big 5 test relies on self-reporting and any individual with their mind on the employment prospect will ensure that the right answers are ticked. That is another reason why I prefer the MBTI as there are no questions with overt choices for being advantageously selected. The MBTI has been used for many decades and there is a common acceptance of the four traits that are measured. That is, extraversion/introversion and the dimension of intuition/ sensing which are based on Jung's earlier work.[12] Thinking/feeling and judging and perceiving which were added later by the Myers Briggs team. There are many forced choice statements for each construct and if an individual may wish to look good to an employer and practise deception on certain questions but they will be caught on others. What is at issue in the MBTI is that we are only receiving information about how the individual is oriented to his world, how he receives information, how he makes decisions and finally how quickly he makes the decisions. None of these variables are particularly useful to work out if a person has a 'difficult personality'.

8 Costa Jr., P.T. and T.A. Widiger (eds) (1994). *Personality Disorders and the Five-Factor Model of Personality*. Washington DC, American Psychological Association.

9 Pauls, C.A. and N.W. Crost (2005). 'Cognitive ability and self-reported efficacy of self-presentation predict faking on personality measures'. *Journal of Individual Differences* 26(4): 194–206.

10 Briggs Myers and Myers (1995).

11 Lester, E., D. Scholfield and P. Chapman (2014). 'Self and Peer Assessment and Dominance during Group Work Using Online Visual Tools'. *Seminar.net* 10(1).

12 C.G. Jung (1971).

The only factor that a potential employer may prefer to have is an extraverted individual. Although many CEOs are introverted types! There is reason to believe that introverts are not viewed favourably as they do not interact well with others, because their own internal world is so rich and diverse. Extraverts like to problem solve together, while Introverts prefer to work on the problem on their own is a good example of biased selection. As there are far fewer introverts than extraverts (it is estimated at only 25 per cent) they are often excluded from prospective jobs solely by this bias. A wise employer, however, will suggest a more rounded profile of staff, and use the different talents of the introverts to offset the dominance of extraversion. Extraversion can easily lead to consensus as they talk so much and gradually others who may disagree may change their view due to overt peer pressure 'around the water cooler'.

The result of this 'personality clash' assignation makes life for the individual extremely difficult being labelled as such. If the MBTI is used, there will be an understanding of how the individual views the world and so on, emphasising the positive attributes of his type, and not focussed on the difficulties (however described) of the person.. This is because there is no MBTI personality type that has a clash with others. There is stress of course which makes the person react differently, particularly if this is over a long period of time.

Furthermore, MBTI is the only test that I am aware of that will indicate to the assessor how that individual will operate if in stress. Here I am referring to long-term stress that has impacted the individual's life. Jung described the inversion of type; this he referred to as the Shadow or the dark side of the individual. In this way an individual will use other less well-used talents to get along in life. For instance, an easy-going extravert who believes that everyone should achieve their true potential may turn into a curmudgeon who blocks all promotions. Given enough stress, this happens.

To me this is an elegant way of explaining human behaviour. The individual is merely stressed, not changed forever. I will come back to this theme later. At this point 'personality clashes' should not be accepted as true explanations of behaviour; it is used as a device to say that the individual cannot work alongside others in the organisation, thus avoiding the blame on poor management.

By the way, I have one final comment about introverts. There are many who like being with people – in fact most do prefer to work in teams – but they do not wish to be told how to think, neither do they need to be instructed on what the consensus is. It is far better to allow the introvert to express his views and out of that may be nuggets of gold, which others have overlooked.

As we mature and develop in life we can own our Shadow side in pleasant rewarding ways. For instance, I am a raging extravert, who as getting on in life, has discovered the beauty of introversion. It is not my strong card, but I appreciate it in all of its depth, and can even spend time on my own quite happily writing, a very solitary experience, which has proved enjoyable. I like to paint watercolours, again as an intuitive, using my sensing side is to my advantage is great. For those who have not developed their dark side and are the same MBTI type as me, would see the writing as boredom, to be only done in spurts between socialising and the painting as too fiddly and intricate to attempt. There is a whole literature on the MBTI, and millions of people have been tested. I highly recommend exploring our different gifts, particularly those that are relevant to the workplace, for instance, Extraversion and the Judging feature of getting the job done. The workplace is typically filled with extraverts and if they are malevolent you will see it fairly quickly, albeit if they are disguised it will take a longer time. Hostility, however, is a feature of the malevolent managers as the co-workers described.

Inconsistency

To work with an individual who is inconsistent by jumping from one positive to negative interaction led to other more hurtful behaviour. This was comprised of two categories anger and disrespect. Anger was mentioned in several references and associated with aggression and impatience and shown by the non-fraudster manager in question:

> *... so when I came back he was angry because I hadn't done what he expected me to do but hadn't verbalised. So that didn't start off really well.*

This is quite common with the malevolent types, and that is that they almost expect the co-workers to read their minds in order to prioritise the co-workers' list of things to do.

Disrespect was perceived in behaviours such as not wanting to listen to colleagues or disregarding colleagues contributions:

> *... he didn't really want to listen to anything you had to say./ ... /*

> *He wouldn't actually care [if I left]; I would not have mattered to him at all.*

Clearly, the malevolent manager has only one view and that is his. And with that aim anyone is disposable. Human Resource practice informs us that to lose an employee is expensive as there is the recruitment then the induction training costs to replace the lost worker. The manager concerned does not expect the co-worker to leave, just do the job and carry on.

So much for the shared characteristics, now the formation of the Tyrant and the Mediocre will be discussed.

Tyrant – Poor Management Practice

This construct is derived from behaviours shown by the non-fraudster managers who used the Tyrant form of Executive Impression Management. They produced poor working environments. The categories to this construct are varied but include practices such as late payment of salaries, poor intake, employment processes and a lack of clear work practices and expectations. Again this is the complete opposite to the Respectful managers. An example of abusive 'testing' of candidates for promotion as shown by this reference:

> *But as time went on … they'd made a mistake and what they thought or planned to do was no longer feasible, so it just meant that they then didn't need two people they needed one. So instead of sort of letting us know this what they decided to do was just to see which one was going to be the better one.*

Another area of contention that Tyrants seem to do is that one manager did not pay salaries on time:

> *I was told by the receptionist and I actually saw emails from my predecessor saying to him, please put my salary in my bank. He didn't even pay their salary on time and all those kinds of things.*

Some small businesses do have cash flow problems and salaries can be left a day or two unpaid when times are tough. However, as the above quote demonstrates, delaying the payments was a permanent feature of this manager. It is saying that employees are not cared for.

Poor intake procedures is another indicator of poor management practice:

> *We agreed to meet for coffee. I don't believe I ever gave him a resume. It was really networked and we agreed to meet for coffee and talk about his firm.*

This manager poached the co-worker from another firm that shared the same specialty service. He approached her at a meeting that her original company put on to meet their suppliers. This sort of practice is despicable and demonstrates the abuse of the original company's hospitality and the worker, who felt compromised. The manager who gives off Tyrant Executive Impression Management is only interested in one thing – himself – and that is the only thing that matters.

Another category of poor management practice with the Tyrant manager was about social interaction being a problem:

> *but I found very quickly that every time I had to interact with him it was problematic …*

He went on to clarify it was my way or the highway type of interaction. Nothing could be doubted or changed to more effective ways.

'Used my own initiative' results from the above lack of clarity. Being imperious which a Tyrant will show leaves a co-worker with little room to manoeuvre:

> *I found, because of his demeanour and the way he was, I found it difficult to go and ask him things.*

Finally another thread in the poor management practice was an example of little or no support and poor office space:

> *It was unfortunate that my work area was in an office where it had the printer and the photocopier and everything so I had people in and out of my office all the time.*

This is often the case in small businesses where resources are minimal. However, this comment came from a co-worker who was able to work in a busy environment but she found that the office was so small it was not feasible to produce satisfactory outcomes until other workers had left the premises.

Lack of Integrity

Another construct to the Tyrant Executive is **Lack of integrity**. It is composed of five categories of data: *strategic positioning of self, hiding, lied, scapegoat* and *trust wouldn't be there.* Several recipients remarked upon **Lack of integrity**; for example:

> *but I feel there were flaws in the way she conducted herself. So her integrity is I think is questionable in my mind.*

This was shown in various ways; one recipient was less than impressed by *strategic positioning for self-gain*:

> *Yes I think it was strategic positioning so that when the time for the incumbent CEO stood down he was the most suitable person that would be considered and the most understanding of what was required for the role.*

One non-fraudster manager was known to *hide* (the co-workers') *things*; as the recipient explained, this took several forms:

> *And the only one that had something to gain was [the manager] so that was very dishonest I think and it's very strange with her because she could hide [my] things.*

Being *lied to* seemed to be an inherent part of this type of openly malevolent Executive Impression Management:

> *When I reflect ... the set of circumstances he put to me wasn't correct, there was someone working in the role when I spoke to him in the November because she left in the December and she was not on probation. She was clearly not on probation.*

Being made a scapegoat was the treatment of one co-worker:

> *... if any trouble, it was going to be me, it would come back on me.*

And with such damaging treatment, trust would disappear.

> *Researcher: If you were receiving care from this person would you have trusted it?*

No, because you would just wonder when it was going to reverse. No I never would have trusted it.

Negative Emotions

Negative emotion is a construct comprising categories describing behaviour as anxiety, disrespectful, unempathetic and viewing people as threats.

When asked about depression, there was one statement that referred to the malevolent non-fraudster manager's own anxiety:

I don't think he was depressed. I think there was an anxiety, I would put it more like an anxiety not a depression.

In contrast to the Respectful Executive impression management, disrespectful behaviour was shown in a number of contexts including behaviour with clients:

We'd just look at each other and think "Whatever!" He didn't know everything but he carried on like he did.

Lacking integrity was also associated with a lack of empathy. One co-worker explained at length the lack of empathy among the Tyrant non-fraudster managers that she had to work with:

Even to me empathy translates to … is derived out of the empathy you feel you want to do the best for them and help them, so if you're messing up the job that you're doing that's actually not helpful to them it might delay things, it might make them suffer financial hardship … so to me you couldn't be particularly empathetic if you then didn't get on and do the job properly …

Giving an ultimatum is seen as being equally unempathetic:

I'm just thinking about my colleague who was from [overseas] … did his law degree and moved out here with his partner and bought a home. My employer was his sponsor and he absolutely pulled the rug from underneath him by … [giving] him some ultimatum, either buy into the business, or I'm selling … But upon leaving, it meant he had no visa, no sponsor and [the colleague] expressed to me … he tried to tell [the manager] the impact on him of the business decision … He

> *couldn't see it even, he couldn't even see what he was doing ... So [the manager] doesn't have regard does he? He doesn't, because he wouldn't have done that. He's his sponsor.*

In a final category, Negative emotions were associated with one manager's tendency to view younger, successful staff as threats:

> *... you sort of felt that she was a little on edge with people younger coming in who were doing really really well.*

This was in line with the fraudster managers who quickly got rid of workers who were seen as threats to their frauds being discovered.

Poor Management Techniques

In contrast to the Respectful Executive, the next major construct is Poor management techniques. It is composed of poor communication, and being left unsupervised.

Poor communication was a problem for several recipients and was discussed in contexts where specific executives appeared unaware of colleagues' need for clear exchanges of ideas and information:

> *When we talked about weaknesses before, he is a very poor communicator, really poor.*

Sloppy work included examples of bills not being paid and recipients' perceptions that an executive was not thorough:

> *He didn't pay his business bills on time, we were always getting calls from credit people, so that would be the only valid thing that I personally took calls on a number of times that he hadn't paid. We didn't even have a relationship with a courier where we could courier documents out which tells me a lot.*

The Making of the Difference of the Tyrant and Mediocre Forms

There are two remaining constructs to the Inconsistent Malevolent format of Executive Impression Management: the Inferior and the Superior types. The information presented here is through the lens of the co-workers as it came out in direct responses to questions asked in the second part of the interview.

The Inferior Type – The Mediocre

It was quite a surprise when the data were reviewed that a manipulative malevolent managerial type of Executive Impression Management emerged. It was completely unexpected. Manipulation is overt but underhanded. As they spend so much time on using the organisation for their own needs, they are classified as Mediocre by their co-workers. Subordinates are ignored if there is no potential use for them.

One subordinate talks about being unsupervised for several years:

> *... I have never felt the supervisory role situation. As the director or CEO he's required to put his final stamp of approval or whatever is required on a particular project or whatever that I have relayed to him in all those roles and currently in the same way as a person who is trying to achieve certain things. So the [managerial] role is almost irrelevant.*

Having lack of supervision is a two-edged sword as the subordinate never knows where the boundaries are and is open to remonstration if the co-worker inadvertently goes out on a limb that is not approved by the manager concerned. 'Guessing what is in my manager's mind' is not a good way of conducting business and an extremely wasteful one at that.

Overall, the Mediocre's own goals come first; these career climbing managers hop from one organisation to another, advancing themselves up the hierarchy openly. They will use all sorts of tricks to do this. They avidly learn the 'how tos' for career advancement. They recognise that upline managers have cronies and wish to join the in-group.

How do I know this? It is not only from the data; unfortunately I was a manager using Mediocre Executive Impression Management. It irks me to write this, but I have to put my hand up. If there were seminars or workshops to learn tips on how to get up the ladder of success I would attend. In those days, success to me was measured in dollars – my salary as compared to others and the budget and wages that were under my control. However, there was a little side to me that was using my management skills that was not measured in those terms, and that was my 25 years of managing voluntary organisations.

These non-profits were small but usually effective in helping their target group. I freely gave my time to assist in this process. This may or may not be a precursor of the changes that had to be made within, but I did try to honestly help as much as I could. Needless to say, the service I gave was nicely noted in my CV, so I wonder if I was so noble after all! I will refer to my experience later to develop this point further.

This manipulative type comes to the fore by being described as wanting to seek other's approval. If he receives the go ahead then he is able to manipulate his audience. In impression management theory, there is no record of someone seeking the audience's approval before they start their social interaction with others. A doctor does not ask his patients if he looks right for the part. If at all, this would be done in front of a mirror at home. It is merely a self-checking device that all is well. Checking with audiences though is outside normal impression management.

Some scholars have developed a theory of social monitoring which explains this audience self-checking process. It can overlay the impression management interaction with their audiences by checking that they are hearing and listening and approving the performance. Kilduff and Day[13] tested whether high self-monitors were able to reach higher levels in the management hierarchy than those who do not. Their article is intriguingly titled: 'Do chameleons get ahead? The effects of self-monitoring on managerial careers'. They found that the answer is yes. Much more research later developed self-monitoring as a personality trait based on Snyder's earlier work.[14] Most scholars believe that self-monitoring is a good thing to do, to check that the message is getting across to their audience for instance. However as Snyder and Gangestad[15] said later that social monitoring maybe used for deceitful purposes, for example checking how well the audience accepted a lie.

In my study, co-workers identified social monitoring as less than good behaviour and it occurred only with one set of managers called Mediocre. Those managers exhibiting Respectful Executive Impression Management had no need to double-check; they knew that their co-workers would willingly listen to what they had to say due to the high degree of trust.

13 Kilduff, M. and D.V. Day (1994). 'Do chameleons get ahead? The effects of self-monitoring on managerial careers'. *Academy of Management* 37(4) : 14–37.

14 Snyder, M. (1974). 'Self-monitoring of expressive behaviour'. *Journal of Personality and Social Psychology* 30(4): 526–37.

15 Gangestad, S. and M. Snyder (2000). 'Self-monitoring: Appraisal and reappraisal'. *Psychological Bulletin* 126(4): 530–55.

It is my contention that social monitoring comes from the negative emotion of fear, something I knew very well from my own childhood. I became in our family the signaller of when things were turning vicious. All I did was monitor my adoptive father's mouth; when it down-turned we were in trouble. That meant all of us were in trouble, as it had no bearing on events or fact. This is a leftover artefact from those days, and I still use it instinctively. Rationally I know I need not do it, as confidence in others requires trust, and I have learnt to trust, but the amygdala in my brain does not know when to stop, given my early conditioning. So given new events I will inevitably monitor for danger signs.

If a manager is fearful, then we will see high social monitoring. What that fear may be about is entirely in his own mind, but nevertheless the audience of co-workers pick it up. As the manager is operating from a negative energy base (using the CAT model), the balance of power between the co-worker and the manager is skewed. In this case the manager feels less power than the co-worker; if not, why monitor? The other Executive Impression Management types do not self-monitor, or more correctly, the co-workers did not notice this happening. It was only apparent in this type.

However, it is still a method of control, using 'power under'. To return to my own experience: it was a way to control my father's anger towards myself, as I could then try to modify my actions to avoid his wrath. This meant others became the scapegoat due to my appeasement or diversionary tactics. He would have been stunned to know that I was manipulative because he felt he was in control, but in reality he was not as I was ducking and weaving to get away from his bad temper.

The Mediocre Executive Impression Management is seen by co-workers as the manager wishing to control from a socially inferior position, the opposite of a position of the Tyrant superiority. This means that the Mediocre manager is more covert in his control of co-workers, but it is still observable. It comes out as attention seeking and asking others about their appearance and image. This is asking others' approval, which is reinforced by a type of social monitoring that is again approval seeking in the recipient's information.

Dealing with attention seeking first:

Researcher: But he did that to gain people's ... what?...

Co-worker: Attention. It was a performance which he possibly could not do anywhere else.

This answer is quite interesting, as the manager could not get away with his manipulations outside the workplace according to his co-worker. Furthermore she saw it as a device to further himself. This is not only observed in this quote but does come up again through his and other Mediocre managers' effort to protect their self-image:

> *He liked to be appropriately dressed, he liked to be recognised in public, he liked to have the respect of the staff but he may not return the same respect to them which was what I got annoyed about. He would expect not to have personal remarks made to him but he could put personal remarks to other people. So he protected his self- image.*

And, in order to do so, one manager concerned took a philosophical position on budgets so as not to break the status quo, and people may think he was not a good manager:

> *Yes, yes. But then it was sometimes, that the choice was unavoidable and the consequences were unavoidable and he took a philosophical position on that. There had to be a certain number and the budget only stretches so far and those that do not get the support of the wider organisation or the stakeholders as they say, we have to do something about the budget to support the ones that are successful.*

Another manager markedly showed outright social monitoring as he would check out a co-worker:

> *It was more when he made an inappropriate remark, ho ho ho, then he would look at me and stop.*

This statement shows how the power exerted by the co-worker is higher than the manager's. In this instance the co-worker's role in the organisation is subordinate to his manager, and ordinarily the co-worker would defer to his superior ranking manager. But no, the opposite happened in this case; the manager received the co-worker's opprobrium and stopped his behaviour entirely due to the scorn showed.

I want to demonstrate this further using the example of another manager who was designated as a Mediocre. He gave an apology to a subordinate co-worker, which is usually a sign of the Respectful Executive Impression Management. In this instance, the manager concerned did a rapid about-turn in order to keep the co-worker on side. So when an apology is given it is important to observe the power relationship. Yes, managers who give off Respectful Executive Impression Management give apologies when wrong, but they do that out of respect for themselves (becoming more self-aware) and the co-worker (trusting the person to accept the apology and it would not be held against them later). In the above example, the co-worker was considered to have some power in the organisation, and the manager felt it was necessary to retain some control of him.

Using quite the opposite tack, are those non-fraudster managers who see themselves as superior through the eyes of the recipients, putting themselves 'above' the co-workers no matter their rank in the organisation, which is now discussed below.

Tyrant Superiority

The main construct in the Tyrant theme is superiority. This is very similar to the construct found in the arrogant Fraudster type of impression management. The categories describe the Tyrant's behaviours such as: could not accept he was wrong, negative power, thought highly of himself and trying to prove that I was incapable.

One co-worker went into some detail over how his manager could not accept he was wrong:

> *It wouldn't matter if he didn't get something quite right he would never really accept or admit that.*

This is entirely different from managers who exude Respectful Executive Impression Management; they are open to the possibility that they could be wrong.

Possibly we have all met this Tyrant type in our previous and/or current employments. Perhaps the admission to any fault is considered to be a sign of weakness and the manager does not want to show his limitations to a co-worker. If that is the case, then the Tyrant misses out on many opportunities to show their co-workers that Tyrants may purely have a different way of getting things done. Having a slave-driver boss or colleague who does not admit his faults is a Tyrant through and through. This means he is at heart malevolent and purely interested with his power over people in the workplace.

There is a danger in recruiting managers who exhibit Tyrant Executive Impression Management as they look promising to be able to obtain high productivity. In fact they cannot keep this up precisely because they are malevolent. The idea is appealing that having a slave-driver in the company will increase effort, but it is not the case not in the long run. It produces short-term results at best, and job fatigue at worst with a high turnover rate in staff. The results that are proffered on a Tyrant's CV must be carefully checked, as often the outcomes may very well not be true or even theirs to credit. Any manager who is worth their salt will never use pressure and strong-arming to increase productivity. It can only be accomplished via the managers who use Respectful Executive Impression Management.

Negative power, another category describing the Tyrant Executive Impression Management, was shown in different ways, including bullying, trying to make colleagues feel powerless and attempting to show people as incapable. Some indicative examples of data that demonstrate the use of negative power include:

> *I would say that day, definitely he was bullying me and that's when I was so upset ...*

The bullying styles of both types of managers are discussed at length later.

Trying to prove that the co-worker was incapable is another subcategory of the construct of Superiority. Promotion is never given to those who merit; it is quite the opposite, it is bestowed upon those who curry favour with the Tyrant. They do this in all sorts of ways. Trying to expose a co-worker's faults was one strategy that one manager and her assistant manager used on this co-worker.

> *They were putting the pressure on trying to prove to me that I was incapable of being promoted.*

However, tricks like this misfire; the motive behind one co-worker's harsh treatment was seen:

> *but I think the idea was not to have me leave, but just for me not to feel I could be promoted.*

Some managers thought so highly of themselves that data in this category were mostly in vivo coded. One was described as having 'hobnobbed' with his connections:

> *I think he advised football clubs, like I think he was a legal advisor to a prominent football club that he was a member of so yeah, I'd say he hobnobbed it with ... but you know kind of full of himself and probably his connections.*

There are another three major categories to the Tyrant's feeling of superiority: being arrogant, being dismissive and abusing power.

Apparently arrogance was seen overtly despite its subtlety:

> *... it could be in subtle ways ... he was an arrogant person ... I have seen him make arrogant remarks.*

Not caring what others think was another aspect of Arrogance:

> *No I can't even say he claimed to be anything, he was just who he was and I guess that's part of the arrogance, you know, you think you know who you are and you don't really care how you are perceived outside of what your own perception of yourself is.*

Also through boasting:

> *It was always there, there was a lot of boasting going on and you always knew she had plenty of money.*

Or by wanting to be the centre of attention:

> *... and she always like to be in the limelight always liked people to look up to her and because she was mature and all of us were that much younger I think she sometimes thought she had to fight harder for that, that could always come across a bit greedy that she always had to be the one in the limelight.*

Some Tyrant managers made arrogant remarks and were excused by the recipient, as in this reference:

> *... it could be in subtle ways but not to the point I would have thought it his personality, he was an arrogant person. I wouldn't see that he was an arrogant person but I have seen him make arrogant remarks ... they were throw away lines.*

Rather than arrogance, some recipients described behaviour as dismissive, as one recipient described:

> *... he just turned around and said to me: "That's nonsense!" or "It does not!" and I thought: Hang on, I practised in that jurisdiction! He was dismissive perhaps. It's like I couldn't possibly know what I was talking about.*

One co-worker remarked about how her executive was always in control of herself and it even extended to her own family.

> *She always seemed to be the same, I mean I saw her with her family, I saw her at social functions but she always seemed the same type of person; she was always in control of herself, always in control. I've seen her with her family she's the same again, so there was no difference really.*

This demonstrates quite clearly the openness of the Tyrant's need for control. It is not covert, it is out in the open for everyone to see, and one assumes, to admire.

It was also noted how an executive could switch on 'the act' as part of her controlling ways:

> *She could be, she could switch it on when she needed to.*
>
> *Well the one example I can give you is where she has just torn one of us off to shred and then a rep would walk in and her whole being would change.*
>
> *"Hello, come in would you like a cup of tea," completely switched.*
>
> *... they [the male reps] used to come and see her anyway, but that's when you'd see a different her altogether yeah. They used to think she was wonderful, lovely. A lovely old lady. Yeah. Well she was to them.*

Abuse of power was also highlighted through actions such as having the last say and needing to always have her own way.

> *I think that she knew she had the strength in that office, she had the last say in that office. She had the power...*

And:

> *I never found out how each [upper echelon executives] participated in me having to resign, never found out. But no, to me there were no morals she would do anything to get her own way and do you know get things the way she wanted then to be.*

The data are quite explicit in their description of the Tyrant format of Executive Impression Management. It is very distinct of the hierarchy climbing Mediocre and will now be compared and discussed.

Comparison of the Two Types of Executive Impression Management the Tyrant Format and the Mediocre

First of all there appears a strong similarity between the non-fraudster managers Arrogant Fraudster and the Likeable Fraudster. All four are types are classified as malevolent. The two superior forms are the arrogant Fraudster and the Tyrant non-fraudster, and the two inferior forms are the Likeable Fraudster and the Mediocre non-fraudster manager.

Looking at the power used to control others, the non-fraudster Executive Impression Management, the Tyrant uses 'power over', while the Mediocre uses 'power under' to control. It would seem to me that Tyrants are more often found in small businesses and the Mediocres in workplaces that have a distinct hierarchy that they can climb. Of course they can occur anywhere, but the Tyrant to maintain his control of others can only do that in his own organisation and get away with it. However, I do know of cases where Tyrants are in control of departments or they head of units and their rudeness tolerated yet still supply the 'goods' in terms of employee performance.

The term slave-driver is couched in a history that is of the past, when our society had slavery and people to control them. Also I have witnessed many a Tyrant in overseas companies where human rights are at a minimum and the Tyrant form of control is admired. We delude ourselves that slave-driving is a feature of past workplaces, like the Dickensian businesses of the nineteenth century, working long hours for a pittance, but it is found in many a workplace in our modern society. The only thing is that we have done is modernised working conditions for the Tyrant to exploit.

Most employees have set work hours, and if required later than the norm are able to claim overtime as payment. In Australia, there are a myriad of work conditions that require extra payments, like working on a Sunday or a public holiday, working shifts and so on. However, none of these apply to managers; they are outside the workplace regulations – as they are agents of the employer business owner. Some professions too are outside workplace regulation, including medicine. Young doctors are subjected to horrendous working conditions often completing 36- or 48-hour shifts as interns in hospitals. They have to endure such shifts as despite their passing their medical degrees, they still have to qualify for their resident status in their internship. This has led to widespread abuse of these young doctors in many countries where no other profession is expected to work such long hours. And it leads to mistakes in hospitals as well as suicides and accidents. It makes you wonder if it were Tyrants who set up such a work design for internees, particular given the rigid thinking that has always haunted hospital consultants since they came into being over the last 150 years. Nowadays with the modernisation of the workplace there should be reforms, but as there are no changes in the US, Canada and European health professions then Tyrants must exist inside. Most would prefer to have medical treatment respectfully given by their health giver, which perhaps points to the lack of control that patients have in these workplaces.

There is one way to find out if there are Tyrants in your profession or workplace: take a look at the regulations. It is easy to evaluate them in terms of respect to the employee. A disrespectful workplace can never be dominated by Respectfuls. They are produced by those who wish to extort the maximum productivity out of their workers. The irony in the Australian workplace is that the trades and allied workers have clearly defined and highly protected work regulations; however, their organisers – trade unions – have a history of disrespect to everyone including any member who questions the system. The building unions in Australia are typically the worst and many a Royal Commission has tried to break their tyrannical hold of the construction workplace. I have belonged to unions in the UK and Canada and support decent workplace conditions, but workplace reforms were never so draconian as I found in Australia.

If Tyrants enforce such exploitation it is Mediocres that uphold it. They will do anything in their interests to do so, and not do anything otherwise. Their *raison d'être* is not to rock the boat so that they can climb up to the top. There is no point supporting changes in the workplace that make it more difficult to realise their ambitions. I came across one such manager who escaped all tests, outside scrutiny and interviews and climbed up from the lowest level in the organisation to one short of the executive class. I am not referring to a mail room boy to successful businessman type of American ideal. He was by no means an entrepreneur, a fact that he would admit himself, just an able Mediocre manager who used the internal promotion apparatus to his advantage. Last time I saw him he was out of his depth but holding on well to his position by getting tenure so nobody could touch him. His subordinates were far more able than him but it did not seem to matter in his organisation or his CEO.

This example gives some support to the Peter principle, in which Laurence Peter states: 'In a hierarchy every employee tends to rise to his level of incompetence ... in time every post tends to be occupied by an employee who is incompetent to carry out its duties ... Work is accomplished by those employees who have not yet reached their level of incompetence.'[16]

The only part of the Principle that I would qualify is that in my view Peter's humorous principle is that it does not apply to every employee, but certainly to the managers who use Mediocre Executive Impression Management.

This has special connotations to interview panels and recruiters. Often the organisation will want internal employees to apply but wish to keep the selection process fair and invite outside applicants. In doing so the internal applicant has an unfair advantage insofar that he will have more knowledge of the business by default than any other candidate. This in turn swings the panel into recruiting someone who knows rather than someone who has more merit. In fact it is my contention that giving the internal applicant the position is the result of a lazy administration, unwilling to train newcomers to the role, despite the obvious advantage that they will perform at a higher level than the internal applicant and pick up knowledge as they go along. However, lazy administrations are indicative of Mediocre managers; why change something that has worked so well for themselves?

Why is this so important? Top positions' energy cascade down the hierarchy, gives the tone of the organisation. This has been explored more recently and in a number of industries; for example, Weber looked at the automobile industries.[17] Tone at the top is seen as critical for effective moral leadership and that the organisation changes and reforms itself accordingly

16 Peter, L.J. and R. Hull (1969). *The Peter Principle: Why Things Always Go Wrong*. New York, William Morrow and Company.

17 Weber, J. (2010). 'Assessing the "tone at the top": The moral reasoning of CEOs in the automobile industry'. *Journal of Business Ethics* 92(2): 167–82.

to the leadership of the CEO and CFO. Therefore if there are CEOs that have achieved their status by using Mediocre Executive Impression Management, the organisation may lose Respectful management and certainly would allow the status quo to continue rather than change into a moral leadership. In my experience I have witnessed many managers expressing Mediocre Executive Impression Management espousing codes of ethics and so on, only to observe that in practice this is not the case. It is dangerous to assume the CEO's annual report is a reflection of who he is (as did Weber). Usually the report is not written by the CEO himself, but rather put together by the policy or Public Relations people and sent up for a signature. Of course, if the organisation is run by a CEO with Respectful Executive Impression Management the opposite would be the case, as the annual report is one way of communicating with stakeholders and shareholders the state of the organisation.

Malevolence Cascades

Recently in September 2014, we have seen the British Tesco food retailer whip up a storm of protest when their quarterly financial reports were seen to be blown out by over £250 million, thus wiping off any profit for that quarter. The new CEO, installed only a matter of weeks before the crisis, has had to suspend eight senior managers and try to desperately save Tesco's from long-term disaster in the stock market as well as in the British High Street. We can use his communications-to see if they are written from the heart or merely public relations' exercises attempting to avert further crises.

After the profit hole was revealed, he wrote in an email to staff (seen by *The Telegraph*): 'Turning our business around will require change in our culture ... We want to work in a business which is open, transparent, fair and honest.'[18] This sounds like the values of a manager giving off Respectful Executive Impression Management; now what remains to be seen is the 'walk with the talk'. If it is malevolent impression management, there will be repercussions in the workforce and the board that will spill out to the attention of the media.

18 French, L. (2014). 'Drastic Dave' takes on Tesco. *European CEO*. London, Tower Business Media.

Effect of Tyrant Executive Impression Management on Co-Workers

These data were collected from the first part of the interview of non-fraudster executive recipients, where they described what happened to them and how they felt working with a manager who gives off what it is now known as Tyrant Executive Impression Management. Whereas at the time of interview, they would have assigned labels such as an 'unfair manager' or put it down to a 'bad experience'. The constructs that emerged are time based: **Before, During** and **After;** see Figure 4.1.

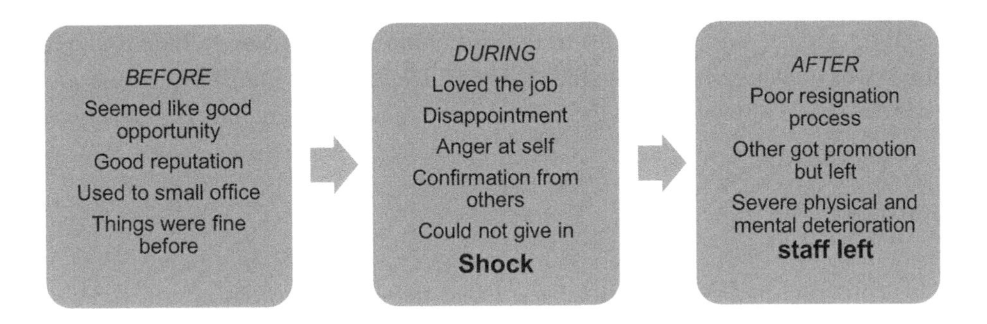

Figure 4.1 Effect of working with an Inconsistent Malevolent Executive: Their stories

Before

Before their employment commenced with the Tyrant Inconsistent Malevolent manager, the recipients reported that they thought that working with their executive seemed like a good opportunity at the time. For instance:

> *I'd always had an underlying desire to return to that environment and that profession at some point in time and there seemed like there might be an opportunity there for me*

In considering the job offer, one co-worker talked about having a good reputation prior to entry into the organisation.

> *I worked for the [previous] company for six years all told, this was the last job I did and I must have been there just over a year so I was quite well known. I had a good reputation with other managers and everything but it was the way it was all done. (reason why she wanted to leave)*

The co-workers felt compelled to explain how they got into this situation. A co-worker said that she was used to small office:

> *It was a very small firm ... since the commencement of my career, I have worked in small firms.*

And finally:

> *Things were fine. (before)*

The co-worker was hooked into the organisation by the Tyrant manager, to be used for their maximum utility to the firm. Others were already in situ when there was a change in management. But all felt that they had to demonstrate that this was a new event for them to work with a Tyrant manager.

During

This construct had several categories: loved the job, disappointment, anger at self, confirmation from others and more mature couldn't give in. In loved the job the co-workers are clear about enjoying their work, what was happening was not due to the work itself:

> *I loved the job, really enjoyed it and the clients.*

However, after working with the inconsistent malevolent manager for a while, disappointment and distress set in:

> *... but it was a disappointment because I actually liked him on first meeting.*

Feeling upset:

> *It used to really upset me because I had worked for the senior partner of a legal firm or closely with him over my career for eighteen years and I was never treated like that. So it was quite out of the ordinary and not what I was used to.*

One recipient felt self-anger being hooked in the way she was:

> *I should've realised that when I met him for coffee one time [before employment] he had little time for me.*

Some co-workers described confirmation from others including colleagues:

> *... and the strange thing is that people around knew because I would often have things said to me, 'We know what's going on', and things like that.*

It turned out that one co-worker was told that her boss had a poor reputation as an employer:

> *... one of [her employers'] friends rang, he said to me ... 'I've known him for years but my wife's known him longer and she reckons she could never work with him.'*

Being an older employee than most in the office, one co-worker said that as she was older than her other co-workers she could not give in to what was happening to her:

> *I was a mature woman. That's why I wouldn't give in you see, the other girl she was a young girl, she was probably twenty-three or something like that.*

And another felt that it was her lengthy experience that allowed her to admit when wrong, which is what her boss could not do, as we now know this is typical of Tyrant managers:

> *and I am someone that's always willing to admit when I've got something wrong. Very happy to kind of admit that and then rectify it.*

One co-worker described shock about the variability of inconsistent malevolent impression management from the senior manager:

> *... which was quite a shock given that, you know, we seemed to establish a good rapport fairly quickly. I think probably in social situations he is very personable, but on a one on one working relationship, no he wasn't.*

A separate reference mentioned this inconsistency as temporal:

Whereas I found he was, maybe he was time poor, but he seemed to get into work early and work quite hard up till lunch time and you never really knew what the afternoon would bring …

After

This construct is composed largely of data categories describing poor resignation processes, other staff left and severe physical and mental deterioration. One recipient at some length explained her resignation process:

[On Monday] I emailed him and told him that his behaviour had upset me and I was going home to think about my situation … But in the meantime I got an email from my boss on the Wednesday, because I had rung in and said I would be off for the rest of this week, I'm unwell. He emailed me the next morning and asked me what the nature of my illness was and told me it was most inconvenient that I was not there … he sent the same email again and said I hadn't responded, would I be in tomorrow? … On the Friday I emailed him and told him there was a medical note coming for the next week and that I was giving a week's notice … I [had to go] to the Advocate for Employment Issues … He paid me I think the following day.

The co-worker went on to say that she never heard from the executive again:

I never heard anything from him, he didn't respond. What can you say if you've behaved in a bad way? There's two things you can say: I'm sorry can we maybe give this another shot, you were doing a good job?" What else can you say, good riddance? You can say sorry and try to work through something or you're not going to even admit you're wrong.

Similar to the effect of the fraudster executives' impression management on staff after the revelation of the fraud, other staff left after working with their Tyrant manager. Their leaving is through considerable harm that had been exerted on them:

One of the previous people left; having counselling because she couldn't cope with how he was. One of the [other] staff members was so intimidated by him, (she was a lawyer), she ended up having counselling and leaving within about a week or two weeks.

One co-worker resigned and found out later that the favoured candidate by her Tyrant manager got promotion:

> *And of course, when I left she did get the promotion but she left a year after me, so I think the whole thing split up after that.*

In the *severe physical and mental deterioration* category, one recipient spoke of her physical and mental reaction:

> *But once I'd left my whole body came up in lumps even in the palms of my hands, I think it was just a reaction, I'd kept so much emotion in and I think I was very close to a nervous breakdown because all I wanted to do was go to bed and curl up in the foetal position.*

It also affected her badly to see workers from the office:

> *... and I wouldn't go out if I had shopping to do I would not go into the town because the office was in the town and at lunch time all the workers would be out doing their shopping, I would not go into the town at that particular time because it affected me so badly I couldn't see any of them.*

The emotional abuse that she received apparently took a long time to recover from:

> *... so it wasn't just what went on there, it was the reaction afterwards, because it took me nine months to get over it. A long time nine months before I felt safe again, and able to just go out when I felt like it and go into the town whenever I wanted to go; not when I thought it was safe to go. Yes it took nine months.*

There was only a few references from the Question section in the interviews about their manager. Out of the black cloud working for a Tyrant there was a silver lining that two co-workers felt that they had received from this experience. One co-worker felt that at least she created an ordered environment for the office, which was not there before her arrival. Another stood up to her boss and felt too that was good for her self-esteem:

> *... one of my colleagues said to me in my first week there, oh I think he's met his match.*

Negative Nuances

Unfortunately most of the data relate to negative feelings. One co-worker said she very guarded and uncomfortable when she worked with her Tyrant senior manager. This intuition turned out to be correct in light of what happened to her, as reported earlier with her mental and physical reactions. Another co-worker referred to the variance of working practice with her Tyrant manager as she was not used to lodging 'wrong' applications only correct ones. And finally, in one category a respondent explained that talking about her experience in the interview reminded her of what he did to her, when realising her face was flushed and she was showing signs of stress. Fortunately, the experience proved cathartic. The recipient reported in response to the interviewer's concerns that by the end of the interview she was feeling much better about the retelling and indeed of the whole episode. No one had taken the time to ask her in depth about her experience before my interview several years later.

This proves a point that exit interviews are very important for the recovery of a person who has suffered at the hands of a Tyrant manager. They provide a forum of validation of their experience especially if this is handled sensitively. This is in addition to the benefits of the information given as to why the resignation. Bullied targets are not all dismissed; many resign before they are pushed. However, it is still a contrived dismissal and it is an opportunity for the target to speak out. Human Resource managers tend to want to keep the peace for the organisation, but there is a duty of care to the employee to know of their rights after exit, for instance the industrial relations court as well as the civil courts for restitution.

Mediocre Managers

There was little said in the interviews about the Mediocre manager concept other than what has been covered earlier in this chapter. Their unique feature is that they are manipulative and usually quite open about it. Their inconsistencies are much more open than the disguised impression management of the fraudsters. At first the fraudsters look consistent but with the Mediocre they are openly inconsistent. They will:

- Openly have favourites.
- Be friendly one day, yet can ignore the next.

- Have strong ambition.
- Measure success in terms of rank in the hierarchy, salary and budget under control.
- Need to control others through their power 'under'.
- Apologise if needing to retain control over someone or situation.
- Lobby for self rather than organisational objectives.
- Are not respected by their co-workers as a manager, respected for rank only.
- Tend to have a CV peppered with organisational or level 'hopping'.
- Are sloppy lazy managers: allow others to run the department, business or non-profit, but highly alert and suspicious when it comes to organisational change or re-design that is not instigated by them.
- Are not self-aware. They think they are but they are not.
- Are reliable looking to the boss, but unreliable to others.

As the Mediocre manager is so underhanded, at first a co-worker can initially be taken in with the Executive Impression Management given. However, over time, and never as long as the fraudsters Executive Impression Management, the overt inconsistencies will soon show up.

Chapter 5
How to Identify a Malevolent Manager

First of all it must be stated that there is continuity in the Executive Impression Management style itself and so the Tyrant cannot change into the Respectful overnight and vice versa. This is an important point to realise, the workplace bound Executive Impression Management is characterised by innate (maybe there will be future research to prove that some of this indeed may be genetic) or purely learned social interaction. It is an ordinary part of ourselves that is so ordinary we do not notice it within ourselves.

Continuity of Executive Impression Management outside the Workplace

Goffman was quite explicit that impression management is how we react to our social world. Taking the hat off as a manager and going home to the family will not induce a different type of social interaction with others, despite the fact that many say to the contrary. Because it is so deep within us, I suspect that a Tyrant at work may equally be a Tyrant at home. I do not see evidence to counter this statement, and certainly no one has yet considered comparing these new Executive Impression Management styles with impression management outside the workplace. It would not make sense to me if a manager giving off Respectful Executive Impression Management at work took on the Tyrant style at home and vice versa. Goffman's work was interrupted by his early death, but impression management stands alone in organisational theory and therefore the Executive Impression Management typology, which is drawn from it, is equally robust. His work remains as a model, therefore the types of impression management that have been drawn from it within the workplace would indicate that there would be a continuity of impression management because it comes from the same individual. Goffman would explain that whereas the actor may give off public expression and this may be different words to what is said in private, it is not going to be markedly different in content from what was said in the two forums. A manager using Respectful Executive Impression Management will always be respectful even in private. The inconsistency would be that he says something disrespectful in private. If that happens the Respectful manager is fooling himself. He is not a Respectful, but probably a Mediocre manager.

Blowing off steam is one context where it could be expected that a manager could utter disrespectful sayings. And we all tend do this when faced with seemingly implacable opponents. However, the opponent is still to be respected because overestimating his worth spreads fear. Underestimating, which is more often the case, creates superiority over a person who has every right to be valued, even if it is in negative terms. If the opponent is respected then there is a fair chance of the interaction succeeding to obtain mutually agreeable objectives. Taking time out to think options through and thinking from the other person's position is far more preferable than ranting or raving to another, although we all do it at different times in our lives. Trained negotiators always treat their targets with respect using trading to reward good behaviour. For instance, in a hostage-taking incident, the negotiations will be about what the perpetrator needs rather than telling him what an idiot he is. This is respect working; no other emotion can create the same results.

A useful template to use in such circumstances of analysing an opponent is the CAT model. Briefly, there are three dimensions to our emotional life. The first is Connection, secondly Appreciation and finally Trust. When we meet someone new, we instantly try to find a connection between ourselves; later, as that connection grows, appreciation of the other person's qualities are quantified, and finally trust grows between the two parties. The positive emotions are Respect or love if we are talking about closer personal relationships, joy or rewards if in the workplace, and confidence as trust grows. The negative emotions are tied at the opposite end of each dimension. Therefore anger is the opposite emotion to love or respect, sadness which leads to envy and greed is the opposite of joy and valuing someone for who they are, and lastly, fear is the opposite of confidence. So respectfully, using this model, a hostage negotiator has to turn the emotion of anger into respect for the individual. While it is never a good thing to lie to someone like this, it is far better to find common ground. Saying things like 'I respect your beliefs', or 'you need to better yourself, or to make yourself heard' are all respectful statements. Appreciating the qualities on both sides is an excellent way to grow enough trust to create a situation to hand over the hostage and in return the hostage taker is received into custody.

Similarly, we can use the CAT model to create a common ground with a malevolent manager. Assessing the manager in these terms will allow the manager to feel comfortable enough to talk about the behaviour at hand.

We must remember that impression management is our outward response to the world that we find ourselves in. It does not exist when we are alone. Therefore a manager may have low self-esteem and does not know it, but in response to others there will be a continuous show of what the person thinks that is required. The low self-esteem may not come out at all to anyone, depending if the individual wishes to maintain secrecy or even 'unknowingness' about the esteem issue. A doctor who is treating you for some ailment is not going to give off impression management about his low self-esteem in that role. The role forces the stereotype of confidence to be exhibited to the patient.

The only way we can truly detect self-esteem is when the role-playing breaks down, which is hardly likely in the five-minute consultations that we have with our general practice medical community. There is an old joke about the last thing you want to hear your brain surgeon say in the middle of your operation is 'Ooops!', which exemplifies that the impression management has to be all embracing. However, the doctor's co-workers will pick up on any discrepancies however slight and however small, and it will be noted and retained as 'unusual'. This will present as an inconsistency, which may be remembered later when it is necessary to review the performance with others. The review can be around the water cooler in the office type of chat, or a performance review, either way, if it is made known to the individual there is an adjustment to be made internally to deal with this now public characteristic.

This can give rise to the psychological pressure of cognitive dissonance within the individual.[1] The idea is that the discordance felt about what is meant to be as regards to what it actually is will create increasing pressure until one day the gap between reality and idealism is so large to be uncontainable and causes a crisis. When reality hits the individual and a fault has to be accepted, it really hurts and causes much upset within.

To give a personal example of this, nearly 20 years ago I was receiving counselling regarding my adoption and trying to recover from the emotional negativity from the break between my mother and me. Innocently, I asked my therapist was there anything else that I should look out for to deal with, as we had gone over some quite intense counselling. She looked at me intently and

1 Festinger, L. (1962). 'Cognitive dissonance'. *Scientific American* 207(4): 93–102.

said 'Adoptees don't trust.' My reaction was 'Of course I trust!' I knew that this was such a fundamental behaviour and I was appalled that she said that to me. I proceeded to give many instances of my trust in others, including attending to difficult issues. My therapist said quietly: 'You don't trust. What you are referring to is relatively superficial, deep down you do not trust people.' I went away and reflected on this for hours on end. Of course I trust people, I justified, I couldn't do my job as a CEO if I didn't trust anyone!

About the same time another wise soul came briefly into my life and mentioned that I do not trust men in or outside work. I felt the same shock. If two people are saying this about me then it has to be true, whether I liked it or not. My self-image was of confidence in others that they would be trustworthy and I easily trusted them. But the reality came to me as quite a shock: these people were right. They had given me a chance to see myself as I truly was. I had a glimpse into my Shadow, and it was not very nice to see. It was a dark place and I was crouching in a corner to protect myself. Cognitive dissonance is not a good feeling at all. I cried and cried in my emotional crisis. This could not be me, but I had to accept it as true – two outsiders saying the same thing was not a coincidence. I was highly motivated to change, as previously my life was miserable and I did not want to go back to that again.

After a while when I became calm, I realised I had to change this, and there was only one way to do it. I began to deconstruct my daily actions, and slowly piece together what was trustful and what was not. Slowly I became more trusting, until years later I feel confident that the outward appearance of me is harmonious with my internal me, that I can trust.

In a workplace the same thing can happen; there can be a breakdown for a person when he realises that what he thought what he was is true is not. The reality is far different. Confronting a workplace behaviour like this has to be done sensitively, and most co-workers will avoid it. Sometimes this will be due to embarrassment, other times it will be due to lack of respect for that person and so on. Many people would not want to deal with the cognitive dissonance breakdown that I had in their office and at best would send the person home, as this, they would say, is not a workplace issue.

Of course they are entirely wrong to do this as it is a workplace matter. Inconsistencies in behaviour are a warning bell to other issues, namely fraud or being malevolent to use the organisation for their own needs. If it is disregarded it is like leaving the office door unlocked at night so that any passer-by can walk in and steal computers and other valuables. When a manager sees a co-worker go through dissonance shock, it is imperative to assist in whatever way possible. Many large organisations have employee assistance plans whereby an employee can receive counselling from trained therapists about their issues. Other organisations may consider paying for outside help or consultants. It is a sign of respect for a co-worker to be assisted in this manner. After all, it is not only the employee who benefits but the company does. A truly reformed co-worker is a good member of the organisation and therefore loyalty, trustworthiness and energy will return. Furthermore, the assistance will never be forgotten by other co-workers and trust is increased.

Managers who use Respectful Executive Impression Management are consistent and kind to everyone equally. They do not put themselves above others, neither do they manipulate. They also have no favourites. Reports from upline managers saw these qualities as well as subordinates. Goffman's consistency was clearly identified. It was only the malevolent managers who were inconsistent. They used subterfuges, blaming and excuses to disguise what they were doing. The malevolent managers came out in the study, clear as daylight, in both data sets the free-fall answers to describe what happened to the semi-structured question components. It was only with these types emerging that the next step of describing a core process could work.

Importance of the Non-fraudsters in the Core Process

By interviewing co-workers of non-fraudsters I struck gold. Not often this happens in research of either type, qualitative or quantitative. If omitted their non-fraudster managers' data into the mix of deconstructed utterances the core process would have been at best led to the identification of two types of fraudster managers. However, with the non-fraudster managers co-workers interviews, the total core process emerged.

The two themes or factors to the core process are the consistency of impression management and the demonstration of power through the giving off or expressing process of impression management to others. Consistency is the most important factor to watch for; the type of manager being observed is further identified by the use of 'power over' or 'power under'.

The Consistency of Respectful Executive Impression Management

Consistency is about walking the talk. A manager who changes his mind about planning, direction, customer service and so on can be still consistent in his impression management and therefore is benign.

With the Respectful Executive Impression Management the situation is defined through a power relationship of equality. The benign impression management's use of power with others is reported as:

> *… he bases them on their own merits and treats everyone equally.*

This treatment is respectful and invites reciprocation from the recipient's own free will:

> *Especially in work like this you wouldn't know that he was the boss. He treats the receptionist the same way he treats his [business] partner. So everyone is easy. Which is nice.*

Equality marks the benign relationship, which in turn induces the control mechanism of consensual voluntary reciprocation:

> *He can be, [persuasive] if he wants something done. I won't say overly, he does it in a nice way.*

Consensual, participative reciprocation, therefore, marks the power of Respectful Executive Impression Management, which co-workers readily enjoy and perform their duties.

Consistent Respectful Executive Impression Management managers employ equality as their control mechanism and rely on consensual voluntary reciprocation. It is a powerful methodology for managing others. This is something that is lost upon malevolent managers who resort to abusive tactics to force others to do what they want to do.

Consistency is present when a new employee feels immediately comfortable with the manager. The work relationship is then established and it does not fail, despite everything. Consistency is seen in a married couple who have been together through thick and thin. One spouse may be angry, saddened or even fearful of one partner's behaviour at times, but this is always quickly dealt with effective conflict resolution and negative feelings disappear fast.

The bottom line is that the couple love each other at a deep level and they know it and therefore value it and maintain the relationship. Each partner can rely on the other's behaviour, knowing that it is consistency that allows trust to develop. This is the secret to managing others using Respectful Executive Impression Management.

Similarly in the workplace the relationship between a consistent manager and a co-worker is able to develop. How can you tell if it is consistency that you feel? The markers are that the manager trusts the co-worker in his competencies and skill sets. After all, that was what the selection process was all about.

When a manager exhibiting Respectful Executive Impression Management makes mistakes he will apologise. With the co-worker making mistakes (we all do) the manager is able to correct without destroying the relationship. This is very important for at least half the population if we are to believe the research on the Myers Briggs Test Inventory. Without going into too much detail, the MBTI tests four dimensions. There is one dimension that looks at how we make decisions: is it on values or is it because of logic? Half the population does it on logic, and the other half make decisions on their values. The latter half tends to be women, but not always. If a person who is mocked for making a mistake, or otherwise devalued, it will hurt that person considerably. The 'Thinking' half, which does include some women, will shrug their shoulders and use logic to accept their error. If they are humiliated for the error, it will hurt whereas the 'Feeling' individuals it will be seen as an attack on their value. It would be like the classroom where a child would be asked what is two plus two: if he answers four, all is well. If he answers three, then the teacher explains why this is wrong, using logic. The teacher is less likely in this early class to shout and scream at the child that morons can add up such an easy sum, than in later classes. So logic becomes acceptable to understand mistakes at an early stage in life to half of the population at least.

This differentiation in attitude to mistakes came to me early in life. At one primary school that I attended, we had an unfortunate child who was less able than the rest of us to cope with arithmetic. I witnessed the humiliation of this poor boy time and time again. He didn't understand and he failed to advance. In those days, if we got something wrong continually we were caned for it. And this poor lad would be whipped on his hand by the teacher on many occasions. If we go forward 50 years or so, that humiliation was still with me. When I caught up with an old school mate from that time, I asked him what happened to the boy. Not much news to be said, but I was quite intrigued that the school friend did not remember the canings to the extent that I did. In fact he shrugged it off saying that was school in the old days, fairly normal behaviour on the part of the teacher. Being caned for mistakes was rationalised as a part of our social history, and no big deal. For me, my internal values of fairness and sympathy to others was transgressed, and stayed with me for a very long time.

Personally I detest being told I have made a mistake, it goes against my sense of harmony and peace, which I prefer as a MBTI Feeling type. I have learned to fight the response of sending out my dragon to defend me breathing fire and brimstone. Even so, it is still heartfelt when I make a mistake. I still hope to be without fault. Clinging to perfection is idiotic, I know that now, but then I could not accept that I am a fallible human being. It is far better for me to accept my faults, rectify them and carry on in life.

Inconsistency with Tyrant Executive Impression Management

I held one director role where I had an open door policy. Anyone could come in and I would give my time to them, despite the fact that it interrupted my work. Later I have come to realise that this was not a satisfactory work methodology but not for the following reason. One afternoon, a technical manager strode into my office and started to rant about something that I was changing, because I was streamlining departmental policy. Many down the hallway heard his shouting, and one or two came to look at what was going on as they went to refill their coffee cups. Everything I said did not calm him down, and at one point I thought he was going to have a heart attack as he was so red in the face with his bellowing. Finally he stopped hurling abuse at me and left my office. People scuttled away out of his path to avoid any further confrontation. It was devastating for me; I lost confidence in my work and wanted to go home early but I could not allow him that victory. However, his violence had hurt me deeply.

I have been on radio chat shows and once talked about this problem in the workplace. The stories that came back were horrifying. If I thought I was hard done by, others' accounts were far worse. There seemed to be many Tyrants out there who consider that it is their right to abuse others. In the study the co-workers who worked with the Tyrant were equally abused with violence manifested when things were going wrong.

Later on, I raised this event in a management communications class, and asked what people would do; even the lecturer was at a loss. Looking back, it may have been better to not have the intensification by asking him to come back later once he was cooled down. However, I believe that my small frame was not suitable to stand up to this tall muscled man who had clearly lost his head. And the fact that he entered my office with malice was unstoppable. He was not reprimanded by his upline manager; everyone carried on as usual. He was a manager using the Tyrant Executive Impression Management to his benefit and got away with it. He never returned to apologise; he probably didn't even think of doing it.

Those hostile people who storm the office and shout and abuse people destroy relationships wherever they tread. In fact, they are not interested in other's relationships with them at all, they just want to have their own needs satisfied immediately. It is the ultimate act of selfishness to act like this in a business. And it is no wonder why co-workers hide from such management, preferring to get on with their jobs rather than incur the wrath of the Tyrant. And so it becomes entrenched as a myth of the organisation to be good by doing everything that the boss wants, or else. The inconsistency of this management style is glaring. The co-worker is either good or bad, and the manager will react accordingly. One point to be noted is that the focus is on the co-worker's behaviour, never the manager's.

The Inconsistency of Mediocre Executive Impression Management

Inconsistency with those managers who use Mediocre Executive Impression Management is quite different. These managers are the arch-manipulators in the workplace. The co-workers recognised that there was manipulation going on; the problem was it seemed unstoppable as well. These managers will give false advice – something that I had to deal once when I was asking my upline manager, who was an academic, to which tertiary education programme should I apply to.

I was told a lot of rubbish and even though it did not seem right, he was a recognised authority in his field was so well known that I meekly followed his advice. I could say that I wasted three years on this 'good' programme, but I cannot say that, as there were a couple of outstanding lecturers who gave us a good foundation of philosophy and an understanding of advanced statistics. There were also a couple of students who questioned everything when they didn't understand, as they were happy to put their heads up above the parapet. I remain indebted to those four people today. This knowledge has stayed with me, and if it wasn't for them I would not have been able to conduct this study and employ a research methodology that has resulted in the emergence of

Executive Impression Management. The advice turned out to be a bonus to me, only because I made it so. It certainly did not enhance my career prospects as no one particularly cared about the qualification I would have received. The programme crumbled on its own, and upon reflection I believe that I was counselled to go there to increase the numbers to assist a colleague in making the programme a success. Therefore, it was never advice for me; it was advice to assist his friend. The fact that I benefited from it was pure serendipity.

These managers manipulate to hold their 'power under' people. To find out that you have been manipulated in a work situation may leave you feeling exhausted and angry, but basically it is the same truth: that seemingly wonderful manager has tricked you covertly into behaviour that suited him and you were 'sucked in'. This destroys all trust and once that goes it can never go back to the relationship that used to be.

When faced with inconsistency people feel that they are treading on thin ice. They don't know where the danger is, although they are aware of something wrong. The individual may make it to the other side of the pond, but it can be at a high cost. What usually happens is that the inconsistent manager trains others to be inconsistent. They use carrots to entice others into following their behaviour.

There can be collusion about conferences. For example, 'Do what I say and you can go to this conference', which is made even more attractive being at a holiday destination. I have seen this many times. One classic case happened to me when the federal government invited community leaders to a meeting to one of our capital cities. I was invited along, gave my input into the policies that were being considered by the government personnel and left on the first flight out. It will not come as a surprise that the government ignored our input entirely, and that some members became co-opted into the government's stand. They were invited to sit on special committees to assist the prime minister in making the retrograde policies. Considering that I actually have a master's in social policy, it beggars belief that these committees were to do real work. Sitting on a PM's committee is extremely career-enhancing as well as fattening of the wages packet. I may sound bitter to the reader – I am not, I accept that this is the way of many managers out there who see no fault in these types of actions. The puppets in this scenario remained so until they were ditched a couple of years later as they had no further use.

Recognising that these methods are that of the Mediocre Executive Impression Management, it is the best tool that one could have to understand the real game that is played. The government wanted to introduce a new and regressive policy. They made it seem like they consulted with community leaders, put them in a five-star hotel and allowed the device of 'listening to the community' to be played out. The problem is that these tricks do not work in the long term, and the new programme was kicked out by a new government who reformed it without reference to the community to become borderline punitive. This is the difference between Mediocre and Tyrant Executive Impression Management; the latter government immediately went ahead and implemented its new regime without consultation, the Mediocres used their power more covertly to control the process to obtain their outcomes.

I have used the above example of what can happen at an inter-organisational level, but I have seen this same exercise repeatedly within organisations, as well as upper management consulting with unions and staff associations mulling over new policies or contracts. The employee representatives may receive many perks in order to co-opt them into their schemes and to introduce a new workplace contract. Some may say that this is not actions of a particular social interaction typology but rather it is plain corruption. The outcome is the same; the corrupters are those who wish to have power over others and use money as ways of getting it.

A consistent manager will lay the terms of the conference 'carrot'; this will always be in terms of performance (past or intended) for the organisation not to the manager himself. A consistent manager gives rewards to those who serve well; an inconsistent manager hands out such carrots for service to him. If you are faced with such a carrot, then remember you are not a donkey and refuse the ploy and do not play along to any other games that the manager wishes you to partake. The result will be that he will shun you and you will end up treading water in some area that is non-career advancing. This is, however, far better than becoming a management toady.

I have seen such toadies end up in CEO positions and have always marvelled how on earth they get there. The answer is simple, of course; the selection panel was predominately made up of similar Mediocre toadies, and select 'the right candidate' for the rewards that the new CEO will hand out later. The recruiter who is of similar style anticipates new work in replacing others who do not suit the new incumbent's way of doing things. The other panel members may be suppliers or customers of the new CEO, all of whom have a vested interest in selecting the right person for themselves, not the organisation. The chairman of the board who is present in the interview may also want such a groveller, and so on. It truly is in the world of managers who exhibit Mediocre Executive Impression Management a case of: 'You scratch my back and I will scratch yours.'

Favouritism is of course naturally inconsistent. We all like to be liked and to get along in this world, but cronyism is a double-edged sword. Today's favourite maybe tomorrow's outcast, and everyone who is clued into the arts of Mediocre Executive Impression Management (Machiavelli wrote the seminal book on this)[2] will know that useful people will be put under the manipulator's wing until his usefulness runs out. At that point he will be dropped as another more useful candidate comes across the 'benefactor's' path. Many have said that patronage has to take place so that artists for instance must be freed from employment to do their art. This was particularly so in the times of Michelangelo and Da Vinci with the courts of Florence, Sienna and Venice. Despite the peak of art obtained, it was still a rich man's pleasure and art was used to demonstrate the royal families' power and success to others. Art did not become the people's prerogative until much later, apart from craftsmen who plied their particular trade in ceramics, jewellery, fabrics and so on. We do not have evidence that people strayed from patronage in defiance, but rather the opposite where the highest patron of the land, for instance the Pope demanded the best artistic work from Michelangelo hence the Sistine Chapel's ceiling which took over four years to complete and has been marvelled at ever since. Patronage networks were important to lead to success, which has been mapped by sociologists since then.[3]

Using the more pejorative word of cronyism,[4] there is a small literature on this malevolent behaviour. There are two types of cronyism: vertical between superior and subordinate, and also horizontal, for instance between like-minded individuals to promote a particular aim. Both forms are unethical yet abound in organisations around the world. I remember one career adviser saying that if you jumped off the work train you would de-rail your career, no matter what the reason was for the action, his point being that out of the network an individual would be forgotten. This is somewhat hard to swallow when illness, study or maternity leave takes you out of the organisation. It is also extremely difficult for parents taking parental leave, usually the mother, and returning to work to find that her position had been downgraded or sidelined due to her

2 Machiavelli, N. (1992). *The Prince*. Boston, W.W. Norton.

3 McLean, P. (2007). *The Art of the Network: Strategic Interaction and Patronage in Renaissance Florence*. Durham, NC, Duke University Press.

4 Khatri, N. and E.W.K. Tsang (2003). 'Antecedents and consequences of cronyism in organizations'. *Journal of Business Ethics* 43(4): 289–303.

absence. When I researched women manager's unemployment[5] many women spoke of similar stories. It demonstrates to me that cronyism is alive and well in many organisations and that they must be run by managers using Mediocre Executive Impression Management.

Treating co-workers with inconsistency is soul destroying and should never be tolerated by anyone in the workplace. Everyone deserves respect no matter who they are; their rank in the hierarchy; no matter how junior or senior they may be.

If the individual is unable to trust his manager then consistent impression management is absent. Also if the manager exudes malevolence to others then it is time to leave because you do not know when it will be your turn for such conduct.

Some people think that they can outwit their manager. This will be mostly not possible as the manager can only be openly inconsistent when support for his behaviour is supported by overt or tacit agreement by others. So any tactic on your part will be ignored or worse still leave you open to be attacked even more. When faced with a manager who uses Mediocre Executive Impression Management remember that he represents the whole organisation, as no upline manager who exhibits Respectful Executive Impression Management would tolerate such nonsense.

The major problem is that this type of manager will confuse you. When you are face to face he will offer you 'respect' and you will accept, reciprocate and feel comfortable. However, the moment your back is turned then the back-stabbing will begin, particularly if he views you as a threat to his position. I have two small scars on my shoulders from removal of moles and I often joked that these are the scars I have received at the hand of such a manager. Like my medically induced scars, the emotional scars last forever if healing does not take place.

Back-stabbing is emotional abuse. It is disrespectful and divisive. If you are faced with a manager saying such things about another, it is up to you to confront the abuse, or more commonly as people do not like confrontation, they will ignore and walk away. A friend may inform you of what is happening, but most times it will come as a nasty surprise when you find out the real opinion of

5 Sheridan, T. (2005). Voicing women managers' unemployment experience in Australia. *The Hidden Toll*. Perth, WA, Women Chiefs of Enterprises International, 1–100.

the manager. In the words that you will hear, disrespect is absent, diminution of your skills and abilities will be said, and scorn will be cast on your work.

Again, I have had this scenario played out on me. I was informed one Friday that the staff wanted a meeting with the chairman of the board with me present on Monday morning. I sweated all through the weekend, but I had no idea what was to come. The chairman had arranged a mutiny; my staff ambushed me and I was asked to resign. It came as quite a shock as I had absolutely no idea that this was going to happen. I knew that there were some issues in the organisation that had to be dealt with, but the organisation was thriving, becoming profitable under my aegis and strategies to win extra contracts had been very successful. I was brought in to save them, and within 18 months I had. Others in the industry honoured such a good result and our organisation was back on the map. I had no intention of leaving, everything was good. Then the manager (the chairman) who was using Mediocre Executive Impression Management put the knife in my back. I left the organisation under a cloud. Some of my staff thought that I must have stolen money as in 15 minutes I was shuffled out of the front door. It was a hideous experience and I could have had a nervous breakdown if it wasn't for my own self-belief and very good friends. This may be an extreme example, but it happens, so it is advisable that any manager who demonstrates this type of impression management is to be avoided at all costs.

I have heard individuals say 'Well at least I know what the manager is truly like, and if you know you are playing with a tarantula then at least you are safe'. Do not fall into this spider's trap because a person not playing their game will get shunted aside or out. I have tried this myself so I feel for the individual who commits to this type of action. If you are not prepared to be equally dangerous to the manager then you will lose and most likely lose badly. I had a shop that was ram-raided by my particular tarantula but having no proof whatsoever I could only give the police my suspicions. And of course the perpetrator got away with it. Occasionally I see bits of my shop reappear but this is many years later, but at least I knew I was right. Pyrrhic victories aside, tarantulas are clever and don't leave such things as evidence lying around. That is why threats are given quietly when no one else is around to witness. It will be your word against his and you will lose due to his power base, whether it be thugs as in my case, or the manager's colleagues or board, in others.

I have also witnessed employees play fire with fire and hold information that would be deleterious to the manager concerned. I always advise that the individual should take it to higher authorities and/or the police if it is illegal activity. Otherwise it is blackmail and the magic of being a blackmailer will soon wear off as the manager starts to plot to get his own back, that is, firing you by usually someone else's hand. Thankfully I have never tried this, but I know others who had done so and paid the ultimate price of becoming unemployed at a mature age. Then the résumé gets truly messy and finding another job will be extremely difficult despite the innocence of the wrongly fired person. The bottom line is don't sink as low as your manager. The best way to deal with this is through leaving but this can only be done if there is another job to go to.

You will know consistency when you see it. It is like a harmony that rings between both of you. This is not about sexual attraction, it is about having similar ideas, goals and aspirations and wanting to do your best for the organisation's sake. That harmony is sought after in this violent world, it is the sound that you need to hear in a job interview and when you enter the workplace and stay there years, as it is the right place for you. It is like your own soul scattered through the organisation when there is harmony, you hear the beautiful sounds and see yourself in so many co-workers. It is a joy to behold. For those lucky people who work in such organisations, please appreciate the rarity of what you have, as millions of others suffer in the workplace and would dearly love to have what is your daily endowment.

Now and then you will come across pockets of consistent managers in larger organisations existing in a microcosm within a workplace full of negativity. Cherish this manager as it means that you are safe as long as he is. Soon as you see threatening behaviour towards this manager it is time to leave, and advising the manager also is the best thing to do. Separation from the general negativity can be by virtue of distance, specialisation or operation. The consistent manager will excel in his job and thereby become a focus of attention by the inconsistent manager's upline or even their colleagues. Head office does not want one area to shine above the rest. It is not without some consideration that these managers are named malevolent, and having someone else show them up for their inefficiencies is a beacon that needs to be extinguished.

Consistency means that the manager will take a natural interest in growing his staff. This can be highly expensive training or it can be an afternoon spent with a particular customer with problems. This is a manifestation of trust so that manager's investment will not only pay off for the organisation but will pay off for the employee concerned. Inconsistent managers by their own selfishness will not give out training haphazardly; it is all to do with carrots and sticks to a contingent of co-opted staff.

Similarly promotion will be a competitive process with a consistent manager. This is due to the fact that the manager is not interested in cronies upstairs but the best that is available for the position. Outside hiring is possible or it can be done internally; whichever is the case, the basis for the selection is on merit, the best person for the job. This includes affirmative action goals and positive discrimination policies that look out for individuals of talent that would otherwise be dismissed for promotion. A consistent manager would want this process: malevolent managers will not, as their world is divided into a 'them and us'; and they distrust anyone who is not of the same gender or ethnic origins. If the world was composed of 80 per cent benign consistent managers, instead of the other way round, we would have a far less of a problem with discrimination, as it means that the employment recruitment process is based on who is best for the job through identifiable evidence.

Power is not about titles and invested authority. I have seen receptionists rule the roost over a largely ineffective staff. It is all about what the co-worker perceives. The receptionist was able to keep her dominance as the rest of the (small) organisation had different tasks to do and no one was there to operationalise the service. Thus the receptionist had power over the intake service to make appointments to incoming clients. She reigned for a long time and I think she is still there. Was this just her commitment to the underfunded NPO? She was praised many times for her dedication by others who did not have to work with her. It was not devotion to duty, as basically her dominance was self-serving. Without going into details she was playing out her anger against a particular section of society and got paid for doing so. There were huge differences in how she operated depending on the client. She had favourites, she bullied in a passive aggressive way, the lot. She was overtly a 'soft mamma' but inside was a heart of ice. She was deprived in her growing up and took her vengeance upon others. This may sound like a very harsh judgement to say, but it was true. And it is also true that despite my resignation from that organisation I have developed compassion for her. Life was cruel to her and in turn she played out the role of punishment upon others unwittingly. However, it does not undo the harm that she has done.

They Know it is Wrong

An interesting observation is that all the malevolent managers chose to adopt the benign characteristics of the Respectful Executive Impression Management; the two types of fraudsters did this to commit fraud and to keep on doing so for a long time. Eventually their façade began to crack under the pressure of time. Imagine a juggler trying to juggle balls in the air. He may not be able to do so hour after hour, it would be too hard to keep up the activity of juggling. The fraudulent managers appear benign, particularly to those who must not suspect their fraudulent activity. And despite different ways of handling employees, they will put on the act if they want to do so. Over time these cracks that appear are considered as oddities and co-workers dismiss these events for just that, seeing the aberrations in the manager's impression management as quirks or idiosyncrasies.

The other two types the Tyrant and the Mediocre Executive Impression Management managers also adopt the benign aspects of Respectful Executive Impression Management, but in their case, it is done openly. The Tyrant's co-workers saw these managers as being nice to clients, and indeed to themselves when they first arrived. One manager was reported as openly recruiting in another organisation, and it was a matter of wooing the person over to work with him. Soon as that happened he dropped the façade; after all, she was working for him now, and need not be worried about her leaving. In this case the treatment doled out was highly abusive and affected the co-worker for several years afterwards, losing confidence in her skills and questioning her judgement. She saw what he did with clients and reported that he was like two different people to his staff. With clients he selectively wined and dined to get their custom. When he returned after the business lunches she would be fearful of which type of person was going to enter the business front door. As long as there were no potential clients around he was openly malevolent to all and sundry including members of his family.

The managers who use Mediocre Executive Impression Management, however, operate in a similar fashion. A respectful front was put on when it was necessary. To understand this further, these managers are openly competitive and have ambition. Therefore they will spend an inordinate amount of time 'buttering up' those employees who may be of use in their upward climb. They also are good networkers, and will use any opportunity to use their network whenever possible. This networking activity is not confined to the managers using the Mediocre type of Executive Impression Management; Respectfuls and the Tyrants will do the same but for different ends. The Tyrant forms would use this to gain clients, to get people to spend money with them. The fraudsters however have little need, as their focus is on how to steal money from their organisation and to cover their tracks. There was reporting of one particular Arrogant fraudster who sat on many committees, but this was not leverage to obtain higher positions, it was merely a celebration of her own superiority; she had no intention to leave her major source of income. Similarly, the fraudulent managers would have friends of their own, but again it was to act the big spender, rather than to use others get to the top. It can be imagined that such spending and ostentation would attract the Tyrant and Mediocre types of managers, but the Mediocre are more interested in rank rather than spending power. A millionaire is of no use to them if they are not part of some organisation of power and control. In the old days this would be the Church or the landed gentry who retained control; a good reference from either would have stood a manager who uses Mediocre Executive Impression Management very well. Charles Dickens described such a character in David Copperfield. Uriah Heep was shown to be full of sickening humility, sycophancy and insincerity, an ugly character indeed. However, most managers who use the Mediocre Executive Impression Management will be far more clever in their obsequious ways to lull a false sense of awe to upper managers and chairmen who hold the strings of power to upline management recruitment in organisations.

If these malevolent managers know how to appear like the managers who exhibit Respectful Executive Impression Management, a question remains as to why they choose not to be like them. After all, if you go through all the charade of how to look good to others, you may as well become one. The answer to this difficult question lies in my own experience as I have only my clients to draw from and I do not wish to use their confidential information.

I have admitted earlier that I know the Mediocre Executive Impression Management type well, as I used to do it. I did this as I thought that this was the way the world worked. I was such a good networker that I felt like I was a vampire going from one event to another in order to meet good contacts. I used to keep a file on these contacts and retain information like their birthdays and so on. I never was terribly good on the file keeping, and it turned out that there are so many shifts in management that it was hard to keep up anyway. At one point, Australia became notorious for its high turnover of CEOs and their non-performance[6] so it was a difficult task to keep track of.

Also I cannot say any of that did me real good anyway. As I went through my recovery and realised what Respectful Executive Impression Management meant I changed my ways. But why did I do this? Apart from the business literature and self-help books of how to be successful, I always took the position that if I was to be successful it meant a high status job. My own drive was related to my separation from my mother as a baby, and that rejection marked

6 Gallagher, D.R. (2004). 'Top management turnover: An analysis of active Australian investment managers'. *Australian Journal of Management* 29(2): 243–74.

my life for over 40 years. For me to be rejected was the worst pain of all, yet I set myself up for rejection time and time again by competing for jobs that were beyond my capabilities, having an inflated sense of my abilities. This was not from a bombastic point of view. I am a very quick learner and knew that given a break I could rise to the job. However, there are not many employers who would take such a risk and particularly these days, as employers will only contract a certain skill set and that is it. Whereas I believed that I could learn on the job, no one else did. The days of the rise from the mail room to CEO have long gone.

Consistent and Authentic Benign Power

If the impression management is inconsistent the recipients' perception is of inequitable power and accordingly, view malevolence towards themselves or other co-workers. This malevolence is seen as divisive, abusive and citing that the executives working to their own needs, rather than those of the organisation.

The only type that is perceived as authentic is the Respectful Executive Impression Management. The recipients' phrase 'What you see is what you get' about the manager in question is a modern way of talking about authenticity. The concept of the Respectful certainly demonstrates support for what is implied by authentic leadership; as Etizioni[7] explains that authenticity is where the outward appearance and the underlying structure are both responsive to human needs. This is supported in the Respectful type; whereas inauthenticity is unresponsive and an institutional front is maintained instead is similar to where the recipients found disparities in the malevolent form. Being authentic is also linked with high self-esteem[8] which was also reflected in the recipients' descriptions of the consistent benign impression management showing respect for and encouraging others.[9] Authentic leaders have also been found to be self-confident, self-aware, reliable and trustworthy.[10] Nonetheless, Ilies et al. advise that: 'However, instances may exist where expressing one's true self results in severe social sanctions, or where projecting a powerful image of one's

7 Etzioni, A. (1968). 'Basic human needs, alienation and inauthenticity'. *American Sociological Review* 33(4): 870–85.

8 Kernis, M.H. (2003). 'Optimal self-esteem and authenticity: Separating fantasy from reality'. *Psychological Inquiry* 14(1): 83–9.

9 Avolio, B.J., W.L. Gardner, F.O. Walumbwa, F. Luthans and D.R. May (2004). 'Unlocking the mask: A look at the process by which authentic leaders impact follower attitudes and behaviors'. *The Leadership Quarterly* 15(6): 801–23.

10 Ilies, R., F.P. Morgeson and J.D. Nahrgang (2005). 'Authentic leadership and eudaemonic well-being: Understanding leader–follower outcomes'. *The Leadership Quarterly* 16(3): 373–94.

true self requires monitoring behaviors for the purpose of self-presentation.'[11] Interestingly, the participants in this study did not observe these two situational responses in the Respectful Executive Impression Management, although several recipients observed that problem clients received short shrift from the executive. Losing some income may not be the serious social sanction that Ilies et al. implied, but whistle-blowers go ahead regardless of social sanctions and pay an enormous personal price to do so: 'In a year-long discussion group of 12 whistle-blowers, all but one lost both his or her job and career, eight lost their homes, seven lost their families, and many suffered from alcoholism and depression at some point after blowing the whistle.'[12] There is therefore some doubt whether the situation of severe social sanctions would actually impinge on Respectful Executive Impression Management to any degree. As for self-monitoring of behaviours in order to modify the impression management, this was observed by two recipients of non-fraudster executives who did not give off Respectful Executive Impression Management in any case. It would seem likely that the Respectful Executive Impression Management does not change under stress or circumstance. One recipient in the study worked with her executive for over 14 years and remarked that there was little change in his impression management, only becoming slightly introverted for a period after a marriage breakdown.

This introversion is explained by the inversion of the individual's MBTI. An extravert will become reclusive under enormous stress. In this case, it was a separation and subsequent divorce of the manager. Note though that the Executive Impression Management remains the same, the manager is reported only as being quieter, not malevolent.

Authenticity therefore is not present for the inconsistent malevolent types. Kernis[13] pointed out that authenticity does not come about through a desire to be real, but is more about the freedom of expressing the self. This observation does fit with the Respectful concept that emerged. It may have developed out of the self-awareness construct of Respectful Executive Impression Management, which is lacking in malevolent managers. There appears to be little self-awareness from the inconsistent malevolent types of Executive Impression Management that was given off to the co-workers of either group, fraudster and non-fraudster executives.

11 Ibid., 380.

12 Clements, L. (2005). 'Whistleblowing: Who, what, when, where, why and how?' *Journal of Forensic Accounting* 6(2): 429–40, at 429.

13 Kernis, M.H. (2003). 'Toward a conceptualization of optimal self-esteem'. *Psychological Inquiry* 14(1): 1–27.

Trust

Authenticity relies on trust. In the Respectful Executive Impression Management not only is the executive giving off trustworthiness, he is also trusting of recipients. Inconsistent malevolent managers, however, are far different. They use impression management upwardly to impute that they are trustworthy; for example, one executive did this through agreeing with all the decisions made by the CEO, never contesting them, which implied that the decisions taken are good decisions. Downwardly though, the managers using inconsistent impression management do not bother with ingratiating impression management with those that they regard as outside their group, and are usually outwardly hostile; this can be done very politely by the Mediocre Executive Impression Management managers, to subordinates.

Whitener et al.[14] explain that trust is a belief that the person will behave benevolently towards them and that trust is formed when the executive exhibits behavioural consistency, behavioural integrity, sharing of control, openness in communication and demonstrated concern for the employee. All of these factors are present in the Respectful Executive Impression Management. For the remaining managers, these concerns are violated, with inconsistencies dominating the impression management.

Trust is the key to what the fraudster is able to project very well upwards with boards and owner-managers, projecting an aura of trust. Even the incompetent manager who was claimed to have 'not enough clue' about committing a large-scale fraud, upper management still trusted him. One fraudster was outwardly very religious. Being religious assumes adherence to a strict moral code. Once the outward impression management of the ethics of religion is given, a deep trust would be formed quicker. Obviously, this particular set of circumstances would only work in a setting that preferred a strict religious moral code. However, most businesses are run in a more secular fashion and assume a moral code in what could be described in an individualist self-interested fashion, but rests on all of society adhering to a commonly agreed set of principles. However, in a conflict view of society several moral codes can exist side by side, for example in the maxim: 'There's one law for the rich and one law for the poor.' Trust is very important. It was found in the question section of the interviews that fraudsters are moderately

14 Whitener, E.M., S.E. Brodt, M.A. Korsgaard and J.M. Werner (1998). 'Managers as initiators of trust: An exchange relationship framework for understanding managerial trustworthy behavior'. *Academy of Management Review* 23(3): 513–30.

more able to be detected as authentic, and possibly this is due to the apparent trustworthiness of the fraudster.

When Trust is Broken

Malevolent management fails to realise what it is like for trust to be broken. They cannot do so as malevolent managers are so willing to break the working relationship in this manner. Let me detail what happens emotionally to a co-worker, superior upline manager and subordinate. Each set of co-workers will play out their emotions in fairly predictable ways.

As said earlier the co-workers in the study felt that their trust was broken by malevolent managers, either fraudulent or not. It is a hidden process as emotions are usually not seen in the workplace. Not allowed to be seen, that is. Trust is the deepest part of forming a relationship with anyone. Using the CAT model, the Connection phase has to be made first then Appreciation of the other's talents and skills take place. Finally, and only finally when the individual concerned feels they can take the next step, trust will form. It is a bit like frost on a window – it only forms when the two other conditions are right. And just as in the case of frost, one hot breath can make it dissolve. For those living in tropical countries, think of making a fire. It can only happen if there is something to burn and a fire-making instrument (matches, lighter and so on). The fire will only take place with those two factors. Just as frost on the window can disappear with one hot breath, so can the fire with one bowl of water poured over it.

Connection and appreciation are two fragile components of our relationship making. Trust is the most fragile. Think of a married couple with one spouse having an affair. When the innocent partner finds out, trust disappears. For the adulterer, even feeling genuine remorse and truly would never stray again, the aggrieved partner remains in a limbo of how on earth can this person be ever trusted again. Workplace relationships are the same. They do not end at 5 p.m. and restart at 9 a.m. This is what most managers are unaware of. That their workplace relationships with others are a committed 24/7 process.

We all have suffered with damaging relationships at work and take the problem home with us. Even if the problem is not discussed it stays with the person until the next encounter in the following days. It is a lasting issue that does not go away; even if shared with others, it is still the same problem. It becomes heavier and heavier. Future relations with the person who cannot be trusted will become taut, casual meetings in the corridors will stop, the usual banter at morning is avoided, even eye contact becomes difficult. The offending manager may not be aware of what is going on.

The pain for the co-worker is awful to bear. It's like a headache that never goes. It begins to spread to create muddled work decisions, which would otherwise be easy. The individual becomes consumed with the problem. Others may notice but cannot really help unless within the confines of a therapeutic relationship. Old wounds of the past re-emerge with the attendant painful feelings. The person may feel that he must leave the workplace due to the lack of trust. Or if they opt to stay will slowly but surely start to exhibit the physical signs of stress, such as a lower immune response; infections are caught easily and create more inflammation than usual. Long-term effects of lack of trust show in inflammatory disease, some say cancer, and certainly heart disease. The emotional effects are not being able to trust anyone again. This spreads from the workplace into the person's relationships at home with his family and friends. The trauma from this may manifest in psychological disturbances with Post Traumatic Stress Disorder (PTSD). Do not think for a moment that PTSD is confined to the war zone. It is not.

PTSD is a terrible condition. The psychiatric diagnosis, according to the DSM IV[15] is made where the individual experiences a risk of serious injury. This injury is seen as physical – we are still waiting for the psychiatric discipline to come to terms with serious emotional injury. Until then, I for one see that broken trust is like a broken limb. It is significant and life-altering. It is distressing to the person concerned and it affects all the activities of their daily life. As broken trust is at endemic proportions the Diagnostic Manual cannot distinguish this as outside human experience. I would like to propose that if this Manual was designed 8,000 years ago, we would have said categorically that broken trust is outside human experience. And yes, I fully agree that this has become so widespread that we are dealing with many people with PTSD.

The resulting behaviours for a person afflicted with PTSD are experiencing flashback memories. I have witnessed hundreds of people who came to me for assistance who were afflicted with this phenomenon. As they recount what happened to them in the workplace they go into trancelike state. They can tell you what clothes they wore, what they were doing immediately before the event and so on. They can recall every detail of the violence that was perpetrated

15 American Psychiatric Association (2013). *Diagnostic and Statistical Manual of Mental Disorders*. Arlington, VA, American Psychiatric Association.

upon them. In recalling the event they feel the same emotions again. Usually it is helplessness, then later, anger and later on they fear that this will happen to them again in the workplace. The aggrieved person may have nightmares following the event, and years later can still have bad dreams that wake them up feeling extremely distressed.

Avoidance of the stressor is another sign of something is terribly wrong. I have seen this myself; where trust is broken with the individual concerned will make excuses for not attending meetings and so on. It feels far safer for them to be hiding in the toilet rather than face the manager. This is the reason why staff with broken trust will leave the organisation quickly – anything to avoid having to work alongside such a manager.

The effect can be so bad that PTSD-affected employees will produce a response of numbing down of feelings. This is a primitive way of protecting against further damaging feelings. Numbed workplace warriors can be seen in almost any organisation. They have lost the battle with their manager and retire to a 'safe' location within the organisation. When approached about inequities in the organisation or other similar problem they will not want to become involved. Often the response will be, 'What else do you expect here?' The wounded person becomes numb in order to continue with working in the place that has duty of care to him and failed miserably.

Broken trust lasts for years, and in many cases a lifetime. To consider that this is only tied to the workplace I would argue is totally erroneous. Because I have taken a different path than my peers in order to meet the needs of my clients I have traversed the delineation of work and home life. It is my experience that all that happens at work permeates into the wider sphere of the individual's relationships.

And of course this makes sense. Psychologists admit that PTSD affects the lives of Vietnam veterans and see the associated psychological distress re-enacted at home. Usually the returned soldier will turn to drink and/or drugs to numb the pain. This will put considerable strain on any relationship that the soldier has. I have come across people who have left their marital relationships and build a cocoon to live on their own. They seldom participate in the workforce ever again due to the risk of having their trust broken.

This has policy implications for the world of employment. Most schemes of unemployment benefits are geared for the person to re-enter the workforce. I must ask the question: 'Would we send untreated war veterans to battle again?'

Yes we used to do that, but in a more enlightened environment, we hesitate and recognise that those involved with war may never go back again due to the psychological harm that has been perpetrated upon them. If we don't send PTSD-affected soldiers back, why do we insist on PTSD-affected co-workers back? And following this line of thought, why isn't the workplace using its duty of care? We go to work these days not expecting to be afflicted with PTSD. If a worker breaks a leg at work, then that person is compensated for this and reduced physical duties upon re-entry may be required. We obviously do not want a re-occurrence of the same event. But we quite happily give stress leave to an employee and expect that person to return to work once again with the (malevolent) manager concerned.

In this part of the chapter I am referring to co-workers and many assume that means subordinates. Unfortunately the malevolent manager can break trust with their upline managers and boards, colleagues as well as their subordinates. This means that the damage is serious for the organisation which will be at risk for losing their human capital and with it their intellectual property. A Respectful manager will preserve and grow the organisation's human capital and intellectual property the Malevolent manager, in terms of Gone with the Wind: 'Does not give a damn'.

So if you are reading this and you do care about your organisation you must stop the breakage of trust in your organisation immediately. Even if you are the office cleaner you can stop the trust-breaking process in a non-violent manner. Make it clear that you will not tolerate such behaviour in the organisation. Take whatever sanctions when you can and if necessary get another job elsewhere which has Respectful management. Why participate in an organisation where you will most likely catch PTSD along with your wages? Withdrawing labour is the most effective tool that unions have employed for well over a century. It has resulted in overreactions by employers firing all concerned but it did put management on notice for fairer wages and work conditions for all.

Withdrawing your labour because management or boards allow malevolent management is an effective tool, only, and if only you have a job offer in writing. Say what you have to say upon your exit. Safely in another job means vindictiveness cannot follow you. If many people did this within an organisation the message will become very clear to those who wish to derive profit from the organisation, for instance shareholders and business owners. The withdrawal must be made with the reason made perfectly clear. One large financial organisation which did not follow up the trust-breaking episode of their fraudster manager lost all of its staff at that branch, and my bet is that they did not have a clue as to why.

You can write your reasons in a letter to the board of directors or the Human Resource manager if he can be trusted. Withdrawal is only effective with stating the reason. Most people, especially those who avoid conflict (I used to be one of these, so I know how it is), will slide out of the organisation without stating the real reasons. If you have PTSD induced from broken trust from a Malevolent manager, it must be clearly stated. In one situation, post my recovery, I went to complain about the lack of duty of care and the existing malevolent management. I was laughed out of the room. However, if all the people who resigned from that one organisation were with me, it would have created a huge shockwave. It would have numbered hundreds of staff. Also there would have been others locked in the organisation who did not know how to leave or fear that there was no other job to go to. Job security locks people into dangerous abusive organisations.

We do not do this with our veterans. If a soldier is diagnosed properly (and early) we do not demand that he immediately goes back into conflict. He is fortunate that he is not locked in to the job contract and the soldier actually receives a pension or similar due to his psychological wounds.

In addition when we get to the point of recognising the violence created in workplaces we will become used to reasons for exiting an organisation on résumés thus: 'Malevolent management'. This means we will be getting to the truth of the matter of why people exit organisations. Apart from reasons of geographic location and better job opportunity, malevolent managers will be high on the list of departure reasons. The sooner the organisation realises it the better.

However, there will be much blaming the victim rather than the shockingly appalling management. One reason that I can see that will stop the naming of what is happening on résumés is the fact that a less than respectful employer will label the candidate as a 'personality problem' and refuse to accept the candidate despite possibly having the best skills and experience for the position. A Respectful Executive Impression Management employer will probe further and will make a decision that is fairer given more evidence. One of the things that can be done for evidence-seeking is to talk to previous co-workers. If everyone labels the candidate as having the same work problem then it is very likely that it is the case. However, if there is evidence that is to the contrary, then further consideration must be given to the candidate in all fairness.

It is possible that poor candidates will start to label all exits due to malevolent management. It takes the spotlight off their own behaviour and blames others. That is why in addition on naming the reason for the exit, follow-up evidence must be provided and balanced with what the co-workers say. It may be unusual for the referee check to be beyond the previous boss, but real insight will be given as to what happened in that workplace, if co-workers are asked. There is nothing wrong in checking the candidate's colleagues or subordinates. We overvalue what the head of the company or department will say and undervalue where the real truth lies and that is with the applicant's close co-workers. We even know of stories where the candidate is given a good reference to 'get him off our hands'. Malevolent managers do not hesitate to lie – and when the shoe is on the other foot when others lie they are outraged that such a thing could happen.

I experienced one job-seeking episode where I would get to interview, perform well and then suddenly everything stalled. It wasn't until several years later that I found out that my previous boss was, as we say in Australia, 'white-anting' me. The reference to termites typifies the process of undermining a reputation. And clearly it was a vindictive act to prevent me from obtaining work in a relatively small marketplace ... The white-anting put fear into these employers' minds and they did not investigate further. I lost one job prospect after another and was none the wiser of what was happening until a couple of years later.

Unfortunately trust-breaking is highly contagious. Once this happens to an individual, he is forced into a choice; either continue to trust and be prepared for the other person to break it once again, or the other choice is never to trust again. I have seen many managers unable to trust again due to the long-term harm that has been perpetrated against them.

Let us now look into these choices in more detail. The lack of trust in others is a self-defeating and primitive way of dealing with the wound of broken trust. This is due to the fact that withdrawing from trust is meant to insulate us against being hurt again. In fact, what happens is that the person is hurting themselves by not allowing trust to form once more. It is a very common effect from the trauma and the ensuing PTSD. The individual becomes hypervigilant on possible trust-making. The memory of how their trust was broken first time around permeates every action and produces a mindset of vigilance of behaviours that look similar. This can be a mere shout from a worker in the office, or several people laughing and the individual does not know what they are laughing about and will assume that it at himself. Either case the unusual behaviour sparks off a shut-down process. It is exactly like a soldier's response to an exploding shell – he ducks for cover instinctively.

What goes on in the mind of someone who cannot trust is that any friendly gesture or invitation to get closer is seen as a threat. It could be a very cleverly veiled threat, but still a threat all the same. Threats cannot be taken lightly, and must be dealt with immediately by taking a defensive course of action. Miscommunication abounds and the person who cannot trust ends up in a very lonely self-isolating place. A person who cannot trust is an island in the middle of the human race. They look the same as others on the outside but when a close up view is taken, the person is an island. This is not the same as paranoia, although it would be easy to confuse the two: not being able to trust is formed on broken trust, whereas paranoia is a psychiatric disorder and can strike at any time and is associated with such disorders as schizophrenia. It usually is caused by feelings of helplessness and victimisation. Broken trust is the direct result of such an action taken at the expense of the individual.

Isolation made me very independent of others, including close family and friends. With co-workers I tended to have the view that they were incompetent and used the phrase that if I wanted a good job done I will have to do it myself. This resulted in hours of overwork that could have been delegated to others. This leads me to another result of broken trust – that of controlling behaviour. It isn't very nice to admit to being controlling, but I was and not terribly proud of it. I used all sorts of tactics to keep everything under control. Again this is a very primitive response to the world, and it is impossible to do. However, that did not stop me, and others too I have witnessed the same, will try to control to the nth degree. This included work, hobbies, my family and so on. Without control I felt vulnerable. It felt like I was naked at a duchess's tea party. This is what broken trust does to a person.

Ultimately I could not face a world where I was not in control. This came out when I was suspected of having a tumour in my throat. It turned out benign and was a huge relief to me, but at the time of not knowing my world spiralled out of control. Illness and disease does that to you, and I have noticed organisations despise sick employees and label the individual as lazy or creating the disease themselves. Malevolent organisations will want to eject the sick person from their ranks as they are a symbol that we are not in control of everything as we hope.

Control is the mark of a malevolent manager as the malevolent trusts no one. The two types of non-fraudster malevolent managers control in different ways and use their impression management to do so. Goffman realised that impression management was a device of social control but as it worked both ways, the actor wanting to control his audience, and the audience wanting to control the actor he did not propose harm in the interaction. But obviously it does so when one party holds more power than the other.

This is shown in the job interview. The actor is the candidate and the audience is the interview panel. If the audience holds more power than the applicant – which it does in this case, it would be demonstrated by a dismissal of the candidate and a 'Next please!' type of response. But if it is truly an interview panel that wishes to select the best candidate, it will be serious about the task at hand and that is where the applicant is in control of performing to the best of his ability to gain the job at hand. For the selection process to work properly, there has to be a balance of power. The interview fails when there is too much power held in either party as control rests with that party and an inefficient social process happens. Obviously, the impression management theory predicts that interviews are equal, and Respectful managers will ensure that the candidate is at ease, that as much information about the job is given, and a fair competition is taking place. An actor-candidate then is required to submit truthful answers, without hyperbole, about previous experience and skills. Both sides regard each other with mutual respect and see the engagement as beneficial to the organisation, rather than particular managers and so on.

If the actor-candidate has broken trust, then all sorts of distortions can take place and may interfere with the demonstration of a person's ability to do the job. Also broken trust on the part of the interview panel will present itself with not knowing what is true and what is not on the information given. The result will be a slanted view of the candidates and the selection would be of who will be best for me. The recruiter wants more work, the manager who wants to look good, and the board member who is only interested in share price and profits.

We all know the outcomes of such poor choices. Misplacement of applicants into wrong job roles double expectations – the overt and the hidden. All of this sets up the broken trust individual for being fired and the broken trust interview panel as trying to get results from a poor match, and when it pans out the individual will be dismissed or stays on as a management toady.

Malevolent managers do not view the human being as irreplaceable, in fact they are expendable. They are quite happy to fire a person and start the interview process once more. This is why a high staff turnover is a sign of malevolent management. It is not simply disgruntled staff leaving; it can be a malevolent manager doing his own agenda interviewing/firing. Managers who use Respectful Executive Impression Management know and appreciate the value of every employee. The selection process is there to make sure that they get the best candidate possible and will include people of different backgrounds and diversity as the Respectful manager knows that this will produce the best outcome for the organisation.

Many people stay within jobs where their trust has been violated and what can happen is that these people can be subsumed or co-opted into operating violence on others. Learning that this is how one gets to the top teaches an immature employee on how to act in the future. Broken trust begets broken trust and it is a very disappointing side effect of the violence that has happened. We know that bullied children at school can end up being bullies themselves in the workplace[16] so this behavioural learning must be stopped once and for all. Promotions should be reviewed with this in mind; destructive activity must not be rewarded.

One reason that employees feel locked in to their workplaces is because of debt. Usually this is in the form of housing mortgages, but can also be for other material things. Locked in employment due to debt is often seen as a third-world problem with people forced to work for a pittance. It is economic enslavement and continues in practice in many countries in the world. The only way to purchase a house is to borrow money for a house mortgage. This ongoing debt over many years certainly had a profound effect on me, and many others who had to put up with malevolent managers in the workplace. They seem to detect who is under the most economic pressure and if it serves them, they will intensify their malevolent behaviour to coerce behaviour that they want from an employee. This of course, is highly immoral and against all respectful values in our society.

Morality

When the semi-structured interview questions were asked outright about managerial morality, there was a mixed response. It was assumed and taken for granted to be in place by the co-workers of the Respectful managers, and in the Question Data part of the concept for the Respectful type there is

16 Haltigan, J. and T. Vaillancourt (2014). 'Joint trajectories of bullying and peer victimization across elementary and middle school and associations with symptoms of psychopathology'. *American Psychological Association* 50(11): 2426–36.

a construct referring to them as having a moral character and being seen to operate ethically. Co-workers talked about moral character in terms of honesty, being generous, doing work in the community, having country values as well as ethics and honour. It would appear also that transformational leaders share characteristics of the executives who exhibit Respectful Executive Impression Management, as Bass and Steidmeier[17] state that if a leader wants to be truly transformational he must exhibit virtue and morality. This is, of course, not likely to happen to any manager giving off inconsistent malevolent Executive Impression Management.

In fact, some of the malevolent managers appeared to be highly immoral to some recipients:

> *... to me there were no morals she would do anything to get her own way and do you know get things the way she wanted them to be.*

The variable in itself was detected slightly more in non-fraudster than fraudster executives. It is only the superior malevolent type: Arrogant Fraudster and the Tyrant who are assigned as immoral (if at all). The relationship of the Likeable Fraudster with their co-workers seem to be so beneficial and strong that morality was assumed, as one co-worker reported:

> *He was honest except for one thing. (the fraud)*

It is most unfortunate that morality and virtue are not the sole domain of Respectful managers.

The fraudster managers are the only ones who try, somewhat successfully, to create the illusion; other types are not worried about disguising or hiding. They are open. Managers using Inconsistent Malevolent impression management do not seem to care if others see their 'bad' behaviour as they feel that they hold the power of the situation (as perceived by the co-workers).

The Respectful Executive Impression Management type does not have any illusory components in it. Some insight may be gained here as the co-workers, as mentioned before, had to be pushed into saying anything further than 'Great!' about what the executive was like to work with. Because the consistency is so strong, 'what you see is what you get' there is almost no need for anything more to be said. It could be argued that this form of Executive Impression

17 Bass and Steidmeier (1999).

Management is the type that is not seen; there is no need for it to be noted as the audience trusts the actor and the actor performs as per expectations.

The managers who use the malevolent types of Executive Impression Management are very different. The recipients found it to be variable and with malicious intent either to themselves or others. Furthermore, the managers who use Inconsistent Malevolent impression management have nothing to hide, it is how they use power in the workplace for their own means.

Tyrant – Illusion

This malevolent type of non-fraudster executive uses disguises when meeting clients – being 'personable' for a short while in order to get their work, later openly dropping the disguise in front of subordinates. He does not care if they see his malevolence; in fact he benefits from it as the staff then live in fear of what he may do. This type of executive is actually inefficient and ineffective and relies on support people to cover up his or her mistakes. But subordinate staff see the malevolence and may even feel targeted by bullying behaviour. As seen earlier, these malevolent superior executives maltreat their staff (through poor work performed due to conflicting demands, overload of work) and results in high turnover of staff.

The Mediocre – Illusion

The illusion for the Mediocre type is different than the Tyrant type, insofar the benign illusion is used outside their safe group, and they feel that they can drop their mask within the confines of their group. Furthermore, there is an air of appeasement to the Inferior that comes out with this observation about the dropping of the illusion in a trusted group:

> *He liked to be appropriately dressed, he liked to be recognised in public, he liked to have the respect of the staff but he may not return the same respect to them [behind their backs] ...*

The group becomes very important for the manager using Mediocre Executive Impression Management, so much so, it led in one case to promotion of the 'in' group:

> *... the most significant thing that I noticed from when he moved from the directors role which gave him his very close knit support group ... within months he was back to having [the same] exclusive group of close staff people around him ...*

But overall, the Tyrant and the Mediocre do not concern themselves with maintaining the disguise like the fraudsters; they have no need to as they are able to use their power in the workplace for their own designs.

As an aside, none of the non-fraudsters' co-workers used the word 'fear' in their reports of the impression management that they received. However, using the CAT model, anxiety and worry are linked with fear. One manager who used Mediocre Executive Impression Management was reported as:

> *Possibly. I don't think he was depressed. I think there was an anxiety, I would put it more like an anxiety not a depression. An anxiety to achieve something in a set time and the anxiety of 'How am I going to do this? I only have this much time left to achieve it and then my opportunity will go.'*

There was one reference about a manager who used Respectful Executive Impression Management, being worried, but it was an outside the workplace issue – a broken marriage, albeit an important one:

> *I think he still was worried about how it was affecting the other party. I think he really did care especially about his kids and how this was affecting them and everything. He was not doubting what he was doing ... it all worked out fine.*

One aspect that is interesting is that two managers who used Respectful Executive Impression Management were reportedly a little withdrawn when under stress and not taking their feelings out in the workplace.

> *... he often seems quiet, under stress, his workload is quite high ... / ... / so that was a little bit tense at sometimes. I think the main thing was the erratic work hours ... but more reserved.*

Which is opposite to a manager who used malevolent Executive Impression Management, who used negative emotions in the workplace when she were stressed:

> *So she put herself in the line of fire in some ways, and then she would get very uptight and you'd see her friend going over and they'd be whispering to each other and annoyed looks on their faces so you knew what was going on, they were having a go. (at the manager)*

All in all, malevolent managers are not good to work with. All the co-workers suffered some emotional abuse if they worked with a Tyrant or a Mediocre Executive Impression Management manager. The problem is that the workers felt something was wrong but had to put up with it until their health had failed. Not knowing who they were dealing with is a hazard for many in the workplace and is explored further in the following chapter.

Chapter 6

The Impression Management Strategies used by Non-fraudster Managers

Respectful Executive Impression Management – The Good Side

This type of Executive Impression Management appears to represent the good side of management with its traits of honesty, trustworthiness and authenticity. It coincides with the characteristics of transformational leadership. As demonstrated earlier the literature shows many empirical studies on leaders demonstrate moral reasoning, ethics and trust, which are the substrata to authenticity.

One of the most important indicators of Respectful Executive Impression Management is being able to apologise. Tucker found that far from being perceived as a weakness, being able to apologise is regarded as an enhanced quality of leadership as it engenders long lasting and trusting relationships.[1] This was certainly the case with co-workers receiving Respectful Executive Impression Management, and it was indicated in the semi-structured interview. Trust comes to the fore once again, as a key factor in the relationship with recipients and their managers.

Being able to apologise implies morality to their co-workers. No fraudster managers were noted as apologetic. However, being able to apologise to others is not the prerogative of Respectful Executive Impression Management, as there was a manager using Mediocre Executive Impression Management who gave an apology to a subordinate about his behaviour. The co-worker was considered to be relatively powerful in the organisation in this case. The co-worker noted that she received the apology, and the manager never said anything derogatory

1 Tucker (2006).

in her presence again. But she noted that it was an appeasement device as he continued his derogatory ways with his inside group.

Impression Management Strategies of Malevolent Executives – The Bad Side

The social psychologist school of impression management is dominated by the view that impression management is used solely for devious reasons. Goffman insists that impression management is present in all social interactions. In fact, Jones and Pittman[2] list four conditions when impression management is entirely absent or minimal: when the person is absorbed in a highly intensive task; when expressing pure emotion, for example joy or fear as it is contained in the moment; ritualised social interaction and in certain situations where the person is engaged in intense heart to heart communication where authenticity and integrity are paramount.

Jones and Pittman went on to produce a classification of strategic impression management levels, upwards and downwards. These are applicable in discussing the malevolent managers. When applied to this group, there are some interesting trends that are noted by the co-workers. In Table 6.1, the impression management strategies are labelled for the non-fraudster malevolent managers in the study, and there were differences in upward and downward impression management strategy.

Table 6.1 Impression management strategies of malevolent managers

	Reported impression management upwards	Strategy upwards type	Reported impression management downwards	Strategy downwards type
Superior	Charming, personable, senior and competence	Self-promotion	Harsh dictator	Intimidation
Inferior	Agree with the boss at all times	Ingratiation	Select group two faces: front stage with others and backstage with select group.	Ingratiation

2 Jones, E.E. and T.S. Pittman (1982). Toward a general theory of strategic self-presentation. *Psychological Perspectives on the Self*, ed. J. Suls. Hillsdale, NJ, Lawrence Erlbaum Associates, 231–62.

Upline Impression Management by Malevolent Managers

Primarily, self-promotion is used by malevolent managers upwards to upline management. There is a careful selection that the manager must deal with. If ingratiation is used, there is a fine line between authenticity and sincerity, or the ingratiation will be seen as sycophantic by upward managers. Self-promotion is based on selling competence. Again, the fine line is that the self-promoter must achieve performance in that competency, or risk being viewed as incompetent. Interestingly, Jones and Pittman remark that the stronger the claim in a malevolent manager the more likely the case that the competence is actually weak. However, they are most likely to get away with it if they in addition to their claims, promote a successful appearance and background.

There is a form of impression management upwards and downwards that was used by one fraudster, and is included as this may very well happen with a non-fraudulent manager who positions his superiority upwards. The exemplification strategy is quite different, derived from 'seizing the high moral ground' and invoking respect by projecting integrity and moral worthiness. An example of this could be within a religious setting. This is fuelled in part by the projection of feelings of guilt and shame if the impression management is unwarranted and is totally strategic to obtain power and control. These malevolent managers can be criticised as being hypocritical or sanctimonious if they overdo it. The example in my study was in fact a fraudster, but he managed to pull off this strategy really well as others were taken in completely. The manager was regarded as a moral person but merely ineffective in his managerial position. Not one of his co-workers suspected that he stole many millions of dollars for his own use. Using the cloak of religion for their own needs has unfortunately been the case with the scandals in various churches for paedophiliac activities, amoral behaviour, stealing the congregation's money, having sexual relations with many women and so on. Each religion has had its own disgrace within its ranks. Not one seems to be immune. And I am sure that this is the case as malevolent people are drawn to the power and control that religious hierarchy gives.

Of the non-fraudster managers, there is a division between those who used self-promotion and those who used ingratiation as described by the co-workers. The division is formed from their attitude to the world; the managers who used Tyrant Executive Impression Management used the superior impression management strategy of self-promotion. The managers who used Mediocre Executive Impression Management used ingratiation.

If the motive of each upwards impression management strategy is taken into account, there is an underlying need for respect from the audiences of self-promoters, whereas the ingratiators want to be liked. Again this helps explain the data as the ingratiators demonstrated clearly to their co-workers that they wanted to be liked, and they showed the same characteristics upwards to their management. However, the ingratiators come into their own in downwards impression management to their subordinates as they stay with the strategy that works for them best, whereas the other non-ingratiators change tactics accordingly.

Downward Impression Management Strategies by Malevolents

The self-promoting malevolent managers use intimidation for subordinates. This is an interesting outcome, as they do appear to not need to have respect from those employees who work with them. It would seem that the more powerful figure (upline management) produces the need for respect, but subordinates produce a need to dominate and abuse by appearing dangerous. If you find a self-promoting manager in the organisation, then look at those co-workers who work with him for intimidation tactics. Einarsen[3] has considered the vexing question of downward intimidation behaviours including: bullying, counterproductive behaviour and managerial aggression in the workplace and refers to this as destructive leadership. Insightfully in 1999, he wrote about the conclusions of an earlier study that: 'The three main reasons [of bullying] were competition concerning status and job positions, envy, and the aggressor being uncertain about his/her self.'[4] Which neatly fits in with the upward self-promoter/ downward intimidator strategies that have been witnessed by co-workers of malevolent managers in this investigation. Furthermore, the interviews with fraud investigators uphold this proposition, as many fraudsters that they have dealt with in the past have been noted as using promotional tactics and simultaneously being bullies to their staff. One investigator felt that about half of the fraudsters that he had dealt with were of this dual impression management strategy type.

The ingratiators on the other hand are more consistent in their impression management strategies. They use ingratiation upward as well as downward, as observed by the recipients in the study. The strategy of downward ingratiation

3 Einarsen, S., M.S. Aasland and A. Skogstad (2007). 'Destructive leadership behaviour: A definition and conceptual model'. *The Leadership Quarterly* 18(3): 207–16.

4 Einarsen, S. (1999). 'The nature and causes of bullying at work'. *International Journal of Manpower* 20(1–2): 16–28, at 20.

by a manager is rewarding as it keeps followers in control and according to one study produced a moderate positive influence on employees.[5] Certainly the fraudster manager who provided drinks after work every day for his staff was able to do this successfully. Earning respect from others is a prime motivation for the malevolents. Tyrants get upset if customers are not impressed, Mediocres are upset if an upline manager ignores their ingratiation. For those co-workers who are subordinate, the managers using Mediocre Executive Impression Management desperately need to gain respect from staff, and will use tactics to obtain this via ingratiation. Thus cliques are born and those in these privileged enclaves are treated well. As opposed to the benefits that are given to the Mediocres' co-workers, the Tyrant merely uses subordinates and colleagues until they wear out. The Tyrant understands the need for respect as they crave it from upline managers and so on, but they dismiss this for those who work with them. In fact it seems that they almost hate their subordinates.

If You Don't Have Respect You Have Hatred

Using the CAT model the opposite of Respect is Anger. This anger can be externalised and others will see this anger in terms of words used describing others as disliking, annoying, frustrating, irritating, being dull-witted and so on. They hardly articulate their anger as their anger. In fact one of the most amazing things is that the individual having anger will then attribute blame to the person concerned and thus absolve all responsibility from himself. For instance, to tell someone that they are annoying puts the onus onto the other person. 'Stop being annoying and we can then get along' is the subtle message. There is no looking at why this 'annoying' behaviour is triggering such an angry response. There can be many underlying reasons, such as the object of the anger is out of the angry person's control and he is angry about his lack of power to coerce that person further. After all, people are only annoying if they are not doing what they are told to do in the way specified. Similarly this process happens of heaping negative adjectives with any other target who refuses to cooperate with the individual. Once a person receives a derogatory label, then in the mind of the individual he is a person to hate.

I happen to have experience this first hand when a 19-year-old great nephew of mine was bashed to death on his way home one night. In the words of the offender 'Don't worry, it's just another chav.' For those outside the realms of

5 Yukl, G. (1992). 'Consequences of influence tactics used with subordinates, peers, and the boss'. *Journal of Applied Psychology* 77(4): 525–35.

current usage, the word 'chav' is derogatory and means white, working class. Only anger can create the emotional sequence that ends in vicious hatred. The target is objectified, separated from the individual self and therefore easily abused. Making a person an object to be ridiculed and laughed at or treated cruelly is within the emotional armour of hatred. This emotion is whipped up in our soldiers and civilian populations at time of war.

We know about propaganda which inevitably fuels hate, we see it in our social media, the press and TV. Propaganda is vilified as it presents a distorted picture. Yet we never stop ourselves from hating others, as we fail to realise that this is equally a distorted picture. Deep within ourselves the dark side or Shadow lurks and controls us in times of stress. The only way to stop your own hatred is to absorb it, recognise it and acknowledge that everyone has this inside them. The next step then is to recognise that this is bad for everyone concerned and have compassion towards yourself. Being human is a hard road to travel on, we are imperfect beings and capable of many destructive actions if we allow the Shadow to take over. There is more about this later in the book.

Objectification is a nasty way of reducing humanity to pawns on a chessboard. There is a feminist literature based on objectification, which outlines in detail the malicious results from this process of lowering self-esteem,[6] to not viewing women as human.[7] Once an individual is reduced in status by the objectification process then he can be used for the perpetrator's own ends and cause misery as the co-workers' needs are not considered. I find it intriguing as to where this process comes from. I believe that it is a modern change in our behaviour. By modern, I am referring to the last 8,000 years. Before then there was no need for objectification. Slavery did not exist. Daily life was about food, capturing it, eating it and developing tools and clothing. We know that spiritual beliefs existed 40,000 years ago from the cave paintings and drawings that have been discovered. If they were like today's primitive societies they would centre on ancestor worship. Deities could live in rocks or special places like natural springs. They were not the fire-breathing malevolent Gods of later religions. It is hard to imagine other than the Golden Rule which is enshrined in all religions: 'Do unto others what you would have done to you'[8] as it is the basis of getting along together.

6 Fredrickson, B.L. and T.-A. Roberts (1997). 'Objectification theory: Toward understanding women's lived experiences and mental health risks'. *Psychology of Women Quarterly* 21(2): 173–206.

7 Mackinnon, C. (2006). *Are Women Human?* Cambridge, MA, Harvard University Press.

8 Bond, K. (1998). 'Religious Beliefs as a Basis for Ethical Decision Making in the Workplace'. Retrieved 1 November 2014, from http://web.archive.org/web/20070703102021/http://www.

It cannot be a quantum leap to consider that this evolves solely from our emotion of Respect, that it is a natural part of us.

Bond makes the point that the rule of reciprocity is a part of all major world's religions, and that it goes far back into time. The Old Testament book of Leviticus is estimated to have been formulated over hundreds of years before it was written down circa 400 BC. Some Bible scholars think that Moses wrote Leviticus as early as 1440 BC.[9]

Hatred does not stop with the target. When the target feels a lack of respect, it creates rebound feelings of rejection, low self-esteem and hatred of oneself and envy of others. This will influence family, co-workers and so on. Therefore the lack of respect snowballs into a maelstrom of self-hate and projection of anger onto others. We are familiar with someone close to us who is unhappy and takes it out on children or those considered less worthy than the unhappy individual.

Costs of Violence in the Workplace

There is no index that measures the cost of violence in the workplace. There are guesses on the cost of bullying but these are restricted to loss of hours rather than taking in the full emotional cost of the abuse that targets suffer. Also bullying can be perpetrated by colleagues as well as subordinates and even if a refined measure for bullying is derived it still will not be accurate. Bullying prevents increases in productivity and usually causes a downward spiral due to other employees' involvement with the issue whether conciliatory or increasing the bullying by being drawn in to by accomplices.

If we were able to derive a measure such as the global peace index for countries, to be applied to workplaces I think it would come somewhat of a surprise for boards and shareholders alike on how much productivity is lost due to the activities of malevolent managers. They assume that the organisation is working at its best, with perhaps one or two trouble spots due to union activity and so on, but it is my view that they would be horrified to see what really goes on and how much value is lost. Economists spend much of their time on providing general measures; it would seem to me that if they

humboldt.edu/~kmb2/paper.html.

9 Smith, J. (2015). 'Leviticus'. Retrieved 17 March 2015, from http://biblehub.com/summary/leviticus/1.htm.

focused on the workplace itself it would lift the veil of secrecy that surrounds such malevolence. This would bring to light the negative effects of the two malevolent styles of management, one being openly chaotic and grasping for power, with the other being equally chaotic but achieving aims through covert manipulation.

I would imagine that any manager exuding Respectful Executive Impression Management would want to know if there is any unnecessary interference with performance, and would welcome such an initiative. Profit alone cannot be the measure due to imperfect markets, the dominance of monopolies, government regulation and so on. But I am sure that if we have a workforce of say 50 people making widgets or providing a widget service, then we could expect to have a measure of how much output we could expect and by extrapolating further how much profit can be expected. My guess is that workplace malevolence costs us billions of dollars per year and wrecks countless people's lives and families. All this for the consumables that we insist upon in life. I think we have our priorities wrong if we insist on a cheap refrigerator and ignore the hidden cost associated with manufacturing it.

In the early nineteenth century Britain and other countries through reasons that seem on the surface at least to be humanitarian, banned slavery. This meant that African slaves were liberated in the British colonies and the United States and they could now work for a wage. Sugar and its add-ons was suddenly freed from the scourge of slavery. Yet consumption increased from 18 pounds per head in 1800, 36 pounds in 1830, to 100 pounds in the twentieth century.[10]

The sugar trade increased without slaves and today most people buying the product will not know about the historical social cost of bringing sugar to their table. Using this analogy into the present day workplace, will the demand say of refrigerators become less due to the abolition of violence in the workplace? The answer is very likely no. Will service industries, manufacturing, natural resource extraction, retail and wholesale trade stop because of non-violence? The same answer applies.

The only reason that violence exists in our workplaces is because we have got used to it. There are scholars and practitioners in non-violence who assert that violence became normal in our society due to the agrarian revolution that began about 8,000 years ago. Prior to this time, social arrangements were in families or clans and were based on mutual cooperation. Without this

10 Ponting, C. (2000). *World History: A New Perspective*. London, Chatto and Windus.

collaboration families did not have sufficient resources to capture and kill large animals. The family had to include others, perhaps blood relatives, for the hunt and in doing so reciprocation in the form of food and products were shared from the animal. Survival was entwined with cooperation. Some scholars argue that there are signs of violence in early Neolithic human remains. These could be explained as warfare between groups for competing resources, but nevertheless the group remained as the dominant social unit and warlike activity is scarce if not almost absent in much of the ancient record.

It is said that the village of Tenganan in Bali has been linked to the Indian state of Orissa through a study of mitochondrial DNA by a team of French scientists, although I have not found an academic record of this event.[11] This means that through the mother's line of genes there is a blood connection to an Indian village in the state of Orissa. This Indian state is on the east side of India, near the Ganges river. But interestingly and somewhat controversially, the oldest known city is not in Mesopotamia but off the coast of north-west India, known as the Gulf of Khambat Cultural Complex. There are claimed remains of a large city, ancient Dwarka, about 5 miles long and 2 miles wide.[12] Artefacts from the underwater site put a date of 9,000 years old. Intriguingly the submarine site includes a granary, which is before the Mesopotamian cities and their culture of growing grain. The oldest known city site in the area is Harappa is on the west side of the subcontinent in Pakistan. Despite being rebuilt many times, the original foundations appear to be at least 4,000 years old but excavations have slowed down due to the military upheaval in the region.

The link with Harrapa and the Soara people in Orissa is that they grow cotton and share the art of fabric weaving. As this was a laborious task, fabrics were made for ceremonial occasions. Whilst I am not an anthropologist I suspect that the peaceful people of Bali, the Bali Mula, are descendants of semi-nomadic people who moved from the advancing agrarian revolution, not wishing to participate as it disturbed their ancient and beloved life. The Bali Mula today live in the cool mountains of Bali, preferring to grow crops of orange trees which fits in with their traditional way of life. They don't pick the fruit, it is harvested by others. They quietly and peacefully grow the trees without disturbance from outside. Another feature of the Soara people is that the women play an integral part in the village, often as shamans and also in the

11 Nick. (2006). 'Indian professor brings Bali and India together'. Retrieved 15 March 2015, from http://www.baliblog.com/travel-tips/bali-daily/indian-professor-brings-bali-and-india-together.html.

12 Gaur, A., S. Sundaresh and S. Tripati (2004). 'An ancient harbour at Dwarka: Study based on the recent underwater explorations'. *Current Science* 86(9): 1256–60.

economic and social life. Instead of clan organisation they have their extended families called Birinda, which consist of descendants from common ancestors of four to five generations. The Saoras' religion is very elaborate and deep rooted. They are polytheist and believe in a large number of deities and ancestral spirits. They practise both slash and burn as well as terraced cultivation with varieties of cereals. Dance and music constitute part and parcel of their rich aesthetic life. The Saora families are polygamous. The total household economy revolves around the woman member who is hardworking and who helps her husband in ploughing and harvesting crops in addition to attending household chores exclusively.

The purpose of this extensive elaboration is that workplaces can exist and do exist that are non-violent. We forget in our busy world that we do not have to follow unthinkingly what is routine in our lives. Non-violence is possible and feasible and not only that, it releases the individual to become highly creative. Creativity in turn solves problems in the workplace, increases production and results in better marketing with more and happier customers. We like to think of inventions as the product of geniuses, but they are actually the effect of creative minds that are freed from ordinary toil. If we can cut the time spent on office politics then that in itself is a compelling reason to stop violence in the workplace.

Violence

The standard definition of violence is defined by the World Health Organisation as:

> *"The intentional use of physical force or power, threatened or actual, against oneself, another person, or against a group or community, that either results in or has a high likelihood of resulting in injury, death, psychological harm, maldevelopment or deprivation."*[13]

Defining violence is important, as there is a long debate on the difference of violence per se and harassment. My own preference is that there is no division, as both are forms of abuse. The Ministry of Justice, New Zealand similarly make no differentiation. 'The definition should be understood to include physical,

13 World Health Organization. (2015). 'Violence prevention, approach and definition'. Retrieved 17 March 2015, from http://www.who.int/violenceprevention/approach/definition/en/.

sexual and psychological abuse (such as the significant abuse of power arising from a dependent relationship, threats, intimidation and neglect).'[14]

In the workplace we see less physical violence these days, although in third-world countries it is present and persistent. Some examples that we hear of are initiation rites that are violent towards the novice. Typically this would be an apprentice joining his first workplace, or more recently the exposure of abuse of personnel in the armed forces. However, we do not recognise other forms of violence so readily.

The World Health Alliance for the prevention of violence reflects, perhaps unintentionally, the view that psychological abuse is less of a problem. Yet during the last 30–40 years that there is more evidence to underline the fact within domestic violence that psychological abuse is far worse and damaging to the individual than physical assault. It has been said that the physical bruises heal, but the psychological abuse does not show and therefore remains unhealed for much longer periods, if ever. There is a fascinating study of the discourse of emotional abuse in the workplace, which highlights what bullied targets feel.[15]

In a national study in Australia regarding unemployed women managers I found that there was a large amount – 40 per cent of women who were targets of bullying.[16] Some of the respondents became so abused that they ended up in psychiatric facilities for treatment with resulting depression and lowered self-esteem and some were suicidal. I was as astonished as many others were, because the 'normal' rate of bullying is around 4–5 per cent in the workplace. These women cited their bullies as being male and female managers and none spoke of bullying upwards or mobbing, a refined form of violence only bullying downwards.

The term bullying was also a shock to understand for me as I had been personally bullied by my CEO for about a year when I was forced to resign for health reasons. I knew that his behaviour was not impartial to me as a director, neither was it respectful; in fact he was actively undermining my authority in

14 Ministry of Justice. (2014). 'Definition of violence'. Retrieved 24 March 2014, from http://www.justice.govt.nz/publications/global-publications/s/safer-communities-action-plan-to-reduce-community-violence-sexual-violence/definition-of-violence.

15 Tracy, S.J. and P. Lutgen-Sandvik (2006). 'Nightmare, demons, and slaves: Exploring the painful metaphors of workplace bullying'. *Management Communication Quarterly* 20(2): 148–85.

16 Sheridan, T. (2005). Voicing women managers' unemployment experience in Australia. *The Hidden Toll*. Perth, WA, Women Chiefs of Enterprises International, 1–100.

my work teams. But I never put two and two together to understand that this was bullying. To me back then, I thought bullying was more about schools and errant prefects meting out unnecessary punishment. It never occurred to me that what was happening to me was bullying. It was not until two years later I read an article on bullying which listed bullying behaviours. Of the 27 indicators I ticked 26, the only behaviour he didn't use was shouting. When I researched this more I went to a government policy office. I was somewhat stunned that my previous CEO had developed a reputation in town and he was one of the worst bosses a person could work with. Despite all my requests for help, not one person assisted me.

If I could not spot bullying then it was a good bet that thousands of others in similar positions would not be able to either. Even today, after public awareness has been raised about bullying in the workplace in the media, there will still remain innocent employees who are targeted every day. One of the reasons why came out of my research that if a target is under the spotlight of Executive Impression Management from a bullying manager that person will very likely not understand what is going on. Maybe even being labelled as gullible or naive by co-workers who do not see the dazzling spotlight of the Executive Impression Management, as it is not focused on them.

I am using here the more distinctive forms of bullying, but there are other behaviours which are equally abusive that are covert and unseen by most people, apart perhaps from the inner circle of the perpetrator's groomed cronies. This insidious form is in my view just as abusive as it wrecks personal judgement, discernment and ultimately trust. If a person's trust is damaged it is like breaking someone's legs – never to be able to walk properly again in any circumstances. Broken trust is so damaging that close personal relationships are affected. Without active intervention from trained therapists the possibility of future life is drastically limited. In my view I don't think that enough emphasis is made in the business world about losing trust. Sure, everyone knows that we must engender trust, but it seems to be purely lip service. This is because people do not realise the primary importance of the oxygen of trust to our emotional lives. Without positive energy in the workplace it is like doubling the workload. It is tortuous and dangerous.

Trust is the energy of the workplace and it is quantified in quality assurance policies and routines. Just think about it for a minute. Trust gives you confidence that others are doing their work. Even a sole trader has to trust others like their accountant to do their bookkeeping and tax submissions properly; they must trust even their customers so that they will pay.

When I came across quality assurance processes such as Deming's Total Quality Management, I was truly impressed.[17] It made me rethink the workplace processes and the importance of documentation for reference. Deming's approach was based on what knowledge that management should know and provide. Again this produces trust as the employee knows who to go to for advice on what to do. Too often in the workplace, managers are ignored as they clearly have not a clue about the problem. Therefore the employee goes to other staff, interferes with their routine by halting for their question, or even worse surfs the Internet for answers. Too often the Internet is used for knowledge but in fact it only shares information. We drown in information and even regard those who have a lot of it in their heads as some kind of genius. For instance quiz nights, or TV quiz shows demonstrate this well. Questions are asked about pieces of information that the participant either knows or does not. Sometimes we see a display of rationalisation by the participant as he negates answers in a multiple question. But it is never true knowledge. Knowledge for the manager is everything intimately related to the business, the production process, their customers and of paramount importance, their staff. Without trust in their employees the manager is severely affected in their performance.

The above illustrates the proposition and research that it takes a new manager about two years to become knowledgeable about his position. Constantly moving managers is never a good idea as they can only learn 'by the seat of their pants' from whatever crisis has hit them in their short career in that department.[18] The rotation is often used as a method to train the manager into a more senior role. I know this happens in many large companies, but it cannot give the manager true expert knowledge as usually the assignment is too short.

Knowledge and how to use it forms trust. If the manager knows that the employee understands his role, then the manager knows that there is no need to interfere. Efficient performance should result. However, what can a middle manager say is called in to settle a complaint about this employee. First of all I have witnessed far too many complaints that are unjustified and develop from envy or greed. But say that the complaint is valid, for instance coming from a customer with no axe to grind that the employee gave poor service. If the manager loses faith in that employee and takes the 'customer is always right' attitude then the staff member is put into an awkward position, without

17 The W Edwards Deming Institute. (2015). 'Edwards Deming the Man'. Retrieved 3 March 2015, from https://www.deming.org/theman/overview.

18 Gabarro, J.J. (2007). 'When a new manager takes charge'. *Harvard Business Review* 85(1): 104–17.

support and without company confidence in him. Actually this lack of trust turns the employee into a scapegoat. Correcting a service improperly given takes time and energy. Far better if the staff member knows his job well and is empowered enough to make choices with difficult customers and he can resolve the problem immediately at the point and time of complaint. It boils down to trust. Most employees operate in a framework of little or no trust. These workplaces are fraught with danger at every move, as the staff member does not know if what he is about to do is to incur the wrath of management.

It is these workplaces that are fertile ground for violence, the reason being that an employee will understand he will get away with it. The managers are off protecting their turf in countless meetings, and the bully or manipulator can go about his business under the radar and not be seen. Similarly the target is unable to get justice for the emotional abuse as it is not observed, quantified or even understood that it is harmful. Often you hear the phrase, 'Well he brought it upon himself' which demonstrates clearly no trust in that individual. I haven't met a single employee that warranted or invited bullying. It is an act from the perpetrator as vengeance, envy or for the sheer delight of making someone's life miserable. In the latter case I was given an explanation for a manager's violent behaviour as: he suffered like that, so now he does it with every single entrant. Where was senior management for goodness sake? Answer is always that they were locked away in meetings and did not wish to see.

In one particular high-level job, 32 hours of my time was soaked up in meetings every week. Where on earth was the time to manage? The organisation's answer was to do those activities after hours. But the employees were at home by then and I could not complete my impossible schedule. What I did was put delegates in place of me in most of my meetings but the backlash of criticisms of 'You don't think we are important enough' soon was rife in the organisation. The irony was: well yes, I did think that they were important enough, so important enough that they could actually manage on their own and resolve their issues. There was little for me to do in these time-guzzlers apart from listen and take notes. I figured that I was an expensive note taker and a summary could always be given to me later if required.

So when does criticism turn into abuse? This issue is a clothing act for violence. Any criticism must be delivered with a solution of how to correct it and present it to the person concerned in a helpful manner. The words stay as corrective and not coercive. When power is being exerted negatively it will always be in the form of abuse. Criticising at the water cooler is not a positive thing to do, and if you experience such a thing then walk away. The reason being is that you are dragged into the violence and become an accomplice.

Many people do not want to participate in emotional abuse in the workplace. However, some do out of fear that the perpetrator will turn on them. Sometimes they are too weak to stand up for themselves, or perceive themselves to be too low in the pecking order to take sides in such a dynamic and they stand there doing nothing. The act of doing nothing is the act of an accomplice. The act of going to a manager about what is happening is an act of trust. Trust therefore is the basis of positive workplaces and the lack of it marks workplaces as difficult to work in.

Comparison of Fraudster and Non-Fraudster Executive Impression Management Types

While this book is not about managerial fraudsters, there is one comparison within the literature that is interesting to discuss. Looking at the semi-structured question responses a number of themes emerged. These are beyond what has already been discussed about the co-workers with regards to their received impression management. The focus here is asking did they observe certain behaviours that common social theories indicate. For instance, psychopathy is noted as being a feature of those people who do not see any boundaries in their behaviour and the theory about them concludes that they would steal if they could do so.

Application of Theory Predictors

The questionnaire covered basic theory indicators of impression management, social psychology, psychopathology and the Red Flags; the data revealed a relationship of recipients' responses such as that shown in (see Figure 6.1).

There are a number of observations that can be made from the co-workers' view. The 'Red Flags' of fraud appeared to reveal little between the two groups of managers. Let me explain further. The Red Flags is an accumulation of work in 1980, which studied known jailed fraudsters.[19] From this quantitative study there grew many indicators that are meant to be looked for, particularly by

19 Romney, M.B., W.S. Albrecht and D.J. Cherrington (1980a). 'Auditors and the detection of fraud'. *Journal of Accountancy* 149(5): 63–9.

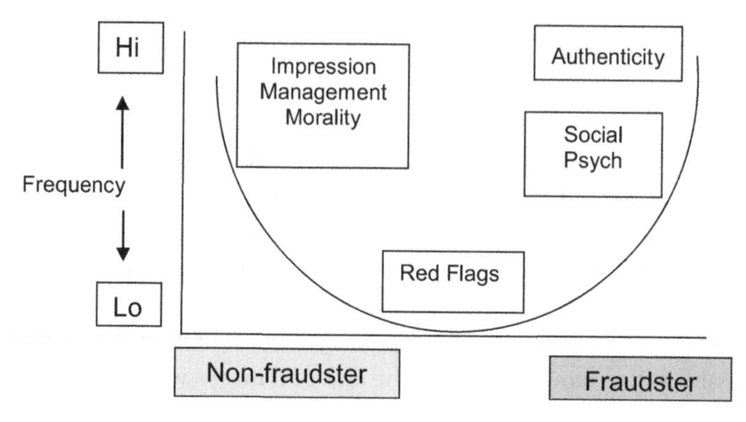

Figure 6.1 The curvilinear relationship of the literature indicators as seen by non-fraudster managers and fraudster managers' co-workers

accountants and auditors, if fraud is suspected.[20] The problem was that they were not all that predictive. Something appears to intervene in the direct link between fraud and the Red Flag personal characteristics. My study gives the answer that all malevolent managers will share these characteristics in varying degrees, fraudster managers and non-fraudster managers alike. Therefore, the original study picked up malevolent characteristics, rather than fraudulent indicators. This is a brand new finding and is being absorbed by the fraud investigation community.

In contrast, the two precepts of impression management, morality and authenticity show some relationship with the two groups of co-workers but in different ways. Morality is more detectable with non-fraudster executives, which is what we would expect, whereas authenticity is more noticeable by co-workers of fraudster managers. As previously discussed, the fraudsters trade more in the currency of trust, which is the foundation of authenticity, than in morality. The other groups of psychopathology and social psychology indicators are only slightly more noticeable with the fraudsters than non-fraudsters.

20 Romney, M.B., W.S. Albrecht and D.J. Cherrington (1980b). 'Red-flagging the white collar criminal: Potential fraud situations have common characteristics, according to a survey of published cases, which can be used as early warning signals to prevent actual acts'. *Management Accounting* 61(9): 51–6.

When looking at individual items the fraudsters and non-fraudster executives demonstrate differently, see Table 6.2 below.

Table 6.2 Top five differences of observations on individual theoretical themes

Theme	Non-fraudster managers
Apologised	Very high
Admit to weaknesses	High
Conscientiousness	Moderate
Work long hours	Moderate
Marital Difficulties	Less Moderate
	Fraudster managers
No one to touch their things	Very high
Surround themselves with 'yes men'	High
Take shortcuts	High
Always right	Moderate
Superiority	Moderate

Overall, non-fraudster managers apologise, admit their weaknesses, are conscientious and work long hours. The latter characteristic is a Red Flag. They also have a 'less moderate' but still have a detection of marital difficulties by the co-workers. The fraudsters are more likely to be wanting people to not touch their office things, for instance, their computer, filing cabinets and so on; this is obviously to hide their thievery, and are more likely to surround themselves with 'yes men', take shortcuts and consider themselves always right and superior to others. The next list in importance of theoretical factors for the fraudsters would be being a good actor, narcissistic, arrogant, variable performance and having no regard for others. It would seem therefore that the co-workers were able to see some of the psychopathic tendencies with this group of fraudsters. The two questions regarding being able to apologise and demonstrating a preference for people to stay away from their things are the better descriptors for this group of non-fraudsters and fraudster managers respectively.

There were some items that bore no indication either way. All managers were considered to be sociable (even though there were at least two who showed signs of introversion), both groups demonstrated moral behaviour and views, and neither group showed overt signs of greed to their co-workers.

Effects of Non-Fraudster Inconsistent Malevolent Impression Management on Co-workers

Basically it is one of confusion. Managers are not behaving as they should be; they say that they are good, but things are not as they seem. This is the effect of the Tyrant and Mediocre Executive Impression Management. The open inconsistency creates fear and anxiety in co-workers; they literally do not know what will happen next.

The content was far less in the study itself, but an outline of the damage that can be created for recipients of this impression management type is seemingly just as much as being a recipient of a fraudster's impression management. Co-workers resigned after the Inconsistent Malevolent impression management was received for several months. They too felt emotions of shock, disappointment and anger at self. They also found out that other staff had left, even the favoured ones, each finding the workplace intolerable. So the effects of working with an executive using Inconsistent Malevolent impression management can be considerable.

If you work with a manager showing Respectful Executive Impression Management, you never feel shock or disappointment with the manager. These managers are not necessarily emotionally present having a high Emotional Quotient,[21] as has been stated in the literature. Psychopaths can easily learn how to appear emotionally present, yet are not benign under their new 'sensitive' exterior; they are in the organisation for themselves, not for others. And when a co-worker receives this type of impression management it will inevitably become apparent over time that the emotional sensitivity expressed is nothing but a trick.

My personal view of the Tyrant Executive Impression Management is that it is the domain of psychopaths and spoilt children who have grown up. The latter if non-psychiatric symptoms are expressed. This is because they have no idea about personal boundaries, as they have never had them imposed, or if they were imposed transgressed them without punishment. Therefore

21 Goleman, D. (1995). *Emotional Intelligence: Why It Can Matter More than IQ*. New York, Bantam Books.

they will show a similar lack of emotion as the psychopath, as they all share the one objective to have power and control over others. This is certainly not restricted to the workplace. Over recent years there has been the uncovering of abuse of minors and children by celebrities. Those who commit such crimes appear to wish the same desire of control over others and are more recently becoming penalised for doing so. The underlying issues are always about power and control.

In the question part of the interviews, co-workers were asked if they had any information regarding the childhoods with the co-workers. Unfortunately there was none at all, therefore there was no determination about maternal attachment disorder. As one of the types of maternal attachment disorder is of the Dismissive (a word that also came up in the co-worker's descriptions), who does not want the help of other care-givers and does not care when the rest of the world disagrees with them. They grow up transgressing social rules so that they can get what they want. I suspect that some of the Tyrants and indeed Arrogant Fraudsters would have this pattern of upbringing.

The surprise though is looking at Table 6.3 below, that the non-impression management theory predictors were not seen by the co-workers; namely, psychopathology, social psychology and the Red Flags. There are some slight differences of the rate of detection between the theories, with the Red Flags the least noticeable by recipients of fraudster executives. Red Flags do not appear to indicate fraudsters. There were two Red Flag predictors showing in the managers using Respectful Executive Impression Management group of co-workers. For example there were still marital difficulties and they worked long hours. Marriages fall apart for various reasons and not all to do with the manager, hence this factor's source is seen as far wider and it would be expected that this Red Flag was seen by their co-workers and due to their needs to make the business successful can work longer hours than others. These two Red Flags could have wasted an investigator's time and effort as they are false positives. Yet to an investigator two Red Flags would be seen as worthwhile to investigate.

When the subgroup of fraudsters is inspected separately there are even fewer signs to their co-workers that they fit within these predictors, but then, they are the masters of disguise out of all the malevolent managers in their Executive Impression Management and this would be expected to some degree. However, when this data were reviewed for the comparison between Respectful Executive Impression Management and all malevolent executives' impression management these predictors were more prominent for the

Table 6.3 Likelihood of managerial fraudsters and non-fraudsters exhibiting signs of different literature based explanations, according to the co-workers

Type of theory	Overall responses	Comment
Impression Management: Morality Authenticity	 Medium Medium	Non-fraudsters are moderately more likely to be more detectable of their morality in recipients' eyes. Fraudsters are moderately more likely to be detected as authentic.
Psychopathology	Low	Fraudsters are slightly more likely to be detected as psychopathic.
Social Psychology	Low	Fraudsters are slightly more likely to be detected using Social Psychological indicators.
Red Flags	Lowest	Fraudsters are only very slightly more likely to be detected through the Red Flag approach.

executives using malevolent impression management. Indeed, recipients of the non-fraudster executives using Tyrant or Mediocre malevolent impression management assigned the list of predictive behaviours in the semi-structured interview guide more to executives using malevolent impression management and not the fraudster group.

The fraud predictors that reflected the malevolent Executive Impression Management the most, are the Social Psychological factors of sociability, persuasibility and manipulation with depression as being the least noticed by the co-workers. This is closely followed by authenticity factors, which reinforces the earlier view that managers use malevolent impression management to engender trust, which they use for their own purposes.

Rehabilitation

There may be cases of turnarounds of Mediocre Executive Impression Management managers (I hold less hope for the Tyrant managers) by intervention at a time of crisis. Indeed I have witnessed this myself, not only within me but others who have come to me who want to change their work lives and live more productively. Many managers who exude the Mediocre Executive Impression Management do not realise how unproductive and unstable their relationships are within the workplace. If this comes to the manager's attention changes can be made to unlearn the ingrained social response and to learn a more positive social interaction. As I have done this myself I know that it takes one to two years to get these new responses ingrained or internalised to the point that now I do not have to think about it.

The reason why I believe there is less hope for the managers who give off the Tyrant Executive Impression Management is that I do not see why they should give up a style of interaction that achieves their goals, no matter how selfish that they may be in the workplace. Co-workers leave damaged, or if they stay they learn to put up with their insufferable behaviour, which means paying a psychological and emotional cost to maintain their job. Ultimately, the subordinates will stay who share the same negative energy (reference to the CAT model) those who have positive energy will leave on their own accord as described here, or be fired within two years. Because it will take this long for a subordinate to leave, as they go through their shock and later withdrawal from their job, it means that the Tyrant's behaviour is reinforced. Always the co-worker is blamed for the departure.

Chapter 7

Methods of Malevolent Managers

Why Do They Choose Malevolence to Get What They Want?

After all, we are told by the management literature that if students learn to do a certain set of behaviours then excellence will result. Surely being a manager who uses Respectful Executive Impression Management would be more appealing than being a Tyrant or Mediocre?

Good Theory is Kept Away from Managers

There is a large segment of literature on leadership as well as the pursuit of excellence.[1] The informed observer can conduct himself to use these behaviours to get the most out of staff. One reason could be that managers actually do not have the literature available, as journals and magazines are too superficial and/or pedantic on aspects of management. Going to business school is seen as an option, particularly the MBA type of courses. Again, it is unlikely that students will be taught good management practice there. In fact there is evidence to the contrary.[2] Not every manager has a management qualification. In the late 1990s in Australia, management was found to be singularly lacking in qualifications and was said to have some of the lowest educated managers in the Western industrialised nations.[3] Twenty years later it is my view that not much has changed.

This is partially due to the new contract-based labour in the workplace. If a person has the right set of skills, ability and experience, a contract is drawn up for limited time with that organisation. Albeit these contracts can be renewed,

1 Peters, T.J. and R.H. Waterman Jr. (1982). *In Search of Excellence: Lessons from America's Best-Run Companies*. New York, Warner Books.

2 Ghoshal, S. (2005). 'Bad management theories are destroying good management practices'. *Academy of Management Learning and Education* 4(1): 75–91.

3 Karpin, D. (1995). *Enterprising Nation: Renewing Australia's Managers to Meet the Challenges of the Asia-Pacific Century*. Canberra, Australian Government Publishing Service.

but essentially post-1992 recession, we have seen a switch from permanent employment to contract employment which is based on hiring explicit skills then releasing them when they are not required. That particular recession saw the beginning of managerial unemployment in droves. This meant that managers were no longer permanent employees as before, they became part of the cost structure that had to be decreased when there is a downswing in business. Before the 1990s, management stayed on, and it was only blue-collar workers who became laid off.[4] This has led to some managers returning to education to receive management qualifications; however, the majority of students in business education are still young and taking the second degree for employment sake. If management school isn't working and the quality literature is not available, there are still other factors that can explain the malevolence which is dealt with later in this book, namely the emergence of violence and the redesigned purpose of management from stewardship to being a self-interested agent of the business owner.

Learning from the Wrong People

The answer to why managers rely on malevolence to get their own way may lie where they learn that it pays off. Generally managers come from a pool of selected individuals who are taught specific management behaviours. The managers using Mediocre Executive Impression Management will have their favourites. These individuals are usually groomed for their future roles so that they will benefit their benefactor. Rewards will be given when satisfactory behaviour using the Mediocre Executive Impression Management creates results of using the organisation for their own needs.

I have seen this time and time again. Many managers have learnt that it is right to have ambitions; to climb over others to reach to the top; to use unfair tactics so that at selection and promotion times these managers use attempts to get the 'right' person in place. I have seen the 'old boys' club' in operation, and also have witnessed discrimination on the grounds of race, gender, disability and ageism. My thoughts are that almost 80 per cent of managers are like this. Managers who use the Tyrant form of Executive Impression Management are only sycophantic when it comes to clients. Many of these I suspect are socialised psychopaths, at the functioning end of psychopathy. They are

4 Groshen, E.L. and D.R. Williams (1992). 'White and blue-collar jobs in the recent recession and recovery: Who's singing the blues?' *Economic Review – Federal Reserve Bank of Cleveland* 28(4): 2–13.

bereft of emotional understanding and are used to getting their own way by sheer bullying.

There appears to be a low percentage of psychopaths in organisations,[5] and they will use their destructive ways to get to positions of power. They do not wait for promotion, they push their own ambition at all times so that any crack in the hierarchy they will use to their own advantage. If, and only if, a person is seen to be useful will they be exploited; however, the objects of their attention are soon discarded once they are of no use anymore. It has been said by Babiak and Hare that they undertake rapid turnover in companies so that they can get to the top quicker.[6] Naked ambition is their way of getting there and they are not ashamed about that fact in any way. They will lie and cheat their way to the top. It is interesting that the co-workers in this study were more able to detect elements of psychopathy than would be expected, but then they had been exposed more than the average worker, particularly with the Arrogant Fraudsters. The psychopath cannot maintain a sociable front to be a Likeable fraudster. One case in the study continued this form of Executive Impression Management for over five years. It would be impossible for them also to be a manager using Respectful Executive Impression Management, no matter how much that they may try to persuade otherwise. So there is strong suspicion on my part as it makes sense that they will be Tyrants of their own organisations, Arrogant Fraudsters or Mediocres who are fast tracking to reach the top.

The problem is that when an individual is on the receiving end of their malevolent impression management it will feel good and true. The individual will be mesmerised. This explains why these managers will get away with their ambitious schemes, as there is really no one to stop their antics.

There are management organisations, but they do not form a regulatory role. The only regulators will be regarding criminal or financial performance regulations in the stock market. There is no one observing and regulating management for their malevolence. Unfortunately the media plays its part in making such people heroes in our culture. We have media magnates who will ensure that this is the case, as they are hardly likely to issue their own bad press. The fights between such magnates may expose harmful activities, and outside journalists may investigate any criminal behaviour. For example, the *News of the World* scandal of 2011, and the Watergate disaster earlier in 1972 which led to the resignation of the US President Nixon. In general these entrepreneurs

5 Morse, G. (2004). 'Executive psychopaths'. *Harvard Business Review* 82(10): 20–22.
6 Babiak, P. and R.D. Hare (2007). *Snakes in Suits*. New York, Harper Collins.

are seen as benign as they generally seem so to their customers in print and the Internet.

The conclusion is that there are many ways that a manager will be educated, not only from their upper management, but the way our culture has formed, that climbing up to the top is still a worthwhile activity, which pays off in power and control as well as in salary. We endorse such behaviour and kowtow to such managers. Wanting an easy life is one such reason, so they usually get away with their malevolent behaviour.

The Forms of Bullying with Tyrant Executive Impression Management

Typically the co-workers reported that open abusive practices were prevalent. Shouting, using verbal abuse, negative comments about the co-workers' output and so on. Emotional abuse beyond general degradation was also noted in the form of criticising, taking credit thus denying the co-worker of praise. In addition, lying and cheating were also observed. The Tyrant Executive Impression Management does not deal with any criticism of their own behaviour, and slams the door on any workplace improvements offered. Employees who do not cooperate with the Tyrant face instant dismissal. This threat hangs over them at all times and is the primary method used to coerce workers to conform. Slave-drivers do not make nice employers, but employees put up with the abuse to ensure that they do not get dismissed and be left unemployed.

Co-workers talked about incredible lengths that a bullying Tyrant would go to. One co-worker had things taken away from her desk and then hidden elsewhere, then later asked for them and then accuse the co-worker of lying. No one is safe from this type of manager. One example in the data was where a daughter of the manager was employed and the same malevolent behaviour was given out to her. Apparently this manager was the same at home as well as in the workplace, abusing everyone until he could get his own way.

The Bullying Ways of Mediocre Executive Impression Management

This type of manager is completely different than the Tyrant. He is not a slave-driver or pushy on deadlines unless his reputation is at stake; he is much more subtle. One notable characteristic of the Mediocre manager is that they will form cliques within the organisation. They seek to belong to them in higher echelons, inside the workplace and outside. Furthermore they also instigate their own circles at work. Everyone will know of these cliques – as it will be part of the tacit knowledge of the workplace, and each employee of course will know if they are inside or outside the group. The exclusivity shown is emotionally abusive and generally there is no rhyme or reason to why the membership takes place; it is only within the Mediocre manager's mind to whom membership is extended. It is the same practice used by the schoolyard gang. If you belonged to that coterie then status was bestowed upon you, and if you were outside then the members would not cooperate with the outsider and turn upon the interloper and in doing so, further abuse the co-worker.

The Mediocres are the masters of office politics, they spread gossip and innuendo about those who they define as competition, and everyone will see this. The openness is remarkable to this divisive conduct. In my own experience I have seen groups of people within the magic circle, and several would-be turncoats and even feed out information if it was to their own advantage. Never underestimate the amount of skulduggery that can be generated out of office politics. The theatre of the manager using Mediocre Executive Impression Management is the total organisation and the audience are useful subordinates and higher-ranking office holders. They run the show and benefit from it in leaping from position to position like a Tarzan in the jungle, as they climb to the top.

Mediocre – as CEO

As CEOs they are cautious not wanting to rock the boat inside or outside. This caution is a weakness when courage is required to deal with internal matters or participate in the wider community. This can affect strategic direction as well as morale with employees. They can be seen as lazy, but they usually are not, as they spend their time plotting and planning for furthering their own ambitions. They will attend many outside functions to do this, and become members of strategic (for themselves) associations so that they can be seen to be helpful to the community. Some will spend their time with charities and non-profit organisations in their effort to look good. I presume that the ultimate accolade would be the British equivalent of a knighthood or OBE, depending which country you are in. In Australia our honours system is very similar to the British and we hand out many a reward to Mediocre managers.

Tyrants rarely receive these awards as they are so obnoxious to most people; however, they still crave the ultimate power over people to elicit respect. One interesting example is that of Robert Maxwell, the media magnate in the UK who confessed that he found men to be too independent and that he preferred to work with women. Sandra Barwick who reported on his wife's autobiography says astutely:

> *All Maxwell's desire for control and power over the helpless ended only in abuse, as hundreds of Mirror pensioners can testify. Prince Charming and the monster so many women glimpsed were never contradictory aspects of his personality. Both incarnations existed for the same purpose, that inexhaustible search for power over others that only fundamentally weak and -yes – that only fundamentally mediocre men desire.*[7]

It raises an interesting point. I cannot imagine that a manager using Respectful Executive Impression Management would remain working for such a man for very long. In fact the CAT model that I have developed predicts a maximum of 24 months that the person with the opposite emotional energy will repel apart, like the wrong ends of a magnet. For example, Robert Maxwell is painted as a manager using Tyrant Executive Impression Management; in fact he was a using the Arrogant Fraudster Executive Impression Management and hid the many breaches of financial conduct until the end when the discovery of the stealing of his employees' pension fund money came to light. Both types are malevolent and a manager using Respectful Executive Impression Management would not stay long. However, the malevolent types will remain, particularly the managers using Mediocre Executive Impression Management. This implies that the organisation itself was run inefficiently, and the proof of that is the final plundering of the pension funds for Maxwell's other failing enterprises. Managers spend more time looking after their own ambitions rather than act as true stewards of the organisation. This means that co-workers have to work in a sea of negativity and productivity inevitably declines.

Being 'two-faced', the manager who uses Mediocre Executive Impression Management is seen by everyone and this makes the manager concerned unreliable to others. If praise is given, the recipient has to work out if it was

7 Berwick, S. (1994). 'The beast and his beauties: Robert Maxwell mesmerised and bullied women. But Betty, his wife for nearly 50 years, remained loyal. Her autobiography will be her first public breach of that loyalty'. *The Independent*, 25 October.

true or false. This leads to untrustworthiness of the manager by the co-workers, except for the naïve and innocent.

Because the literature treats bullying as one perpetrator profile, it is hard to understand what is going on with some behaviour indicators, and others which are not so commonly used. Some definitions are broad as in the notion of violence happens when the target feels hurt, angry and most tellingly of all, powerless. This is exactly the objective of the malevolent managers; they simply use different ways to achieve their aim of power and control of others. The manager using Tyrant or Mediocre Executive Impression Management gains control using many ways as described in Table 7.1. It is important for the person investigating the bullying to be aware that there are two different modus operandi. Once the style is defined then the next step of what to do about it comes into operation, and again there are two different approaches that must be used. If we use the eight management behaviours as defined by Quinn,[8] we can see how the malevolent manager responds. Innovator, broker, producer, director, coordinator, monitor, facilitator and mentor, are the roles required for efficient management and it can be seen that these malevolent managers fall far short.

It is noted in the literature that bullies are '... weak, mean-spirited people who display hurtful and destructive behaviour ... Many bullies become managers because of the position of power and as such, no one is likely to check up on their behaviour ... and often think that they are a law unto themselves.'[9]

Often the Tyrant learns ways of bullying within the parameters of an organisation. For instance, in a public civil service, he may not be allowed to shout at people due to the civil service regulations and culture, whereas in military service this is the norm.

Similarly Mediocre learns ways of bullying that is more acceptable within the culture. Again this can be the result of cultural norms and therefore learns to shout and rage at subordinates in the armed forces. But there is another source of learning open to the Mediocre but not the Tyrant. It can also be the result of management training and reading management 'expert' books and media. This is one reason for my earlier book on managerial fraud not to contain all the behaviours that will be seen by co-workers by managerial

8 Quinn, R.E. (1988). *Beyond Rational Management*. San Francisco, Jossey-Bass Publishers.
9 Gonthier, G. and K. Morrisey (2002). *Rude Awakenings: Overcoming the Civility Crisis in the Workplace*. Chicago, IL, Dearborn Trade.

Table 7.1 **Comparing the bullying styles of managers using the Tyrant and the Mediocre Executive Impression Management**

Tyrant	Mediocre
Openly offensive, using obscenities in front of others	Watchful, Machiavellian in approach, passive aggressive
Intimidates by threat of job loss	Calculates to push the person out
Humiliates	Evaluates, takes credit for work done by target
Openly degrades	Sabotages and undermines
Ridicules openly	Ridicules covertly with in-group
Insults	Damning with faint praise
Yelling or screaming abuse	Never outwardly yells. Abusive statements made unbeknownst to the target
Belittling of opinions	Backstabbing
Constant criticism	Feigns politeness or even friendship
Undermining of work performance	Actually relies on target to perform, to make the manager look good. Never acknowledges, unless politically expedient.
Increasing demands	No demands. No guidance
Unreasonable monitoring, using co-workers to spy	No monitoring if co-worker seen as powerful. Otherwise target is simply ignored
Unreasonably angry direct to the target	'Blows off steam' later
Treating the target as incompetent and telling everyone	Micromanaging if wanting the target to leave
Impossible deadlines	No deadlines, assumes that the co-worker will attend to them. Blames the target if not achieved.
Increasing demands	Will pass on increasing demands only if politically wise to do so, then blames the higher manager in doing so
Isolation from others	In-group expands
Do what I say, not what I do	Unexplained job changes
Ignoring the target's advice	Will only accept advice if political to do so
Give menial tasks to talented staff	Assigning meaningless tasks, sideways moves
Lying to cover up own behaviour	Lying to obliquely coerce target to do things
Putting target under duress	Impedes target receiving information from others
Blames directly and indiscriminately	Uses meetings to show up inadequacies of target. Often indirectly and circuitously

fraudsters. This is because fraudsters learn how to behave to avoid suspicion. Psychopaths are quick and adept at learning a new suite of behaviours for them to cover up their deceitful behaviour. Tyrants learn open ways of behaving violently and unfortunately both forms are reinforced by our culture where violence, open or passive aggressive is supported as a way of getting results. Such films that depict the offender as being right to achieve results through violence support this. A Tyrant will always believe that they are right; there is no remorse in their behaviour as they sincerely believe that they have done nothing wrong.

The Mediocres will use Respectful behaviours if this is ruled as necessary by upper management. If, for example, there is a practice of apologising within the organisation, he may choose to apologise but this will be done without sincerity, despite looking like it. An example of this was mentioned by one of the co-workers in the study. The co-worker accepted the apology as given and did not consider further. The result was that the manager continued with his offensive behaviour but not in front of the co-worker, ostensibly complying with the apology. The Mediocre rose to the top of the organisation and reigned politically correct and conservatively until it was time for him to leave. His in-group were placed in higher-ranking roles and supported him openly in the organisation. Meetings with his coterie to abuse others as they had previously done became within work hours. Accordingly, non-clique members were not promoted. And so the cycle of abuse continued at a different level in the organisation, and took up more work time than before.

Often this behaviour is excused by the CEO as his or her intolerance of poor work performance. Others, particularly important more powerful others, around the manager, are persuaded that there is a performance issue with the target, while what really is going on is organised abuse. The parallel to domestic violence is quite extraordinarily similar, as the perpetrator in that situation is usually able to convince all around him (including the victim) that it is the victim's fault as to why the punishment is meted out.

Indeed, the victims of white collar bullying are most likely to be women, as well as young people, casual or temporary workers, contractors and trainees. All would be considered to have a less powerful and transient status to the bullying manager, and therefore easy targets. It is known that the most usual workplace for this behaviour to occur is education, health services and public administration.

The perpetrators thrive on bullying those who are vulnerable or those that they feel professionally threatened by. If challenged a bully will often defend himself saying that his verbal abuse is a joke, and the target does not have a sense of humour. More often than not an experienced bully of either type will cite non-performance as the central problem. Therefore evidence gathering of performance can be critical.

My own experience with a Tyrant boss was with an older CEO who had learnt that corporate rules forbade shouting at employees, so he used all the other devices known to Mediocres as well as what came naturally to his Executive Impression Management type. Therefore it is important to know that the above Table 7.1 can be a total list for a manager who is experienced enough.

I was drafted into the organisation to facilitate change management from a civil service to a competitive market based organisation. I was well qualified for the job and I was enthusiastically embraced by staff and the board. My first few months were hectic and many instances of putting out fires with disgruntled employees and unions. Also, my CEO told me that as part of my duties I had to micromanage a well-known trouble-maker. No other resources were given with this demand and I had to personally do it. I informed the person concerned that my remit was to keep a close eye on him, and that as it was impossible for me to do that, I would rely upon his time sheets, which I needed every Friday. These were dutifully sent in and I reviewed them. I was hauled over the coals later when the CEO found out that I was not doing as instructed. His anger was blatant and called me a few names out of earshot of anyone else. I had to do what he requested, that was my job, doing what I was told to do.

Then one of my finance managers made a mistake on the organisation's balance sheet. Once again I was called into his office to be berated for my lack of micromanagement of the accounts department. This put some fear in me and I started to review the spreadsheets from my department after hours as there was not enough time in the day. Several things began to happen. My daughter was complaining about eating fast foods, as I was always so late getting home. I noticed that my managers began to report direct to the CEO and that I was being sabotaged at every turn.

The point that I want to make here is that I never once thought that this was bullying. As my stress mounted I began to be fearful of the consequences of my being fired. I had a 'double' mortgage due to a divorce and I was stuck in a job that I tried to stay on top of. Bullying to me was represented by the apocryphal stories told about what happened to young trade apprentices upon starting and during their apprenticeship. These were centred on physical abuse and were unrelated in my mind to what was happening to me. However, it was bullying, an act of violence that seems to be ubiquitous in the workplace. From counselling hundreds of managers I know that this is extant in the workplace and there is little available to help a person to recover from such terrible violence.

Chapter 8

Confronting the Malevolent Manager – The Careful Process of Unmasking

One point that has to be made perfectly clear: only managers using Respectful Executive Impression Management are violence-free. All the other types will inevitably use violence as demonstrated in the modes of bullying described earlier. The direct violence is the product of the Tyrant and passive aggression will be the domain of the Mediocre. Knowing that all malevolent managers are bullies must be understood; the abuse may be kept quiet by the targets who ultimately will suffer and may leave the organisation. One statistic used is that 27 per cent have current or past direct experience with abusive conduct at work.

To approach a malevolent manager about his behaviour is not to be done in haste. The following steps have to be taken before any interview. Firstly there has to be a collection of evidence to the reported behaviour. This type of evidence has to be written notations of all interaction. Emails are the best format for recording conversations, as everything is documented. Even if the conversation was oral, and without witnesses, a written record as such is still useful. It will remain at the very least a testament to how the co-worker felt at the time. Even a distorted perception is worthy of consideration and analysis.

After the grievance has been documented, and preliminary evidence is taken the next step is to conduct 360-degree interviews or a survey to collect information about the manager concerned, to verify bullying or other malevolent acts. This can only be done in confidence, with the guarantee that none of the information will be given or leaked to the manager. There are many previous cases of reprisals on people who report their managers for bad behaviour. Such whistle-blowers will be targeted further by any malevolent manager. A way to overcome the perception of a witch hunt is to institute such surveys for all managers within the organisation. This is more work but highly effective for finding malevolent managers. People are sometimes surprised about finding pockets of malevolence; others more intuitive would have felt uneasy but with no reference as to why. A 360-survey implemented in confidence is the only way to find such managers. The survey questions cannot be feeble. We are talking about investigating if there is violence going on in the workplace and have to be direct to invite information. Here are some sample questions:

- Have you ever felt hurt and angry with your manager?
- Does your manager have favourites?
- Have you ever witnessed your manager lying?
- Do you feel that you are receiving the correct level of supervision and content?
- Does your manager send you on training courses?

These questions are dichotomous. They invite a yes or no answer. Regardless, further information has to be elicited so a 'Please explain' or 'Your comments please' are useful. Collect the data and review it with the following in mind.

One aside is that a vindictive employee of any status who has decided that this manager should be ousted can use the instrument for supplying false information. Therefore, any negative commentary must be separately investigated. Negativity is sign of a malevolent manager who exists or in the making, never let this situation develop into a full-blown malevolent manager.

If the 360-degree survey information received is diverse, then it is likely that the original co-worker may have difficulties himself, for instance lack of self-esteem, which may be shored up through assertiveness training. If the information that comes back is on the same theme and, of course, with different words then it is very likely that the complaint is true. One thing that was very noticeable with the Tyrant and Mediocre managers is that they were quite open about their malevolent behaviour, even to the point of justifying it by blaming the 'system' or the complainant's inefficiencies. So all who are surveyed are able to witness it; they may not understand it, or excuse it, but nevertheless it is apparent.

The third step is to go back to the target of the manager's behaviour and give support in every way possible. Those with a valid complaint may not be the strongest employee and will need support to continue with the process. After all, it is very likely that the manager concerned may have the right to hire and fire and will quickly do that without any compunction. Malevolent managers get rid of obstacles to their power and control, so counselling the target on compliance gives less chance for a dismissal. The interview with the malevolent manager has to be conducted carefully and mindful of the typology that will present itself.

Confrontation of the Abusive Behaviour by a Manager Using Tyrant Executive Impression Management

A manager that uses Tyrant Executive Impression Management will assume superiority in the interview. However, even with the most obnoxious there is an equally valid threat to him to be dismissed for unseemly conduct. If the manager is the CEO, then the chairman of the board must be informed and present at the interview. Advice has been given in the past to never get in the way of the CEO and his chairman. This is to prevent actions being taken out on the investigator as well as the target. However, if there is a chairman using Respectful Executive Impression Management then there is every chance that he will cooperate and either get rid of the CEO using Tyrant Executive Impression Management or remove him from the area concerned. Employment must be on the condition that all employees are treated with respect, which malevolent managers seem to forget in the heat of their battle for domination. Therefore, dismissing a CEO on these grounds can be undertaken. The Tyrant CEO, however, will invoke and resort to litigation. He will not take it lightly that his superior ways are not wanted. That is one of the reasons why the evidence gathering must be extensive and not relying on hearsay. The notes will be used as evidence in court, or if the organisation is fortunate for settlement purposes. Tyrants do not like being publicly undermined, and will have a seething sense of injustice to display to all the wrongdoings of the organisation.

Many organisations do not want negative publicity from such a public row, and cave in to giving very generous handshake packages to be rid of such a nuisance. A chairman using Respectful Executive Impression Management will not be so intimidated and will draw the line and let the civil courts decide. A chairperson who is using Mediocre Executive Impression Management will get rid of the nuisance CEO by automatically giving in to his demands or worse still ignore the evidence and keep the CEO in his position, using excuses of that he has made the organisation what it is today by his direction – read slave driving. Furthermore a chairperson who is using Tyrant Executive Impression

Management will get rid of the CEO at any excuse so that he can remain the ultimate power in the organisation.

If these steps fail to work with the malevolent manager, and he is allowed to get away with his behaviour, then it is time for not only the target, but the investigator, if employed by the same organisation, to be looking for other employment. It is a warning sign of the true nature of the organisation and must be heeded.

I have found in my practice that opposite emotional energy does not attract, despite the commonly held belief that opposites attract. The sayings refer to complementarity aspects of personality, skills and experience, but not to a person's emotional energy. Opposites in emotional energy struggle to stay together unless there is some other tie that binds them together. For instance, in a marriage parents may stay together because of their children. Sometimes employees find themselves stuck in a negative organisation due to responsibilities to pay the mortgage and so on, but it is always at a cost to the positive energy employee who must find a strategy to stay stress-free in the remainder of his internal or external contract with the organisation. The only people I have found who maintain themselves stress-free are Buddhist monks or saints. However, they spend so much time to their devotions that a Tyrant employer would dismiss either of them simply because they do not spend all their time at work. A manager using Mediocre Executive Impression Management, however, will judge from a distance, and despite his own misgivings with the employee will keep the person on if it is politically wise. No manager using Mediocre Executive Impression Management would want to dismiss a popular saint in their ranks. However, they would if the worker was a non-entity.

Normally, a malevolent manager and an employee showing respect will part within 24 months. If it lasts longer than that, it is due to some diffidence from the respectful person who may in fact be denying that he may not be as respectful as he thinks. I have developed this latter theme later in the book, because one feature of the malevolent managers is that they do not actually see themselves as malevolent to others. They will admit to being ambitious or skilful at accruing resources (like stealing) but they will generally not admit that what they do hurts others. When you hear the phrase 'You must be a fool not to ...' it will come from the mouth of a malevolent intentioned person, who sees that it his right to obtain the most power and control as he possibly can. Sometimes you will hear the words: 'Forgive me, I have ...' but these are the words of someone who is trying to manipulate the system, including you.

Confrontation of the Abusive Behaviour by a Manager Using Mediocre Executive Impression Management

This type of manager will use everything in his power to stop an investigation. These actions include diverting attention away from him by saying others are worse in their behaviour. Also they may try to pull strings to get attention from higher echelon to intervene. They will be cognisant of the rules and they will draw upon legal expertise if they do not. They will not necessarily be litigious, but will use such forums as industrial relations courts, anonymous letters to the press and so on. This behaviour is very different from those who have a legitimate cause; what they are doing is attempting to prevent the confrontation over their behaviour.

It is almost like catching an eel on a fishing hook: the manager will wriggle and squirm like crazy rather than address the fact that his actions are bullying and need redress. This is another reason why it is necessary to have as much evidence as possible to confront the manager, as the response will be excuse after excuse. One very popular way out for a manager using Mediocre Executive Impression Management is to assert that the target deserved such treatment. One thing that has to be made clear is that no one deserves to be abused in the workplace and that exclusion of activities or omission to intervene is just as abusive as sticking the co-worker's head down the toilet. Blaming the victim is never an excuse for behaviour; in fact it demonstrates that this quality that is being rebuked may very well be the factor within the manager's own personality that is being projected onto unfortunate others.

General Hints to Tackle a Malevolent Manager

Once a complaint is heard about bullying, there has to be duty of care given to both sides. The investigation and subsequent interview has to be done carefully and not effected as a witch hunt. Most malevolent managers think that they are in the right, and to find out otherwise is a strain to their perception of life. There is one type, the Likeable Fraudster who upon confrontation will attempt to commit suicide. Likeable Fraudsters are masters at manipulation and will have their whole department or unit on their side. If this behaviour is confronted to demonstrate clearly that this not benign behaviour or respectful to others, it is a twisted attempt to curry favour and so on. The Likeable Fraudster and here I will include the Mediocre managers, can pull the plug as to be known for who they really are, as it is too damaging for them to live with. Nervous breakdowns have occurred due to this type of cognitive dissonance, as referred to earlier[1] and the manager may very well need intense counselling to divert his attention away from self-destructive acts to taking managerial responsibilities seriously.

Always have a witness during the confrontation interview. It is important to have someone who is trustworthy to be in the same room. This witness can verify events later, if things get out of control. Some managers are violent; some will smoulder and ruminate on vengeance upon the target and the investigator; some may go to the media and conduct vitriolic campaigns to rectify the injustice. A witness, preferably senior and understanding of this type of behaviour is best to have at hand to aid the interview. Moreover, if the manager concerned is prepared to accept, it is good to record the events by video or audio recording.

With the interview and evidence there must be a plan of action, which must be agreed to. This can include confidential therapeutic counselling, a move to a different unit or department, or shadowing by a senior manager or outside consultant to observe and feedback the behaviour to the manager himself. Or alternatively a warning is given that if this behaviour is reported once more by anyone, then dismissal will take place. An apology must be given to the target before witnesses as well as a written apology. A written apology is almost better than face to face, as it can be used later as evidence if the no-bullying rule is breached. The apology must be inspected before it is given so that the words remain respectful and do not push the manager into blaming and other avoidance tactics.

In some jurisdictions this may have to be three warnings before dismissal, but my preference is for two only. The reason is that the first warning is the boundary setting, assuming the manager was not aware of what he was doing. Or if he was aware of the intention to hurt, then re-training of that behaviour to stop. The second warning is there to say it is dismissal time, as the boundary set previously has been violated. This has to be declared in no uncertain terms to the manager, that bullying behaviour is not tolerated in any form, and any transgression will cause instant dismissal.

Finally, the revelation of bullying in the workplace can induce employees to leave, and this issue has to be managed sensitively. This is because the violence is seen to be tacitly agreed upon by management in general. It creates distrust in management, and co-workers' own ability to build relationships

1 Festinger (1962).

in the workplace based on trust is broken. That is why it is important to act immediately to gather evidence upon an initial complaint. By gathering evidence it shows that management does care about such ethical violations. But this is not enough on its own, there has to be an outcome. As discussed earlier this may be a dismissal or re-training or transfer. All that needs be done is that a general message is sent out to all staff, including the board that bullying is not tolerated within the organisation, and that this is the outcome, briefly and simply stated.

Chapter 9

How to Choose a Manager Who Uses Respectful Executive Impression Management

In order to choose a manager who uses Respectful Executive Impression Management, it is important to understand your own self thoroughly. If this does not happen, choices are prone to your inner self's projection of internal negativity. This can mean that an otherwise positive energy manager is disputed and denigrated as being the positive person that he is, due to false perceptions projected from the self.

As mentioned earlier, the theory of the self is very much a philosophical debate and even though some consensus may arise, it may not be the true state of the self. Goffman referred to it as a state of nothingness that only appears when impression management occurs; others impute from this, rightly or wrongly, the moral self that lies within.

As Goffman states that impression management is purely a representation of self, it implies the true self lies within. This self, however, may not be totally desirable to the individual. Leary and Kowalski[1] refer to desired and undesired representations. Also they say that there is a public self and a private self. In addition, they refer to the literature that includes both the private and public self, and this points to the Lockean sense of self as the moderator of behaviour, the arbiter of ethics:

> *Our model explicitly highlights points of connection between the private self and impression management. Three such points are paramount. First, one's standards for self-evaluation are implicated both in motivating impression-relevant behavior and in determining the form*

1 Leary, M.R. and R.M. Kowalski (1990). 'Impression management: A literature review and two-component model'. *Psychological Bulletin* 107(1): 34–47.

that impression management takes. Second, one's private self-concept has an impact on one's self-presentational choices. Third, one's desired and undesired selves channel the impressions one attempts to convey.[2]

The self being divided into two, with a public and secret face despite giving us clarification does more to confuse. Is it not accepted that there is only one true self, warts and all? Baumeister was quite explicit about the sense of self in social-psychological usage when dealing with the concept of impression management.[3] He states that the concept '... does not imply that the self is created only by impressing others. A "true", "real", or "private" self is constructed not by self-presentation but through one's choices and performances. Creating the self is a matter of self-presentation only insofar as it is concerned with establishing and maintaining one's *public* self, that is the image of oneself that exists in the minds of others'.[4]

To access the hidden self, the true self, not what we think we are, but what truly lies within us, is a difficult process. However, it is made easier through compassionate (as opposed to critical) self-analysis and meditation. At this point I would like to include from a personal email that I received from Gede Prama, a world-acknowledged Buddhist teacher who wrote to me about the Long Journey of Making the Unconscious Conscious.[5]

While law and society try to change people by rejecting their negative sides, meditation changes people by accepting them as they are.

Entering unconsciousness is like entering the dark rooms in our house that [has] never be opened for years. Doubt, fear, anxiety are there. And meditation teaches us to enter these dark rooms slow but sure. That's why one definition of meditation is to be face to face with the reality as they are. That is also the reason why in perfection stage of meditation, people are guided to 'accept, flow, smile' to all blessings of this moment. Those who grow deep in meditation know, what people called as the frightening dark rooms of unconsciousness is only rope which is mistakenly [seen as a] snake ... While the commoners struggle to be kind and full of love, the masters who come to the stage of insight,

2 Ibid., 44.
3 Baumeister, R.F. (1982). 'A self-presentational view of social phenomena'. *Psychological Bulletin* 91(1): 3–26.
4 Ibid., 4.
5 Prama, G. (2014). Long Journey of Making the Unconscious Conscious.

their natural nature is kindness. Love, kindness, honesty become their natural nature. That is the experience of many enlightened masters.

This knowledge is life-giving to our souls – our inner selves. Nowadays we do know that meditation reduces stress and counteracts the increased adrenaline that courses through our bodies when we are under stress. In fact, we only have two devices to reduce stress: meditation and strong physical exercise.[6] I can only advocate that taking up meditation is the easier thing to do within the workplace: take a five-minute comfort break, lock yourself in the toilet, close your eyes and breathe! Every person that I have counselled I have taught the basics of meditation so that they have a useful tool when out in the workforce again. Not everyone can go out and take a 20-minute jog, but everyone can stop and meditate and within 10 minutes feel relaxed and de-stressed. Wilson offers other techniques as well to minimise the stressful experience, but out of all of them, he encourages meditation.

Meditation can deal with anything, especially when an individual faced with a manager openly manipulating co-workers. Goffman saw this type of manipulation, when he later stated that people try to contrive situations in which they interact. A case in point is his discussion of fabrications, where people are led to believe that a particular situation exists, when in fact it does not.[7] This would be the in the repertoire of the Tyrant more than the Mediocre, but can be learnt by the latter if in a toxic culture. Co-workers are given false deadlines and when they produce the work on time and at great personal cost, he laughs at them for being so gullible. Lies are told and believed, scams and rorts exist for the same reason, an open manipulation of the truth to extort money.

We try, mostly in vain, to prevent this manipulation by scanning a manager's face to look for signs of lies and untruths being said. The face, Goffman says, is the place of authenticity, which people look to when searching for clues of authenticity. The face is the issuer of words that people measure; however, with a malevolent manager, it also is stage managed to give the right impression. It is the place where the self and the world meet. Authenticity, Deighton states,[8] must therefore be present. However, this only applies to the manager using Respectful Executive Impression Management; the other managers will produce the right face for their malevolent purpose.

6 Wilson, P. (1995). *The Little Book of Calm*. London, Penguin Books.
7 Goffman, E. (1974). *Frame Analysis: An Essay on the Organization of Experience*. Boston, MA, University Press of New England.
8 Deighton, J. (2004). 'The presentation of self in the information age'. *HBS Marketing Research Paper No. 04–02* April(2): 1–18.

The Self Being Represented by the Face

Deighton takes this one step further. He recognises that the face is the place where emotions show reactions to the other actors. However, it is not a one-way deliverer of information, where the face shows and reflects the actions of the social situation. It is a two-way process. The face reacting to, as well as posing, to the audience, should measure authenticity. The managers using Mediocre Executive Impression Management would know how to bring the right face to their audience. Goffman's writings on face work explore this reciprocity of saving and giving face:

> *It seems to be a characteristic obligation of many social relationships that each of the members guarantees to support a given face of the other members in given situations ... A social relationship, then, can be seen as a way in which the person is more than ordinarily forced to trust his self-image and face to the tact and good conduct of others.*[9]

Goffman predicted that if an individual does not live up to the promise, then that person will be held in disrepute. The self-presentation therefore is meant to be of the hidden self. However, this totally fails within an organisation where power and control is invested in management hierarchies.

The Hidden Self

When stress occurs individual beliefs about the world change.[10] The non-fraudster Executive Impression Management data are peppered with references about an 'us and them' fracturing of their world, whereas the Respectful Executive Impression Management's view is one of cohesion.

The co-workers of Tyrant and Mediocre impression management reported this in many ways, e.g., favouritism, being exclusionary to others and high pressure tactics. The world is a partitioned place to these managers and their only way of dealing with it is to divide and conquer with the use of violence. It is the way that this person has learnt to deal with the world. Goffman is most insistent that impression management is dealing on the outer of the self,

9 Goffman, E. (1967). *Interaction Ritual: Essays on Face-to-Face Behavior*. New York, Pantheon Books, 42.

10 Bandura, A., G.V. Caprara, C. Barbaranelli, C. Pastorelli and C. Regalia (2001). 'Sociocognitive self-regulatory mechanisms governing transgressive behavior'. *Journal of Personality and Social Psychology* 80(1): 125–35.

with the world as the self knows it. But this is not a private self or a public self. It is *how* individuals make sense of their world. The interesting thing about this aspect is that it is non-blaming. The individual grows up learning these tools to protect himself from incursions by others. Therefore, the individual is in fact feels weaker than others around him. The Tyrant learns to dominate, the Mediocre learns to contrive. Despite the Tyrant's intimidation, underneath there is a weak notion of self. Even psychopaths are said to have this inner core.[11]

THE SELF: THE ARROGANT FRAUDSTER

A staged confidence game requires all the performance of normality. Indeed, as this investigation has found out, in the co-workers' eyes the Arrogant Fraudster Executive Impression Management displays cracks in the veneer of the disguise over time. What is seen is not a powerful character who is trustworthy and authentic; rather co-workers see, albeit momentarily, fear which is accorded by Goffman as an indicator of weak character. These fraudsters are still operating within their impression management type, disguising their view of a highly fractured world using the mask of Respectful Executive Impression Management. This is the contrivance that gives them away. If the Arrogant Fraudster used the open Tyrant Executive impression management, the fraudster would not have had the cracks appearing, as this Executive Impression Management is closer to his true self. The problem of course is that an ordinary organisation would not normally hire him, as Tyrants are less than attractive to a selection panel looking for a particular expertise. The fractured attitudes of self-promotion and downwards intimidation would not be tolerated. However, a fraudster using The Arrogant Fraudster type of Executive Impression Management uses the disguise in the belief that this disguise will work better than his true hidden self.

THE SELF: THE TYRANT EXECUTIVE

The Tyrant Executive Impression Management is based on openness too, but in a negative fashion, as one recipient remarked:

> *What you see is what you don't get.*

The manager using Tyrant Executive Impression Management does not have to bother with being authentic, trustworthy or moral. Despite the self being a

11 Tamayo, A. and F. Raymond (1977). 'Self-concept of psychopaths'. *Journal of Psychology* 97(1): 71–8.

private moral space, it is the self's activities (such as malevolent impression management) that attract judgements of good or bad from co-workers as they appear not to care what others make of them. If I can turn to an example here, Steve Jobs was the central and dominant manager of Apple Inc. He outraged many employees and left many disgruntled co-workers in his wake. Despite all that was terrible about his management behaviour he was driven to provide computers, laptops and later phones that were beyond compare to the world. Jobs was an adoptee and I can certainly understand his behaviour as a way of controlling his environment. He used the Tyrant Executive Impression Management, whereas I used the Mediocre Executive Impression Management: there was little difference between the two of us, both wanting to control what could hurt us – other people, and both with a drive to make our mark on this world. This drive is to offset the primal wound of being separated from our mothers, which is felt in the form of cruel rejection. Therefore, to be accepted by others becomes first and foremost drive in our hidden selves.

Apart from the millions of dollars that do mark the difference between us, I can sympathise and empathise with his style of management. This is where Goffman steps in as he would say that the Executive Impression Management is purely a social behaviour of the inner self that maybe hidden even from the individual himself. Unfortunately Jobs was unable to reconcile his loss of his mother, and passed away never knowing that compassion is the way for the self to recover. One of the most healing statements that was said to me from an adoption counsellor was: 'It has nothing to do with you.' It refers to all of the pain of rejection that was felt so keenly by us adoptees and retained throughout our lives. This is one of the most compassionate statements I have ever come across. Once this truth sinks in, an adoptee was well on the road to recovery. Being accidentally hurt in life is a fairly normal experience, but most will respond with 'S**t happens.' Earthquakes, volcanic eruptions, floods, hurricanes happen, and of those who are caught in these natural disasters are not blamed for their deaths and wounds. However, adoptees do, and will continue to do so until they either recover or die. Jobs gave us Apple and Pixar: I have written this book. My intent is to help others with this new theory to explain the violence of the workplace. I am no longer plotting and scheming to be the best (read well-paid) CEO in the world. Thankfully, I gave that up nearly 20 years ago. When my management interaction changed to that of the respectful type, that goal quickly disappeared.

THE SELF: THE MEDIOCRE MANAGER

The manager using the Mediocre Executive Impression Management is at heart a person who feels that he has no control, that no one will listen to him, that the only way to gain being heard is for this anxious individual is to manipulate people into doing what it wants. This sense of self can occur through the early maternal attachment of Anxiety, that is, a child who learns that his behaviour is dependent on his mother taking every turn to give him attention that he craves. This is an impossible task of a mother, particularly if there are other factors involved, such as domestic violence or perceived severe threats to the mother's well-being to create over-protective behaviours. The infant learns to focus on the mother and uses attention-seeking behaviours to receive his mother's notice. Growing up, these behaviours become reinforced with illnesses, ordinary events that school kids get involved with and so on. The individual craves the attention that he used to receive from his mother, but displaces that onto friends and his teachers and later from his spouse or life partner in later life. He learns that some social behaviour is rewarded, like high marks at school or university, and others receive social sanction and these are to be avoided. Once they get to be managers and have power in their workplace, they continue to use these behaviours. Deep inside though, they are anxious individuals, unhappy that they do not receive social attention as is their due. Hence the manipulative construct is used time and time again.

THE SELF: THE RESPECTFUL EXECUTIVE

As seen earlier, underneath the malevolent managers Executive Impression Management one would *expect* to see a weak person not a strong character. Similarly, the self of a manager showing Respectful Executive Impression Management would be *expected* to be a strong character. However, this may not be the case. For example, an individual could use Respectful Executive Impression Management, yet be weak, despite the impression management offering goodness, trust and authenticity to recipients. In fact, the Emperor in the fairy tale of the Emperor's New Clothes, was described as being a good and trusted ruler, but the tailors found his one weakness, his love of high fashion and exploited it for their own ends. Displaying Respectful Executive Impression Management does not automatically mean that the individual is good. It only means that he or she is showing consistency, trustworthiness and morality in their impression management to people. They may in fact have other reasons for their benign behaviour; for instance the road to heaven is said to be paved with good deeds. In fact, the individual may only be doing these kind acts for his own salvation. This good person may well be merely strategic, and not doing kind actions out of the goodness of his being and caring for others. Similarly, for the Likeable Fraudster it was the bond that had to be made with certain staff to get away with his stealing, and the Mediocre Executive his clique who continually gave sycophantic attention to his behaviour.

The Real Character Underneath

The real character according to Goffman is only revealed at 'fateful moments'. This moment is a crisis whereby the future of the individual is at stake. For instance, we hear of stories of martyrs who gave their lives for others. Their characters were of enormous strength, so strong that they were able to withstand the threat of their very being. We hear of mothers defending their children against wild beasts, of pilots who are prepared to risk their lives to save their passengers and so on. Weak individuals would show fear and with the fraudsters they showed fear at the moment of discovery of their frauds. For the non-fraudster managers, we have no such data from the co-workers. They did not see their manager undergo a crisis, so there cannot be any determination out of the data. However, it is arguable, particularly in the light of the explanations of the malevolent non-fraudster managers' behaviour, that they would have weak characters, as their notions of self are weak. In accordance with the information of the managers who use Respectful Executive Impression Management we could expect to see strong character formation.

Goffman considered that the character was instilled in the person and was unlikely to change over time.[12] However, there are some indicators for the managers using Tyrant and Mediocre Executive Impression Management that indicate their internal weakness. There are four categories of impression management approaches if an individual is 'found out' in a public predicament.[13] These include using excuses, justifications, concessions and denial. It would be expected and is confirmed in this investigation that the malevolent managers (Tyrant and Mediocre as well as the Arrogant and Likeable Fraudsters) would use these strategies. A manager using Respectful Executive Impression Management would be expected to only use apologies,[14] which implies genuine self-awareness and humility to learn. This too was confirmed in the data. It is only Respectfuls who genuinely apologise.

12 Goffman (1967).

13 Konovsky, M.A. and F. Jaster (1989). '"Blaming the victim" and other ways business men and women account for questionable behaviour'. *Journal of Business Ethics* 8(5): 391–8.

14 Tucker (2006).

Selection Interviews

Using an indicator such as apologising is a bit difficult to obtain in an interview. It can be done, but may give false positives for finding out if the candidate is truly a manager using Respectful Executive Impression Management due to the capacity of other types to astutely use the apology in their favour. It is far better to conduct due diligence in interviewing co-workers to verify. The caveat as mentioned earlier is that a manager using Mediocre Executive Impression Management may use an apology if it is warranted in a given situation. Even, unfortunately, Tyrants have been known to have an apology to be squeezed out of them. President Nixon did not apologise for the disgraceful break-in at the offices of his opposing political party in 1972. The Watergate incident caused Nixon's downfall, which he strongly denied despite evidence to the contrary. It was not until the famous David Frost interview some years later that he apologised to the American people for his behaviour. Similarly US President Clinton admitted his sexual liaison with a member of staff in 1998; however he did not publicly apologise until after his impeachment.

Whilst many people knew of the wrongdoings, which were widely reported in the press and TV, not receiving an apology until some years later, disrupts our social desire for harmony. We all know what Respectful Executive Impression Management means as we all subscribe to it, even if secretly we do not agree. That was the problem with the co-workers of the managers who used Respectful Executive Impression Management, they knew what they saw and once the words of Good and Great were used, there was nothing more to be said, as we all recognise what they mean. A good manager is exactly that – good. If they are less than that we demand an apology. However, with the advance of violence in the workplace, millions have been deprived of such an apology. The fact that we all think of ourselves as good, then it leaves us wide open for deceit, as for many of us, we are deceiving ourselves.

And that's why knowing yourself is so important. Once we can do that, we can truly recognise goodness in others, as we can see it within ourselves, no matter how sinful and vile we may be. Hitler banned all experimentation on animals, and for this he was seen as having at least one good point. The fact that he allowed experimentation on humans is abhorrent, but he loved animals and was a committed vegetarian. This does not excuse his heinous behaviour, but it is a challenge to our image of him. One of our deep values is that we are rational human beings; to have such a fact about Hitler is at odds with the behaviours that we condemn. In fact, we can only conclude that he was not rational in his behaviour. That label fits with our image of the warlord.

To be less than rational is to live outside our known world. We give pejoratives to those who are not rational. Idiot, crazy, mad and imbecile are some words that we use for those who are irrational. However, this is the key to understanding ourselves, we are truly not rational beings.

Management Rationality

One of the greatest delusions of almost all present day life is that humans behave rationally. What will happen to most readers being presented with this statement is immediate refutation, as Western thought is dominated by the delusion of rationality. To say otherwise is illogical and deeper than that, it is incomprehensible. To believe that human behaviour is irrational speaks of anarchy and again, at a lower level lies madness.

There are many examples at the macro level can be given about so-called rational decisions that history has now shown to be otherwise. The launching of the crusades to save Jerusalem in the 1100s were made in the name of God. The Islamic defenders of Jerusalem also called upon the same God and both sides slaughtered tens of thousands in his name. Many people today will say that this is not very representative of the modern world, but they excuse similar irrational behaviour with thousands of people being killed when the Western world gathered together to wipe out the 'weapons of mass destruction', in the name of the very same God.

Islam has a different prophet than Christianity but both religions believe in the same God. Even the Jewish nation shares many prophets with both of these religions and still adhere to worshipping the same overall being. Yet there has been war after war in the Middle East. A rough calculation of the number of deaths from war in the Middle East during 1945 to 1999 covers 48 conflicts and an approximate total of 2.5 million deaths. It could not be stated that every person killed believed in the same God. Yet all of these conflicts had God central to the war. It was believed that it was God's will to enforce whatever the point was of the conflict.

Peace seems to be steadfastly avoided, yet peace is the most rational way to live after all. There is no need for pointless killing, no displacement of populations into refugee camps and walled areas to protect the inmates from others. A rational sensible world means eradication of poverty and disease, tolerance of beliefs and respect for each other. Presently advertising drives consumerism, multinationals and monopolistic organisations reap rewards of billions of dollars and happiness is shaped by the media, which mostly is in the hands of a few magnates who wish to control the thought process of their 'informed' readership, enforced by social media and gossip.

Ideas of 'Enoughism' and non-violence are seen as idealistic fantasies and unachievable dreams.[15] Wars are justified, as do the greater widening of the gap between rich and poor, individuals and nation states. This is far from a wonderful world. Poverty and disease still rule life for most people on this planet. Millions of children die from malaria, dysentery before they are 5 years old. The cushioned first world does not see this at all, apart from an occasional news item or advertising from a charity. The world population currently stands at 7 billion people. According to the United Nations' Department of Economic and Social Affairs by 2050 the number will be well over 9.5 billion. Where are the economic and social resources to support such numbers? Does this mean that globally the extra 2 billion people are condemned to poverty, lack of education, disease and malnutrition? In Western Europe there is a sharp decline of replacement babies being born and already there are signs of a decreasing population. The recent recession of 2007/8 is not totally responsible for the decline in house values in rural Western Europe; there are fundamentally too many houses for too few people. This is particularly true for France and Italy. However, immigration from more populous and economically disadvantaged countries is maintaining overall numbers. Traditionally though, immigrants are not attracted to rural areas; they follow where the work is, which is predominantly urban conurbations. These areas become a type of shanty town with older apartment buildings reminiscent of the tenement buildings of the Victorian era in England, with overcrowding and lack of sanitation adding to the newcomer's burden.

Lack of rationality provides not only an unequal distribution on resources but economic displacement of the refugee. Today refugees have to go through a process of legitimisation to be accepted by the new country or be transferred back to their old one. The horror of war is the result of irrationality completely and utterly.

Turning to the workplace, that is, the micro level irrationality reigns supreme. This not only results in failed business, but 'successful' ones too. Monopolistic and oligopolistic organisations have preferred treatment or hold superior positions in closed markets to new entrants. The rationalist economy

15 Kurlansky, M. (2007). *Nonviolence: The History of a Dangerous Idea*. London, Vintage; Naish, J. (2008). *Enough*. London, Hodder and Stoughton.

determined by the twin factors of supply and demand is only an ideal and does not truly exist. Stock market ups and downs are more due to gossip and fear than cause and effect.

Strategic management and decision-making are also products of irrationality rather than true independent processes free from value-laden assumptions. If an organisation is lucky enough to be in the right place and right time then it may be successful despite irrational decisions made by the business owners. Non-profits emerge to fulfil areas of need for the disadvantaged but they do not exist in a perfect marketplace either. Their success depends on governmental support and/or public donations. People donate primarily to those who have sensorial loss for instance the blind and the deaf rather than what is perceived as self-imposed disadvantages like addiction, unclean and unsafe housing, no recipients appreciating or deferring to the Lady Bountiful of altruism.

Values that exist in our workplace concern with greed, hatred and fear. These promote avaricious behaviour for wages entitlements and bonuses, bullying and discrimination respectively. This is the perfect environment for malevolent managers to thrive. They do not want respect, equality and non-discriminatory policies; they use the organisation for their own selfish gains and nothing else can be expected. They learn to say the talk but do not uphold it in their actions.

This in itself, the not walking the talk is the best indicator for malevolent management. However, our culture and the media push us into further consumerism that it becomes difficult to say stop. Surrounded by the rotten petri dishes of imperfect organisms the respectful managers and co-workers are drowned by the madness of irrationality.

Personally I think it is time to stop the merry-go-round of reason being used for justifying selfish acts. Organisations must become responsible for their internal as well as external actions. Management has to step off into the unknown world of respect for others and joy of working with people who want to be there to assist in any way possible to make the organisation work.

I can give many examples of how it works. My recent work with setting up a social enterprise in northern Bali is one such instance. People step up when they see something that they can do, and do it to the best of their ability, for instance the marketing function, operations management and so on. Others learn how to make the handicrafts and provide the wanted items for informed customers who enjoy hand crafted items rather than the machined output of things that we tend to clutter our homes with. Language is picked up from each other so that they can talk to customers. Some of the women work long hours for small rewards but know that one day soon they will receive the fruits of their labour. There is respect for every participant, laughter rules meetings, common sense is listened to and practicalities are met. There is no argument about who is given what: everyone knows how the money is distributed, with the woman who made the item receiving 50 per cent of the sale price.

There is no doubt in my mind that my task has been made easier in setting up the enterprise as I am surrounded by a culture of respect. The original inhabitants of Bali lived in this northern region, ignoring the swampy lowlands of the south. It is their culture, which has been handed down the generations so that a social enterprise such as this is able to thrive. To do anything as revolutionary as asking for respect in the workplace in the first world is immensely difficult.

I know this first hand as at one time I was a research consultant for small business generation and development and was asked to produce ideas for micro business financing for Western Australia. The Grameen Bank[16] finances small businesses with no collateral. The self-administered finance scheme is open to peer review and if repayments are not on time, the peer group then investigates why and assists the individual in repaying the loan. One default in their circle is too hard to bear so everything is done to make the micro enterprise work. The bank has very low rates of failure and default, and accordingly has had immense success connecting the world's poorest with the resources they need. Micro business financing has been lagging behind the Grameen Bank's example and certainly the government that I was assisting at the time felt it was too radical an idea to take forward, despite the fact that it was operational in Canada and parts of Europe. Later I implemented a very small microfinance scheme in Perth with a charity that supports the homeless, and from that a micro-savings scheme, both with support from the Perth Rotary Club.

Such far-reaching ideas for the workplace can be operated; it only requires the willpower and a minimum of resources. Examples have been around a long time for management buy-outs.[17] They have proved to be good long-term businesses in the hands of those managers who, I have observed, usually

16 Grameen Foundation. (2015). 'What We Do – Financial Services'. Retrieved 23 February 2015, from http://www.grameenfoundation.org/what-we-do/financial-services/.

17 European Private Equity and Venture Capital Association (2001). European Buyout Success Stories: Special Paper. Zaventem, Belgium, European Private Equity and Venture Capital Association.

emit Respectful Executive Impression Management. If it is a matter of a quick buck to be made, then the enterprise will falter and co-workers will become unemployed. And one little side note to add here is that a managers who set up their own business generally take themselves out of the job market for good. This is because the former business-operator will know too much about managing a business and will be greatly feared by most employers who do not want a new applicant to take over their business.

Nevertheless there are pockets of respectful workplaces run by respectful managers that do exist and if you are lucky enough to work for one of those organisations then stay where you are and develop and blossom with the company. However, most readers will have experience of the malevolent workplace and have their own stories to tell about the ridiculous way decisions are made, how selfish the managers are and how uncaring the organisation is.

The words 'No one is indispensable' are used as a threat to keep co-workers in line, to maintain control by withdrawing the job from the incumbent if he threatens to destabilise the current workplace. I am quite sure that those words are never spoken in a respectful workplace. In the process of creating art-forms, the co-worker is not dispensable. Their art is themselves; lose the creators and all is lost. This would apply to the graphics industry, the magazine media, blog authorship and so on. To lose the creator means losing the intellectual property and the art of what can be created.

The same goes for organisations that rely on offering service or communicating with their customers. Lose the customer interface and the business will go downhill, unless propped up by other mechanisms beyond the workplace, for example, bureaucracies and skewed marketplaces. To risk losing creative personnel is like playing Russian Roulette, the gun of failure is pointing to the business owners and the lack of respect shown to the artistic creator is firing the gun. No one likes to be considered as replaceable. Each and every one feels that their self is different from others' selves. The mind and soul is integrated into one body which must be respected if not, then abuse occurs. Society shows respect as each child is born with balloons, gifts, flowers and the same respect is shown when the individual dies, more flowers and attending the funeral. Why then, in the workplace, millions of workers from 9 to 5 are shown disrespect?

Powerful entities do not interfere with the birth or death processes as these are out of their control, that is, out of their power. However, soon as the child is at an age to work, then the machinery starts rolling only stopping until retirement – if that person is lucky enough to live in a developed country, or finally at death. Treating individuals with disrespect is morally wrong and unethical. Individuals owning up to being amoral and unethical are few and far between, this is because it is shameful to go against social mores. Far better to lie and go about their daily business abusing co-workers. Being amoral and unethical is often a judgement laid against organisations and their managers, but never owned up to and the lies are written into the ethics statement pinned up in reception.

Why can't organisations own up to their behaviour? It is because to state what the practices are like in reality will dissuade their customers as well as suppliers from entering into commerce with them. There are whole armies of Public Relations people who exist to cover up any anomalies or deflect public opinion against them. Their very existence points to the fact that organisations do not conform to social values expected. There are many examples: the Union Carbide gas explosion in 1984 has killed over 16,000 people and caused over half a million injuries. The Chernobyl nuclear meltdown in 1986, Exxon Valdez leaking over 40 million litres of oil into the Pacific Ocean near the US coast in 1989, and more recently in 2013 the collapse of the Ali Enterprises garment factory in Bangladesh are breaches of those values. The companies and some of their employees concerned have been brought to court and found to be negligent in their actions. Using such extreme examples is easy it may be said, but there are similar costs with allowing bullying in the workplace. The Workplace Bullying Institute puts the cost per company as: '*Turnover + Opportunity Lost + Absenteeism + Presenteeism + Legal Defense Cost + Dispute Res. + Trial Costs + Settlements + Workers Compensation/Disability Fraud Investigation = The Routine Cost of Allowing Bullies to Harm Others with Impunity.*'[18]

The breaches of moral and ethical behaviour are many far beyond the extent of this book, but the point is made, every day organisations abuse and damage their employees, their families and others, and include damage to our environment through their negligence. It must be time for this irrational behaviour to stop. If not now, what will it take for society to say stop these transgressions of our social values and instil respect?

18 Workplace Bullying Institute. (2014). 'Estimating the Costs of Workplace Bullying'. Retrieved 14 May 2014, from http://www.workplacebullying.org/2014/04/24/costs/.

The Exalted Management Status

I am sure I am not alone to have had a work experience when the upline management to not turn out as well as I had expected. It is quite curious really, as the relationship is unique among our social connections. Family members are always the same, with their idiosyncratic ways; love them or hate them they just are like that. Some will remember birthdays and Christmas, others will not. Explanations to why their behaviour is remiss are often proffered by other family members who are older and wiser. Usually the advice is to leave the relative alone, rather than be hurt by their behaviour.

Friends tend to be loyal and trustworthy. If later their actions lead to behaviour untoward to the friendship, then they simply are no longer a friend. There is a choice to be made: the friend drifts away or becomes an enemy. However, at any time in life, current friends are kind, sharing and always there to listen when there are problems. Enemies do the reverse, are unkind, only share negative information or seek revenge or validation of their negativity. Enemies' relationships are as strong as friendships, albeit they are negative. Again there is a choice to be made: either be caught up in the spiral of hatred or ignore. Usually the latter is best in the long run, to defuse the strength of the negative connection.

When growing up, educational settings with their teachers and principals can make life difficult for the student for extraneous reasons or even those which are relevant. Again there are choices to be made: attend another institution or opt out of the educational system altogether.

The rest of the world is composed of individuals who largely do not affect your life. In every setting there is a choice to the participation within the relationship. Family, friends, enemies, schools are part of our social life, and as the child grows up in our Westernised society he learns to make choices. In many families, however, there is one relationship that is seen as non-negotiable by parents with their children and that is with religion. But even then, by the time of adulthood, many will choose to stay or leave the means of worship and form their own beliefs elsewhere.

The Workplace is a Different Culture of Power, Control and Violence

However, when you attend a workplace everything is different. So different that to some it comes as quite a shock that the only choice is to work or not work. To choose to not work compromises relationships with others by not being able to participate in such basic commodities such as shelter and health care. It could be said that it threatens life itself. Of course there are sub-markets that a person may participate in, such as begging, gangs, drugs, prostitution, but all are workplaces as casual as they may be. A person who does nothing all day long is often despised for doing exactly that. They are seen as a threat to society. Many prefer not to see homeless in their neighbourhood. Neither do they wish to see the loosely defined workplaces operating on their doorsteps. It is far better that they plied their trade elsewhere. Legislation can be passed to make these acts unlawful, but all this does it seems, is to drive these activities underground. Their customers will know exactly where they are, despite the law being upheld.

Looking at lawful work, an individual's persona and status is delineated and demarcated by their occupation. This is particularly so for males who have generally participate in the workforce for longer periods than females who have household and care duties. Women are more likely to work part-time, take time out for caring others and retire earlier. Although this dynamic is changing due to the complexity of finding and retaining employment, as contract or casual labour increases. Just as the question of what will you do when you grow up defines a child's horizon, the question of *what* do you do defines class and or status and therefore relationships with others.

We live in a society that is dominated by work, which is usually within structured workplaces. This has not always been the case. Underdeveloped countries often have high unemployment rates among males. The answer to this is meant to be economic development; however, not all economic development is good usually ending up with exploited workers to supply the Western industrialised world with cheaper goods. Once a nation's workers realise that they are underpaid, and are organised enough to demand more wages, the industry is moved elsewhere to a supply of cheaper workers. Right now we are in the midst of a manufacturing economy provided by Chinese workers, who are vastly underpaid compared to the first world. Their managers are equally underpaid, and are as much exploited as the employees. True they can enjoy a better standard of living but it is hardly one that would match our managers' standard.

When it All Began

This has not always been the case of human activity. Before economies were born, there were communal activities based on finding food, making clothes and worshipping spirits or ancestors. Where food was abundant, society became less nomadic, time was more devoted to develop building skills and rudimentary shelters appeared instead of nomadic tents made out of animal skins. However, the late Holocene climate changed rapidly cooler for several centuries and this forced migration to food sources of warmer climates. It is reputed as causing the eradication of the Mesopotamia area and pushed the locals into irrigating crops. This required a larger labour force than just a few families could offer and simultaneously God Kings came to power with complex hierarchies and replaced peaceful democracies within family groups that had flourished before. Townships were born and thereafter cities developed. The rest they say is history.

I suspect that this climactic event 8,000 years ago caused the beginning of management. Labour needed to be organised for purposes of grain growing, food and shelter needed to be paid for. In return for their labour, food and shelter was provided. This was later withdrawn so that the individuals had to build their own shelter and a monetary system replacing the direct connection of a person with his food, developed.

With management came violence, and many times it was organised violence. Brian Ferguson, an anthropologist, came to the conclusion that there are five factors for warfare to develop.[19] This was based on a review of anthropological excavations. All of which had no real visual presence of killings or murders until about 10,000–8,000 years ago. Shifting from nomadic way of life to settlements created a greater tie to local resources than otherwise was the case. No longer could families move away from fiercer tribes. As families settled and subsequent populations increased, there came more competition for these resources. The hierarchies that began to form felt they needed to protect their own interests from others. And trading with others far away became another factor for defending or even war creating to secure their supplies. Lastly there is the effect of climate change, which puts increasing pressure on the population to survive. Warfare is large-scale violence and emerged at the same time as managers. Managers did not start wars, it was always their upline managers (Kings, elders, leaders) who chose to do so, and their subordinate managers carried out their orders.

19 Ferguson, R.B. (2003). 'The birth of war'. *Natural History Magazine*, July/August, 28–35.

We have evolved with our family relationships, religious and tribal obligations. Generally these relationships have been founded on mutual respect. Parents knew that they would be looked after by their children in later life. Reaching adulthood, which was then about 12–14 years old; each gender had their own initiation and knowledge to learn to collect food and provide shelter and run their lives according to their beliefs and practice.

Management interfered with these natural processes. As workplaces became prevalent and stable, managers were installed to supervise the growing and gathering of crops and other food supplies. The community leader had to have power invested in him to take on such a role, and accordingly took on divine right. In this way, power was obtained over the people. No one could doubt the new ways of the king as to do so was to doubt the very existence of God. This demonstrates the power of belief systems with Neolithic peoples.

Using this artifice the labourers were forced into production to benefit the king. As the king could not be everywhere, trusted men, and it was always men, were designated as managers to supervise. Management had an affiliated and attributed investment of divine right of the God King. Gone was mutual respect. It was replaced by the use of power over people to meet the ends of selfish and greedy God Kings. The reward for doing so was to obtain food and shelter and for some slavery.

It is quite possible that management relations came about differently than any other social relationship. Managers became a new stratum to society. Previously, familial groups of humans developed mutual respect, the God King's management destroyed that respect and in its void begat violence. For those people who became bankrupt in this system ended up in slavery. Domestic relationships were destroyed and men held power over their chattels: their women and children. To speak differently, to think otherwise, meant imprisonment or death.

Thus the whole of society changed to what it is today, violence based on avarice and conspicuous consumption. Wars became merely, and still are, attempts to secure long-distance supplies; the petroleum supply was fought for by the Americans and most of Western Europe in Iraq and Iran in the 1990s and early 2000s, also the processes of jealousy and greed, for instance the European wars of the mediaeval period onwards. Groups were demonised in this process and therefore became an excuse to wipe these opposing groups out.

With management, lands were taken from the populace; for instance, the Enclosure Acts of England were directly from the greed of land owning interests, the semi God Kings of England, who in turn 'obeyed' the English monarchy with paying taxes. In order for this to be accomplished an army of gamekeepers, farm managers, yeomanry were installed to look after the interests of the landowners.

Agriculture became the first workplace, concomitant with the trades that developed their own skills with metals and fabrics and later buildings. The guild of the tradesmen were organisations to keep the standards of work high and the knowledge of the trade secret. If an individual did not belong to a guild, then their work was not recognised as prime quality and therefore could only be sold as cheap goods. Again the power over people was used to keep control of certain knowledge.

Landowners ensured that the patrilineal system of inheritance kept their women out of the workplace to stay locked within the home. Primogeniture also ensured that other sons than the first born would also be sent to occupations such as the military and religious orders. Thus the feudal landowners had control through direct familial lines the concept of God Kings and war when required to obey the orders of the monarch. All of which was enforced by violence overtly or covertly by selected men.

As the economy grew so did management. Every workplace has management in it. Even the smallest workplaces, management will be there; however it will be invested in the owner. Today, everywhere we look, workplaces have managers or owner-managers. It has become an accepted part of our lives that we do not question it. Yet it is actually an alien relationship that has been thrust upon us by primordial God Kings.

To understand this more fully, I have researched this fact with the 'primitive' Bali Mula people. They are the original people of Bali. Their workplaces have expanded too, for instance growing oranges, weaving fabric and so on. All of this is done on a mutual respect basis. Their belief system is based on ancestor worship and nature provides all that is necessary to live, therefore nature must be protected and worshipped also. They do not believe in a fire-breathing God, neither are their elders invested with power from God. The CEO of the clan is two people; they rule together and make decisions on what has gone before, with the ancient writings of previous elders and what is right and respectful today.

Consequently they are peaceful people, and do not use violence upon each other. Mutual respect reigns, and therefore there is no management role in the workplace; basically they are self-managed work teams. They are able to self-manage as they trust each other, and management knowledge is not invested in one particular person. Older members of the work team train the younger members and impart knowledge willingly so that the next generation will be working at peak performance. They do not sell their land as it is for their children and their children's children. There is no violence to be seen or heard, apart from the legacy of animal sacrifice to appease the spirits of nature and their wise ancestors.

Unfortunately self-managed work teams are not the norm in the Western workplace. This is despite the fact that they increase production, reduce costs and give the business a competitive advantage. They can be found in some IT businesses, for example Google, with virtual work teams using the Internet and in some more enlightened businesses.[20] Most workplaces, however, are hierarchical and not based on trust.

In England in the nineteenth century most workplaces were dismal, patriarchal and authoritarian. Strict rules and regulations made life difficult and all were enforced by the threat of cut in pay or dismissal. This has been described as the transactional method of management. This methodology exists today in most workplaces. Rules may be softened, but when cut to the chase, the elements of punishment are the same. True, there were attempts at better working conditions with unionised labour. Furthermore there were a scattering of benign paternalistic employers such as the Cadbury factory and the town-site in Bournville as a notable example. But the majority of the workforce is locked in to the transactional style of management where there is no interest in providing good working conditions and respect for each other.

Meanwhile no one else holds such power despite efforts with normative transformational management models, management training and leadership development. The last two are major industries in the academic world, intending to give the student a competitive edge in the job market. Unfortunately even the best education can be undone as they are co-opted into power elites of organisations.

20 Manz, C.C. and H.P. Sims (1987). 'Leading workers to lead themselves: The external leadership of self-managing work teams'. *Administrative Science Quarterly* 32(1): 106–30.

Evidence that points to the newness of the relationship is that there has to be rules and regulations to give knowledge of what can and cannot be done. Families do not have complex rules, neither does religion really as all of them are based on the golden rule 'Do unto others what you would have done to you.' Our relationships' foundation is on mutual trust outside the workplace. Friends are trusted, family members are trusted, spouses are trusted and even religious figures are trusted. Or meant to be. The presence of violence over the last 8,000 years has eroded much of that trust, however; like a parable or fairy tale it is the theory that is interwoven into our social consciousness.

Reciprocity is another social rule that is absent from the average workplace. This is referring to genuine appropriate payment for work done, if there were true reciprocity there would be automatically fair and equal wages. Women are still underpaid today after one hundred years of social awareness. Profits could be shared with employees, beyond share buying schemes, which essentially prop up the share price in stock markets. True profit sharing is very rare to be found. The early cooperative retail shop movement is an example. However, 'profit' can be what is left after the owners' cut and payments for other goods with direct benefit to the owner, for instance cars and housing subsidies.

Being authentic is another value that can be scarce in the workplace, that each party trusts the other that they are who they say they are. And with authenticity is morality. Working in organisations that are immoral still exists today; for instance cigarette manufacturers and those industries that use asbestos despite the known and proven health risks. Inauthentic organisations are to be found in the media where truth is at risk due to owner interests.

Another indicator of the newness of the power invested in managers to our psyche is that most of us resent being told what to do; it feels that adults are treated like children. When we feel the exertion of authoritarianism we rebel. However, this is more to do with recent history of flexing our psychological muscles after the two world wars than anyone defining the workplace as now a liberal place to be.

So the manager is a manager, and their relationship with each employee is vital. Vital is a word that means life-giving, and it is true being employed is life-giving. In most of the world these days the manager holds power over to hire or dismiss, or if they are not directly responsible for dismissal, their recommendation will. No one else holds such power in your life. Family members who you do not wish to stay close to become distant and therefore play a lesser part in your life, they hold little power over you once you have become an adult. Friends may come or go, but they are still a reliable bunch of people, albeit small, that you can trust. They too do not hold power over you. Getting married and having responsibility for children is just that, a responsibility. Your children cannot fire you and make you unemployed. It is only your manager who can do that. And that leads to a set of bewildering set of circumstances that is not learned earlier.

Many of us stay stuck within the bad/poor manager workplaces and we put up with it. We have heard about the urban myth that frogs do not jump out of the boiling pot as they have got used to the increasing heat. But humans do know when things are bad for them and yet do not leave an emotionally abusive workplace. The reason why is that the manager holds abnormally high power over the employee's life, holding the employee's ability to house and feed his family. When it is taken away from you in an unfair or constructed dismissal, the reality will confirm to you the life-giving element to being employed.

Chapter 10

How to Instil Respect in your Workplace Despite Malevolent Managers and your Position in the Organisation

There are things that you can do to increase the amount of respect in your workplace. Each one may seem obvious, but it is worth mentioning here.

- Use only respectful words to others.
- Be cool and be kind.
- Save your letting off steam for outside.
- Insist in meetings that respect is shown to everyone.
- No one can be really fired for seeking respect.

If you keep this up relentlessly, one of two things will happen, others will follow your example or if this becomes noticed by a malevolent manager, you may risk being dismissed. But as the last point says, there is no case for dismissal for incurring respect. If you feel that you have come under the microscope from a malevolent manager start looking for another job, or move internally away from the antagonist. This is all far away from how things ought to be.

When you first walk into a job you will be meeting your co-workers and your manager. He (if you are at a lower rank chances are that he may actually be a she, but forgive me to continue saying he) may introduce you himself but may not. In most cases the initial meeting is an introduction to the power relationship, although you may not recognise it. I never did, apart from when I saw the senior title indicating the higher authority.

If you are like me I blithely walk into a new job thinking "Great! I have made it!" as I have had an extremely varied career I have said this every time since I left school. I have said this even when I worked in a factory working on the floor in harsh environment. I remember thinking I have no idea what this will be like, but at least I will be getting good money. I know I am an optimist so perhaps this demonstrates the character trait, however, everyone else that I know also feels the same when entering a new job.

Among the emotions felt is a bit of nervousness about performance, touched with a dash of 'will I be good enough'? Of course, looking back I was good enough always, I have never had a performance issue from my point of view, and later from my staff I was generally liked and people usually did not want me to leave. Feeling nervous about your performance is normal. After all, you have survived an application process with an interview panel and résumé submission and they have checked your references, and here you are. A new paycheck to come in and a new chapter to begin.

Even with the most hurtful of bosses I never suspected anything when I walked through the door of the workplace. Everyone had a smile on their faces and said welcome in so many words. I was shown my workplace a desk or factory bench and shown what I was meant to do. If I was lucky I would have a duty statement, but more often there was none available. From thereon I muddled through, learnt the job and started producing quickly what was required. In this process there would be several meetings informal or formal with my manager. Always the masks were firmly in place. It was outside of my contact with my manager that I learnt the awful truth.

There were several characteristics of these malevolent workplaces that I think are worth discussing so that you will be warned of poor management.

Being Hired against the Immediate Manager's Wishes

Often there is an interview panel to the jobs that I have achieved. At the interview there is naturally the immediate manager, as he will know the most about the job in hand. He will ask certain questions that will be tough, but as I knew the tasks could answer appropriately. As the selection process is competitive there are other candidates. What is not known to any of us but later comes out, the immediate manager has his pet interviewee. By the way I have heard this done despite the fact that the favourite does not meet the Essential selection criteria. Usually an excuse is given (from the manager) to cover this lack of skills and the rest of the interview panel are made to agree, unless the selection is extremely formal that is, for instance, a high government departmental position and open to public scrutiny.

The Favourite Candidate Loses

As the recruitment process to be any good must select the best available applicant for the job. When I get the approval I am overjoyed but little do I know that my win is seen as a loss to the manager concerned. From opening the door as I entered the workplace to when I eventually left and closed the door behind me, the whole experience had been daunted by the sabotaging behaviour of both the manager and the unsuccessful candidate – who in both cases where this happened to me, were directly responsible to me.

A String of other People in that Position

If you find out that there have been predecessors in your position and they haven't lasted too long, or they are criticised about their behaviour, this is a warning sign of malevolent management and you must take heed. Do not believe that this is true. In fact a good starting point is to evaluate what you are being told as a projection of the person who is giving you this advice. The theory goes that if an individual despises a trait in others then this is likely to be in his own suite of behaviours, but the person does not want to recognise it or acknowledge it.[1] If you receive different opinions to what was originally said, then take it that each person is projecting their own dark negativity and the target may in fact be innocent of the charges laid. In organisations one has to be aware that there is no trial of innocence until proved guilty, it is the other way round and maybe the actual reason why the incumbent left.

Vacancy Caused by Reorganisation

Another tactic to hide the above is that the organisation will be or is reorganised. Look for the underlying reasons for the reorganisation. In one job I had, it was ostensibly to save money, as it was 3 management roles combined into one. The thinking really was one of control that the new person was to exert on 3 separate warring departments and to make a barely functioning arm into a

1 Freud, S. (1990). *Case Histories II*. New York, Penguin Random House.

more elevated status to manage the business planning function. My position was fundamentally a transactional role – which was not what I thought was the objective, neither the Chairman's or anyone else on the interview panel. I was not able to achieve the transactional outcomes of dobbing in people who were viewed as terrorists in the organisation (I kid you not), taking out sanctions against certain targeted people, and generally get the middle management to toe the company line by enforcement of rules and regulations.

My duty statement was laid out in secretive meetings, where no minutes were taken and no others were present or able to witness. This is despite the fact that I had a written duty statement and against which criteria I was recruited for. My boss wanted me to be a carrier of information to him from the other departments and to get rid of any personnel who thought otherwise, or as put vaguely 'against the re-organisation'. The dream of a job as sold to me by the panel and recruiters turned into a nightmare, which ended up in a Mexican standoff. I ostensibly followed orders but did not to my subordinates, concentrating more on efficiency and effectiveness and creating trusting relationships within and between the siloed functions to increase productivity.

Enslavement by Meetings

To be enslaved by meetings was astonishing for me to experience, as I was bit of a go-getter, lets get things done type person. As mentioned earlier, I totalled my meetings hours per week and found that it was 32, this is without the unofficial bumping into people in the corridor type of meeting which usually was more urgent and important than sitting in meetings all day long. With only 8 hours a week to do my work I soon felt like I was in an ever-increasing avalanche of work, reports to read and emails.

There is a time and place for meetings, but this was an impossible load. Most of the meetings were rubber-stamping what already had been done. The meetings in which my boss was present were stiff and formal, made to be less formal by talking about sport. I would sit there watching the precious minutes slide by until we could get back to business. A meeting on average took about an hour. With the boss it would lean towards two hours sometimes three. Then there were minutes to be read and agendas to prepare on top of the meeting itself.

I am a fan of using the one page agenda, minute summary and action list. To me it is far a far quicker process and boiled down to actions and who is doing what. This went down like a lead balloon for my colleagues who really had to conform or lose their jobs. I merely lost my job.

The Guise of a Not for Profit

I have also a working background of social services as I have mentioned earlier. In fact I put in 25 years worth of voluntary management with not for profit organisations (NPOs). The work was unpaid but usually rewarding in the outcomes of the services that were operating. The mantra of the NPO sector in the years when I worked was to get the NPO to be more business like. This meant accountants and lawyers were drafted onto boards, when usually the difficulty of the NPO laid in marketing and operationalization. Tendering for government contracts became the norm instead of an allocation of money per year.

Tendering for contracts is essentially good marketing. If you cannot sell the premise of the NPO then it would become a dead duck. The NPO would always have an administration staff and they were the ones to prepare the profit and loss statements, balance sheets, to do the payroll and to pay creditors. The Board's accountants saw the world in terms of balance sheets and the lawyers in terms of contracts. Management meetings became stuck with the various parties' pet areas and stake outs would last many hours.

There is a mix up of values in some NPOs, the management board wants numbers and the staff want outcomes for their clients. One expects that NPOs may be good places to work, but do not confuse 'doing good' meaning being nice to people within the organisation. NPOs are littered with passive aggressive bullies and mediocre managers who are there as a rung up the corporate ladder. The 'do gooders' are useless at stopping the corporate meltdown, all they want to do is to keep their service going and help as many clients as possible. They are not interested in office politics other than maintaining their client service. This is when they will aid and abet the better prospect who will win the good fight regardless of values shown.

The above comments are also relevant to sectors which deliver health and education services. Bullying is prominent in both sectors and to not be advised that this is such, is akin to sending people on board a ship without life jackets. NPOs are not nice places to work neither are the health and education areas. They attract women more than men as the work is seen as more fulfilling. Men who join these services are seen as soft by the outside world and some of them are, but don't think that all are the same. I have witnessed women bullying and males. Either gender can be unpleasant and the emotional abuse grinds down the efficiency and effectiveness of the service delivery.

Some of the worst cases I have seen is in University settings. Each department has its own agenda, which may be opposed to the faculty's agenda, which again may be entirely different from the University's administration. This is typical across the board with power plays and courses rising and sinking with the power balance. Again, do not believe that noble causes will be filled with good people. It does not happen. Staff can be present for all sorts of reasons and many little to do with being of service to the customers, students or patients. I often think that they are there because the health and education sectors are actually sheltered workshops, many of the people employed would have a very difficult time outside where their little empires would be less tolerated. At times I am surprised by a pocket of resistance where outstanding service is given without a blink of an eyelid. These places should be held up as shining examples to all, given Oscars for their service delivery. But they are ignored in the power play of malevolent managers who are only there to service their own needs and not of the customer.

Chapter 11
Sharing is Caring

How to Rate your Workplace

As we know workplaces vary enormously. From the hustle and bustle of a factory floor to well-lit beautiful individual offices. It is quite surprising the environments that we can tolerate to earn our living inside or outside buildings. Organisations of course, vary intent as well: there are profit making companies large and small, regulating public sector departments and ministries as well as the variety of non-profits.

Organisational structures can vary with steep hierarchies with well-defined ranks to flat almost linear structures of self-managed work teams and cooperatives. Many organisations have multiple sites, and of course some of these sites may be in different countries, multinationals and huge conglomerates. Internal to the structure are individuals who manage the organisation, from the chairman of the board, CEO or managing director down to the supervisory level. We know that there are five types of managerial Executive Impression Management and some managers may be goal oriented hard task masters, while others (usually aimed at the Respectfuls) could be considered as too easy going. Salaries and wages will differ from one job to another; some employees are treated fairly, some are not. We still have unequal pay by gender and lack of recognition of work/family balance as well as unease over unethical companies; for example old-growth forest-felling companies or those who manufacture cigarettes and so on.

Until now, it has been virtually impossible to compare. Executive Impression Management has given us the five different types of managers, four of whom will run workplaces to achieve their own aims of power and control, and we know that they will use violent methods to obtain this, no matter how subtle the control mechanisms. If we put this against another set of variables of emotional energy, then we have a powerful indicator to the type of workplace it truly is. Co-workers can measure their workplace for themselves, or human resources can undertake such a measurement across their workplace.

The way through this is to seek out information on how workers respond to their workplace, similar to how tourists respond to hotels overseas. Tourists will feel that their satisfaction will be the highest as economic theory informs us, with the person's needs met. However, one person's preferences may be another's dislike For instance, being in a busy tourist area may not suit the individual seeking quiet and peace in their holiday hotel. But when all the ratings of that particular hotel are averaged, an observer can then make judgements about the hotel and whether to book it or not. All this is very necessary information to make better and informed decisions on spending that vacation dollar or euro than just chancing a hotel blindly.

Just as hotels are rated in stars, workplaces can do so on the criteria that is set out and standardised. For instance, the difference between a four-star and a five-star hotel these days is having a swimming pool. There are indices used by businesses already, such as the Rate of Return of Investment, and the Corporate Responsibility Index promoted by Business in the Community. But what is missing is an evaluation of the workplace and its management. It is management that makes a good workplace different from a bad workplace, no matter what industry or country.

Similarly we can draw conclusions about our workplaces. And if we add up the levels of satisfaction, not only a meaningful percentage value can be assigned but an average rating can be given. An outside observer can then make judgements about which workplaces are the happiest and furthermore, non-violent.

This information is completely missing from a job search point of view. Many people get caught landing in unhappy workplaces as they have walked in blindly, without this vital information. I use to advise unemployed managers to get information about the company before an application for employment is submitted. There is simply no time to be wasted on inefficient, ineffective organisations that are ruled by malevolent management. But this information is very difficult to get. These days though, we have the Internet with all of its social media. And although it makes life a little easier to research a business, there is no standardisation of information that makes sense of the disparate pieces of research. In economic terms, the job market is an imperfect marketplace; it is challenged by lack of information which is mostly one-way, that is, an information flow from candidate (résumé) to employer, and if the company is large enough it will print an Annual Report, which is glossed up to shine its best even in bad years. How can a person make a life decision without such vital knowledge?

In my early days after leaving school, options such as banking, the civil service, teaching and nursing were the standard aims of female school leavers. All were considered as 'respectable' occupations and that employment would inevitably bring happiness, through certainty of wages and secure employment. As I was in the middle of my teenage rebellion, I was disgusted with these options and wanted to be an artist. The only way to be paid an income from that arena was to be a commercial artist, an occupation that has been completely reorganised by computer graphics. It took about four years for me to realise that there was no such job for me that would make me happy, and finally studied for a degree to increase my job options. From there onwards I tried to find workplaces that were good, and I floundered from job to job as it was hopeless, despite my abilities and array of accumulating experience. For me an opportunity to follow my artistic whims was never there and it has become a hobby rather than any source of income. By the way, nobody knew that my real mother and my aunt were accomplished artists at that time; my adoptive parents didn't have a clue of what I could do. So there was zero guidance and hence the boring options that I was given. And I am rather pleased that the artistic bent has carried down the generations from me. However, many of us end up in occupations that we become expert in but it is happenstance if this work is fulfilling or not. Hence my preoccupation with the workplace and its management. I could shuffle papers all day long if I was in a happy workplace, but it would be something impossible to achieve with a slave-drive boss or mediocre manager. We know these types now, but we had no indicators then.

If we could put together the index we could measure this vital information. For instance, would you join a company that is known to have a low satisfaction (unhappy) rating? For many people the answer would be no. Some might still battle on, believing that it will not affect them. That is OK, as that is their choice, but for those who prefer to work in happier situations, it does matter. Stress will occur shortly after arrival in a malevolent workplace, as their needs are not being met, and with that come the longer-term harmful effects of stress on their health with lower immune responses and more illness, physical and mental. After all, most people spend at least eight hours a day in their workplace and if they are unhappy that equates to one third of their lives. Considering that one third will be spent sleeping, the remaining time will be spent worrying about their work – after work hours!

So how can the illusory idea of happiness be measured? I propose that it can be done through measuring people's emotional response to their workplace. My own theory of emotional energy (the CAT model) makes this index possible. And as I have been developing this over 15 years, I know how well it works. The three major dimensions of emotions that people feel are that of connection, those of appreciation and finally those linked with trust. It is these three themes that are developed in the star rating system so that a better assessment can take place.

We know that managers with Respectful Executive Impression Management enable a feeling of respect with employees; the other types do not, so it will be felt by people, and has been done so through my research in developing the types. Feeling connected in a workplace is paramount. The second emotional energy dimension is Appreciation and it is measured on how an individual feels about their tangible rewards such as salary, wages, perks of the job, allowances; and the more intangible recognition such as being thanked, employee of the month awards and so on for the work that is done. There is a large literature on rewards and far from me to replace it, but simply, an employee feels better about a workplace if there are just rewards. This knocks out favouritism – the trump card of the manager using Mediocre Executive Impression Management. It also says much about the amount of the reward. We have no McDonald's Big Mac indicator of the price of currencies around the world equivalent; instead, we can measure of how a person feels about being appreciated in their workplace.

Trust is measured by the feelings of confidence that a worker will have in a workplace. This can be represented in terms of appropriate levels of supervision, being developed with training, high autonomy, being able to speak up even if it is bad news about the work or organisation. A workplace driven by fear will never have pride in the product or service delivered, or autonomy to do a good job. Micromanagement rather than supervision, makes the individual feel even more stressed. So Appreciation wraps up this area that the four malevolent types exert control of. At best individuals are never appreciated, unless there is some value to the managers themselves.

Broader psychological theory has it that if an individual is feeling angry, sad and fearful which are the negative energy sides of the dimensions, it will result in stress. This will push the worker further into feeling unhappy about his workplace. The rating has to rely on honest measures of how an individual feels, then it can be a true reflection of the workplace. Outside observers can type the managers within an organisation, and together with the employee questioned about these three dimensions, a profile can be put together.

Disparate Ratings

What if a person rates an organisation low and yet others rate it highly? There are several comments about this possibility. Employees could be forced to rate high and against their true feelings; it could result in a skewed average rating. Such a breach must be investigated. If it is a true reflection, it could be that a bully has targeted the individual, and that the unhappiness is created by this harmful practice. This outcome would verify the individual's instincts and create an awareness of what is truly going on. Finally it could be down to the possibility that a person may have some difficulties integrating into a workplace and checking this out with professional help; for instance, employee assistance counselling may be of assistance. Never overlook the person that scores differently than anyone else. This individual may be able to tell what is really going on, but has not the courage to speak up. Confidentiality issues must be addressed, but this still can be approached delicately.

So answering the questions of:

- How well do you feel respected in your workplace?
- How well are you appreciated in your workplace?
- How well are you are confident in your workplace?

will give an accurate reflection of how happy (satisfied) or unhappy (dissatisfied) are in your workplace. To give an example: a person rates the questions after reading and understanding what is being measured by assigning 1 to 5 points, the higher the points the happier the person is.

- How well do you feel respected in your workplace? (4 points)
- How well are you appreciated in your workplace? (2 points)
- How well are you confident in your workplace? (1 point)

This gives a total of 7 points. Divide by 3, and we have 2.33 as an overall indicator of this person's satisfaction with his workplace. As 5 is the highest score, if an organisation came out at 2.33, it is an indicator that all is not well within, and this should act as a spur to action by the human resources department if not management itself.

Why should workplaces be measured? It can be a good reality check for an employee to see how others view the workplace. Also it gives a measure of how employees feel about the workplace, very important information when a jobseeker or applicant is considering future employment with the company. Being honest with assessments will help incoming workers decide on whether or not to continue with their application and look elsewhere.

Probably the biggest effect will be on workplace management, likely as not to improve their game. Shareholders would be interested, as well as investors. It is a very important measure of how well management is working, as they can compare their own workplace to other workplaces within the organisation and other workplaces within the industry or country. This means it is a highly valued piece of management information that is rarely produced in organisational development, management performance reviews or even reflected in the stock market share price.

Companies promote themselves on their best work practices so an index like this will be received well by the community. Personally, I think it is time that this move is made for several reasons. It will:

- decrease violence in the workplace;
- produce higher productivity and efficiency within;
- will theoretically produce lower priced goods and services;
- training times would be less for job candidates as there would be informed and enthusiastic to join and implement best practice;
- there will be savings across the board for re-training malevolent managers – as there will be fewer in the organisation;
- lower cost employee assistance programs;
- less time for human resource teams being diverted away from their core business of supporting management.

An index like this can give the incoming candidate faith in the organisation knowing that it is a respectful workplace run by respectful management. It would also be reassuring to those stakeholders who are ethical in their shareholdings. Knock-on effects will be for families and children as their work/

family time will be less of a problem in a respectful workplace. The business case is easy to make; what is needed is the courage to implement such an index across the workplace.

If the result of the index is low, the company is going to be very less likely to promote this fact, so it will be omitted from their website and corporate information. However, the reverse will be true. Those with good to excellent scores will promote this piece of information to give them an edge in the competing market for talent. These companies will stand out like lighthouses on stony rocks. They offer protection against abusive workplaces and beam out their respect for employees.

In a perfect world of perfect information this is the missing piece of the jigsaw for organisations. The Internet has become the medium for perfect information; the only thing that is needed is for the job applicant to be computer savvy. These days that includes every youngster and many workers. The older work groups are learning to use the computer, or have access to family members who do, to gain this information. One little number not seen on a website destroys the myth that our workplaces are safe, and that management is 'good'.

Talent acquisition is becoming more of a problem as the workforce ages in the Western industrialised democracies. In population terms, the baby-boomers will last for several more decades then drop out of the workforce. This means that younger people will be sought after to replace them. As there is not enough to go around in the economy, recruiting labour will be problematic. Answers like drafting in third-world labour are short term, even these groups are becoming more knowledgeable than their forebears. Australia for instance gives a special visa for entry for skilled workers from Asia in particular. It is not a full residence visa, which the likes of me immigrated on, but a time-limited exploitation of their labour and then they are returned to their country.

In Europe the expansion of the European Union has meant that there are other new populations with higher rates of unemployment. For instance Turkey is a candidate country seeking admission to the EU has a long history of supplying unskilled labour to Germany. This was true also for Portugal and Spain, but is now true for the newer members such as Poland and Romania who seek jobs in the older established European community. Canada relies on immigration to supply a younger workforce, but the US has virtually closed its borders to prevent immigration from the south. Essentially all countries will have a shortage of skilled labour in the next two decades and job applicants will have a more exalted status than what they have now.

Being in Australia has given me insight to the oil and gas skilled labour force, as the larger recruitment firms who specialise in this industry know all the available candidates across the world. Given that most of the industry has to be skilled we have witnessed here already the shortage of labour and the resulting competition to hire skilled labour. In this industry, a job seeker has no trouble at all, as compared to other industries, in finding out what is offered by the various oil companies. In fact poaching of labour is common and in an effort to prevent this, 'golden handcuff' type of contracts are already in place.

This situation is a preview of things to come. Already recruitment firms are becoming global, job seekers upload their résumés online, state their preferences of work and companies go from there. Soon as the labour market shrinks, getting human resources will be very difficult. Therefore bad management cannot deter an organisation for their access to a labour pool. The more strategic organisations will advertise that their workplaces are respectful and will attract the right candidates.

I think that this is the time to call for such an index to be implemented. Violence in the workplace is merely a new concept that we have had to live with; it is not innate to us. Living harmoniously is innate; we like getting on with each other and we do not like conflict. If we did like violence, then we would have been like this from time immemorial.

For 8,000 years our workplaces have been dominated by managers, most of them malevolent, but thankfully some are Respectful and do manage their co-workers well. They are the link to the future. Yes we can have hierarchies, multinationals and complex organisations. But they are truly unworkable in the future if they only hire managers using Mediocre and Tyrant Executive Impression Management. Slowly, malevolent managers will not be able to find work. They will be faced with having to change their ways or risk unemployment. I know that the Mediocre managers are the most likely to be able to change; the Tyrants, however, have this behaviour ingrained into their early childhood or personality. The Tyrants, I believe, are only a small percentage of managers and perhaps now we can see them as a dying breed. There is simply no place for a manager to flout the rules and rule by violence and fear. The driving force for this massive change not will not come from strategic business plans; it will be from the factory floor as well as the sumptuous office. We all need respect in our work lives. It is part of our human rights to have respect, and the workplace has been overlooked because it is one of the last bastions of violence in our society.

The means to make this happen will be the Internet providing information about the Respectful workplaces. The Internet is open to all, it is free, and even with the cheapest mobile phones in the third world, there is built-in capability to access the Internet. Nokia has been the leader in this wave of technology to Asia, Africa and South America. When I work in Bali I use a Nokia with this feature. I was astounded that such a low-cost phone would have it, but it has been proved that farmers use it for weather and soil conditions for their crops, and radio stations that give local information, are accessible as well. The price is so low that a working person could buy one at the cost of a few weeks of poverty-line wages. It means that information is now becoming available to far more people than ever before. Mobile phones are ubiquitous, nearly everyone has access. An interesting statistic is:

> *There are almost as many cell-phone subscriptions (6.8 billion) as there are people on this earth (seven billion) – and it took a little more than 20 years for that to happen. In 2013, there were some 96 cell-phone service subscriptions for every 100 people in the world.*[1]

Fernholz continues to say that even in Africa, 63 per cent of the population have a mobile phone subscription. This means that ultimately the Internet will rule the world. Encyclopedic sites like Wikipedia carry at the moment nearly 5 million articles in English alone, let alone the host of other languages that are provided.

It is often said that knowledge is power. The Latin form is '*scientia potential est*' was written for the first time in the 1668 version of the work *Leviathan* by Thomas Hobbes, who was secretary to Francis Bacon, as a young man.[2] At that time in the seventeenth century, knowledge was in oral or printed books or pamphlet format. Now it is digital and more people than ever have access. In Neolithic times, knowledge was confined to family groups, in oral tradition. This meant all that there was to know was available. This included information about the workplace – where to hunt and how to conduct the hunt. The temporary manager of the hunt had to be respectful or others would

---

1 Fernholz, T. (2015). 'More people around the world have cell phones than ever had landlines'. *Quartz*. Retrieved 25 February 2015, from http://qz.com/179897/more-people-around-the-world-have-cell-phones-than-ever-had-land-lines/.

2 'Thomas Hobbes' (2015). *Stanford Encyclopedia of Philosophy*. Retrieved 10 June 2015, from http://plato.stanford.edu/entries/hobbes/.

not join the hunt for food. Therefore respect was innate in the workplace and information on how to select the hunt manager would have been handed down from generation to generation. A malevolent manager could not exist then as no one would put up with their harmful ways.

Tyrants are Becoming Fewer?

It is true that smaller organisations can still be the stronghold of Tyrant, but I am ever hopeful that employees will walk out as soon as they realise that the boss is not as wonderful as he was trying to make out at the job interview. However, they prey on people who are used to such domination. To me this is why such cultures of obedience to the family head or community ruler will allow Tyrants to rule in Asia, more than those cultures that are more sophisticated in their understanding of human rights.

Considering that human rights as a set of principles were set up over the last few centuries in the West, and further defined in the United Nations Declaration of Human Rights in 1947 to stop human suffering after two world wars, that galvanised leaders to stop such abuse. The Declaration has not stopped wars altogether, but has acted with some effectiveness to prevent war through peace negotiations and to curtail them. However, it is normative in regard to its rights, and just as much a person is to be treated with respect and dignity, this right does not stop at the workplace door.

The insidious growth of information spread by the Internet has meant that such ideas about mutual respect in the workplace are beginning to supplant such tyrannical behaviour in Asian businesses. While Singapore may have more of a paternalistic authoritarian society, its workplaces are more contemporary and therefore, particularly with ex-pat workers, they will be influenced by the trend of mutual respect taking place elsewhere. Indonesia has more free democratic elections, which is no mean feat with its populations distributed across 13,000 islands in the archipelago, and again information about good workplaces is available online and many of the larger companies will try to imitate.

Asian small business is inevitably family-based and one would expect them to be more authoritarian. It is commonplace that long hours and little pay is the price of creating some economic security for their family. However, the Bali Mula, the indigenous people in Bali, have businesses that are family-based yet they are still respectful as indeed all their relations within their culture. However, human rights abuses loom large in Asia and expecting respect in the workplace is not so easily achieved. Nonetheless, it is inevitable that this notion of respect will filter through.

For us in the Western industrialised economies, there is no barrier to implementing such measures, apart from the ingrained pattern of violence that has formed in the last few thousand years. There is a whole literature that espouses better management techniques. Similarly there is scholastic interest in making better managers fed by a battalion of business schools and their academics. What they are overlooking is the basic premise of power and control of others. If humans can give up the need for power over others, then we will have a far more comfortable and successful life. This would lead to a real consensus based culture, and not one that is driven by violence of the conflict model of society.

It is the conflict theorists that hold the view of industrialised society having irreconcilable conflict. Marx and others were on the right path, despite the red herring of planned economies and resulting totalitarianism. Foucault was correct in asserting that there is power in discourse. And this was used for the power elites to control the less powerful, that is, most of society. The conflict is in the form of violence and is found in every theatre of everyday life. My focus is the workplace, and I have accidentally unearthed violence in my research about fraudsters. What I have discovered is that it is not the form of the organisation, for example, small business, multinationals, government departments – it is the management that dictates if violence is present and allowed to be used in them.

Manipulative managers who say, 'do as I do and you will be successful', have hidden violence from our very eyes. The reality is there is no peace at the top if violence has been used to get there. Factions will form and fight with each other, competing for attention and wanting favours bestowed upon them. I have met plenty of such CEOs; they feel that once that they are there, it will be glorious with all of that power and control. However, the story is different for many of them as their legacy in the organisation is one of abuse, no matter which way it is said.

Malevolent managers stay malevolent; they do not change once they have reached the top. Once they achieve that, they are ripe for poaching by head-hunters into another organisation to 'lead'. They leap willingly for the right salary and perks packages, as they feel with this is more money is more control. Their lack of success in the next company demonstrates that it is only be their abusive ways that they can be successful. Instil abuse at the top in a respectfully managed organisation and the CEO will be asked to leave within 24 months. In a mediocre managed organisation, there will be many a sleepless night fending off Machiavellian moves by subordinate managers. A tyrant at the top though can rule his roost with a heavy and draconian hand. Managers will be dismissed who buck against the imposed tyranny. The Tyrant CEO is only interested in one thing and that is total power. Even they become unstuck as the climate changes in their marketplace, or through political moderation (they see it as interference) or through other means. History is littered with despots that ruled and either cheated by death or at the hands of malevolent management. 'Et tu, Brute' were Julius Caesar's last words in Shakespeare's play as he realised that his closest friend was among the assassins who killed him. Treachery is rife among thieves, and so it is with malevolent management.

Thinking that this sort of activity does not pay off is denying the strength of power that comes to the malevolent manager. There is the saying that 'All power corrupts', but that is totally untrue with a Respectful Manager. John Dalberg-Acton in 1887 wrote that 'Power tends to corrupt, and absolute power corrupts absolutely. Great men are almost always bad men.'[3]

I have always had trouble with this dictum. I know that there is a possibility of Respectful managers to get to the top; however, many get stabbed in the back along the way or do not use the Machiavellian instincts that are honed in the malevolent managers. It is the malevolent ones who when they get to the top show their true colours. Power corrupts them every inch of the way to the top; nothing is changed and nothing is new behaviour. Being under the spotlight emphasises their malevolence as shown by many a top politician when they are toppled.

However, there are a few examples of Respectful managers becoming good CEOs in the political sphere, and one such example would be Nelson Mandela. He joined the African National Congress in 1942 and after a life term in prison he eventually became the president of South Africa. His preferred duties were putting South Africa on the economic stage after years of international exploitation. Even to the end of his life he was trying to engender peace and acceptance, which are clearly not the acts of a malevolent. As the BBC reported:

> *On his 89th birthday, he formed The Elders, a group of leading world figures, to offer their expertise and guidance 'to tackle some of the*

3 Dalberg-Acton, J. (1907). Letter to Bishop Mandell Creighton, 5th April, 1887. *Historical Essays and Studies*, ed. J.N. Figgis and *R.V. Laurence*. London, Macmillan.

> *world's toughest problems'. Possibly his most noteworthy intervention of recent years came early in 2005, following the death of his surviving son, Makgatho. At a time when taboos still surrounded the Aids epidemic, Mr Mandela announced that his son had died of Aids, and urged South Africans to talk about Aids 'to make it appear like a normal illness'.*[4]

Nelson Mandela is a magnificent example of a great man, using Respectful Executive Impression Management even when imprisoned for many years. Every act was to serve his people, it was beyond self.

There are examples of day-to-day Respectful Executive Impression Management. It is now only a matter of cancelling the white noise of the malevolents to see which manager is truly an honour to work with.

4 BBC (2013). 'Nelson Mandela's Life and Times'. *BBC News Africa*. Retrieved 25 February 2015, from http://www.bbc.com/news/world-africa-12305154/.

Conclusion

It has been a long journey of discovery in this book. The accidental findings of the non-fraudster malevolent managers are an eye opener. By using social theory to look at the daily interactions of managers, I was able to establish that Goffman's impression management theory was the only vehicle to fit the investigation. There are a plethora of theories mostly built on shaky foundations of quantitative hypothesis testing as social scientists endeavour to understand human behaviour. Very few have predictive value, merely describing what is. For instance, say a manager is narcissistic. Can we then say that all of the manager's acts to his co-workers will be that of narcissism? No, we cannot. Most of his actions may be narcissistic, but we cannot predict all.

However, with the new core process of Executive Impression Management that establishes the malevolent types managers who use Tyrant and Mediocre Executive Impression Management we can safely predict that all actions will be malevolent. These managers use the organisation to fulfil their own needs. They are not interested in the truth, as they will lie; they are not interested in trustworthiness as they will betray. Co-workers are there to be used as pawns in the larger game of power and control in the workplace. It is the power that they gain as they climb up the hierarchies that they thirst after. They are abusive and therefore violent. They do not care about others' welfare. It is their fixation on money, rank and control that drives their weak egos to outwit others to attempt to demonstrate that how strong they are. Little do they realise that they are playing a false game, one that was historically given to them as stewards of organisations.

Managers came into being approximately 8,000 years ago. There was no need for them to exist earlier, and there is no historical record to the contrary. The role of steward for another higher ranking human, leader or God King has allowed them to subvert their power onto themselves. Investing control of others for their own gain.

Among the grovelling Mediocre and slave-driver Tyrants, there are to be found islands of integrity and independence, that is those managers using Respectful Executive Impression Management. When entering a workplace a young employee expects to find those managers, but the likelihood has decreased substantially over the millennia until today when we have too many malevolent managers in the workplace.

Managers who use Respectful Executive Impression Management are hard-working, good to work with, and they practise good management techniques. Their consistent impression management demonstrate that they are truly individuals of integrity, honesty and trustworthiness. They care about their co-workers, colleagues, their superiors and subordinates. These managers are able to draw out efficient production of products or services and run successful organisations in terms of delivery and profit. Their impression management is authentic; they regard others as they regard themselves, with respect. There is no self-service, no use of the organisation for their own gain. In fact they inspire others to work as hard as themselves.

The malevolent managers are dangerous and hazardous to a co-worker's health, physically and emotionally. Their inconsistent Executive Impression Management leaves co-workers shocked and confused. They tell lies when it suits them, and the managers using Mediocre Executive Impression Management will have favourites and cronies. The managers using Tyrant Executive Impression Management do not care one iota about their workers and will drive them into the ground, squeezing every last action out of them.

These malevolent managers will use terms like personality clashes to dismiss individuals who are seen as a threat. Poor work performance is another tactic used to get rid of a troublesome, that is, nonconforming employee. They have no interest in appearing like a Respectful manager, except perhaps at recruitment and selection time. Their poor management practices are inefficient and produce shoddy work or ineffective services. They are not interested in investing employees for the future of the organisation. They are only interested in their own career gains. The malevolent managers have no need to hide their actions, they manipulate, subvert the organisation for their own agenda.

The effect on employees is dreadful. Violence is used to control them. Their tactics are to be abhorred as they create great harm to their targets. Tyrants will bully others through domination techniques: Mediocre managers will use more manipulative bullying tactics of exclusion and back-stabbing. All the bullying tactics can be learned by the other type, and if the culture allows, will make Tyrants more manipulative and Mediocres more overt in their control and exertion of power over people.

Normally, Tyrants use intimidation to control their subordinates, while Mediocres will use ingratiation. In fact the Mediocres find that ingratiation works so well as a method of control that they use it upwards to their superiors. Tyrants are more clever insofar that they self-promote so they make themselves a necessary part of the organisation. Sometimes they are recruited to obtain a production target. They may be successful in the short run; however, they drive co-workers into the ground with their persistent pressure and deadlines. Mediocres through their presentation of being all things to all men will be hired as they seem exemplary in their performance. The reality is far from their show, with many employees psychologically and emotionally harmed by their devious methods.

Hiring a manager using Respectful Executive Impression Management is the best option for recruiting or promoting. By talking to their co-workers, a good understanding of their impression management will be gained and will act as confirmation for their selection. Respectfuls are in short supply, however, as they have often been the targets of other malevolent managers and being less driven for success, will prefer to stay with their employees producing excellence, than grabbing power as a CEO, as their counterparts do. Managers who use Respectful Executive Impression Management must be encouraged and supported in the workplace so that the organisation can grow and develop in meeting the needs of its customers.

Malevolent managers are everywhere, and now given the tool of Executive Impression Management, the reader can interpret the confusing signals that are given off by their managers and discern who these managers truly are. They cannot help themselves in being inconsistent and needing power and control. These two markers are the basis of the core process of Executive Impression Management and can be easily seen by their co-workers. Managers using Respectful Executive Impression Management will always treat co-workers as equals and will be consistent in their social interactions with others in the workplace.

The last chapter 'Sharing is Caring' is written as a methodology to overcome these malevolent managers who dominate our workplaces. It uses the peaceful means of spreading information to others about workplace management. The indicators are how well the employee feels about being connected into their organisation, how well he is appreciated and finally how well is he trusted. The dimensions are scored out of 5 points and the average is a score of the individual's emotional energy. Add all the employees' scores and divide by the number of people partaking in the process and the score will represent how comfortable people feel in the workplace. An organisation with high scores will want to promote this on their websites, which allows job seekers to assess where the managers using Respectful Executive Impression Management predominate. Shareholders will want to see how their investments are performing as well as chairmen of boards and CEOs. This together with other factors of shortage of labour in the next few decades will dictate Respectful Management in the workplace.

To be connected, appreciated and trusted is everyone's right in the workplace. It is time to insist this for every employee. I propose that now we know about these types of malevolent managers and how they can be identified, we can use the Internet to allow the marketplace to work on sufficient information about workplace management.

All this can be done peacefully and without violence. If enough people are inspired to have respect in the workplace, then now is the time for change.

Appendix A

The CAT model.

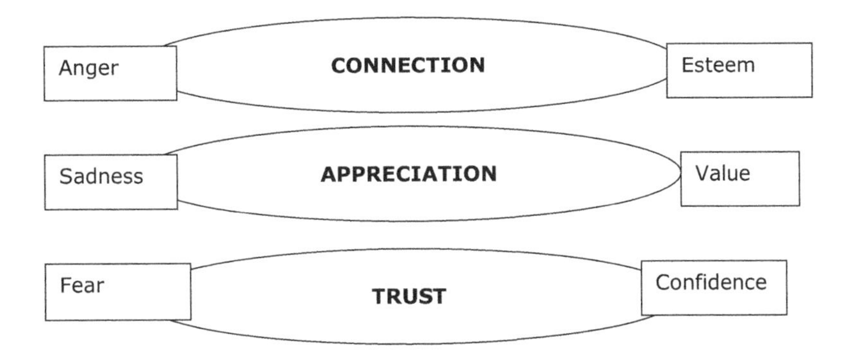

The basis of the model is formed through understanding emotions and how they can be aggregated into 3 dimensions, very similar to how all the colours on an artist's palette, therefore the painting, are derived from 3 primary colours.

Appendix B

This is from an email that Gede Prama has sent to me in 2015 about how our negative selves fail to heal using our traditional methodologies. He recommends meditation as a way to accept our faults as a natural part of ourselves.

> *It has been long recognized that our actions (including negative ones) are partly unconscious. In conventional Freudian psychology, all emotions that are repressed will be thrown into the unconsciousness. In Jungian psychology, it will become our shadow along the journey. Those who learn eastern psychology, this will become our karma that will affect us later.*
>
> *Whatever framework you use, it is hard to deny that some parts of our actions and decisions cannot be explained logically and systematically. Some experts in decision making like James G. March explicitly explained this in his book Decisions and Organization. For that reason, psychologist Carl G. Jung discovered the terminology of synchronicity (meaningful coincidences).*
>
> *Implicit in these findings, the scientific world also accept the part of human actions and decisions which are unconscious. Inspired by this, it is worth to briefly explore the whole efforts of human beings to move from the dark sides of unconsciousness to the bright sides of consciousness.*
>
> *Religion versus Psychology*
>
> *As we all know, religions tried to eliminate the negative impact of negative emotions by repressing us. Under the threats of hell and sin, religions prohibit us to do this and that. Even through religions have threatened us for thousand years, crime and fraud are still remain in the society.*
>
> *Psychology on the other hand recommend to us not to repress but to express negative emotions healthily. Writing, painting, singing, playing, discussing are parts of the way to express negative emotions.*

And as we can see in society, not all psychological interventions are successful to reduce crime and fraud…

Like other kind of medicines, meditation also does not heal all diseases. The unique approach of meditation (in perfection stage, not in the developmental stage), people are changed by being accepted.

References

American Psychiatric Association (1994) *Diagnostic and Statistical Manual of Mental Disorders*. Washington DC, American Psychiatric Association.

—— (2013). *Diagnostic and Statistical Manual of Mental Disorders*. Arlington, VA, American Psychiatric Association.

Anderson, A., J. Park and S. Jack (2007). 'Entrepreneurial social capital'. *International Small Business Journal* 25(3): 245–72.

Ang, I. (1995). I'm a feminist but ... 'Other' women and postnational feminism. *Transitions: New Australian Feminisms*, ed. B. Caine and R. Pringle. St Leonards, NSW, Allen & Unwin, 57–73.

Ashforth, B.E. and V. Anand (2003). 'The normalization of corruption in organizations'. *Research in Organizational Behavior* 25: 1–52.

Avolio, B.J. and B.M. Bass (1999). 'Re-examining the components of transformational and transactional leadership using the Multifactor Leadership Questionnaire'. *Journal of Occupational & Organizational Psychology* 72(4): 441–62.

Avolio, B.J., W.L. Gardner, F.O. Walumbwa, F. Luthans and D.R. May (2004). 'Unlocking the mask: A look at the process by which authentic leaders impact follower attitudes and behaviors'. *The Leadership Quarterly* 15(6): 801–23.

Babiak, P. and R.D. Hare (2007). *Snakes in Suits*. New York, Harper Collins.

Bandura, A., G.V. Caprara, C. Barbaranelli, C. Pastorelli and C. Regalia (2001). 'Sociocognitive self-regulatory mechanisms governing transgressive behavior'. *Journal of Personality and Social Psychology* 80(1): 125–35.

Bass, B.M. and P. Steidmeier (1999). 'Ethics, character, and authentic transformational leadership behaviour'. *The Leadership Quarterly* 10(2): 181–217.

Baumeister, R.F. (1982). 'A self-presentational view of social phenomena'. *Psychological Bulletin* 91(1): 3–26.

BBC (2013). 'Nelson Mandela's Life and Times'. *BBC News Africa*. Retrieved 25 February 2015, from http://www.bbc.com/news/world-africa-12305154/.

Berwick, S. (1994). 'The beast and his beauties: Robert Maxwell mesmerised and bullied women. But Betty, his wife for nearly 50 years, remained loyal. Her autobiography will be her first public breach of that loyalty'. *The Independent*, 25 October.

Björkqvist, K. (2001). 'Social defeat as a stressor in humans'. *Physiology & Behavior* 73(3): 435–42.

Blau, P.M. (1964). *Exchange and Power in Social Life*. New York, John Wiley and Sons.

Bond, K. (1998). 'Religious Beliefs as a Basis for Ethical Decision Making in the Workplace'. Retrieved 1 November 2014, from http://web.archive.org/web/20070703102021/http://www.humboldt.edu/~kmb2/paper.html.

Boston Globe (2008). 'FBI reports rise in mortgage fraud'. *Boston Globe*, C.4.

Briggs Myers, I. and P.B. Myers (1995). *Gifts Differing: Understanding Personality Type*. Mountain View, CA, Davies-Black Publishing.

Brinkmann, J. (2001). 'On business ethics and moralism'. *Business Ethics: A European Review* 10(4): 311–19.

Broughton, T.A. (1995). Some notes on the art of lying. *The Best Writing on Writing*, ed. J. Heffron. New York, Story Press, 1–14.

Burns, J. (2004). 'Godless capitalism: Ayn Rand and the Conservative movement'. *Modern Intellectual History* 1(3): 359–85.

Carr, A.Z. (1968). 'Is business bluffing unethical?' *Harvard Business Review* 46(1): 143–53.

Cioffi, F. (1994). 'Porky-Talky. Review of *A Pack of Lies: Towards a Sociology of Lying*'. *London Review of Books* 16(18): 16.

Clements, L. (2005). 'Whistleblowing: Who, what, when, where, why and how?' *Journal of Forensic Accounting* 6(2): 429–40.

Coleman, J.S. (1990). Social Capital. *Foundations of Social Theory*. Cambridge, MA, Harvard University Press, 300–12.

Conger, J.A. (1990). 'The dark side of leadership'. *Organizational Dynamics* 19(2): 44–56.

Connell, J., N. Ferres and T. Travaglione (2003). 'Engendering trust in manager-subordinate relationships: Predictors and outcomes'. *Personnel Review* 32(5): 569–87.

Connell, R.W. (1977). *Ruling Class Ruling Structure*. Cambridge, Cambridge University Press.

Costa Jr., P.T. and T.A. Widiger (eds) (1994). *Personality Disorders and the Five-Factor Model of Personality*. Washington DC, American Psychological Association.

Cressey, D. (1973). *Other People's Money: A Study in the Social Psychology of Embezzlement*. Montclair, NJ, Patterson-Smith.

Dalberg-Acton, J. (1907). Letter to Bishop Mandell Creighton, 5th April, 1887. *Historical Essays and Studies*, ed. J.N. Figgis and *R.V. Laurence*. London, Macmillan.

Davis, J.H., F.D. Schoorman and L. Donaldson (1997). 'Towards a stewardship theory of management'. *Academy of Management* 22(1): 20–47.

Deighton, J. (2004). 'The presentation of self in the information age'. *HBS Marketing Research Paper No. 04–02* April(2): 1–18.

Drucker, P.F. (1999). *Management Challenges for the 21st Century*. Oxford, Butterworth-Heinemann.

Easton, B.H. (1980). *Social Policy and the Welfare State in New Zealand*. Auckland, Allen & Unwin.

Einarsen, S. (1999). 'The nature and causes of bullying at work'. *International Journal of Manpower* 20(1–2): 16–28.

Einarsen, S., M.S. Aasland and A. Skogstad (2007). 'Destructive leadership behaviour: A definition and conceptual model'. *The Leadership Quarterly* 18(3): 207–16.

Eisenhart, K.M. (1989). 'Agency theory: An assessment and review'. *Academy of Management* 14(1): 57–74.

Etzioni, A. (1968). 'Basic human needs, alienation and inauthenticity'. *American Sociological Review* 33(4): 870–85.

European Private Equity and Venture Capital Association (2001). European Buyout Success Stories: Special Paper. Zaventem, Belgium, European Private Equity and Venture Capital Association.

Ferguson, R.B. (2003). 'The birth of war'. *Natural History Magazine,* July/ August, 28–35.

Fernholz, T. (2015). 'More people around the world have cell phones than ever had landlines'. *Quartz.* Retrieved 25 February 2015, from http://qz.com/179897/more-people-around-the-world-have-cell-phones-than-ever-had-land-lines/.

Festinger, L. (1962). 'Cognitive dissonance'. *Scientific American* 207(4): 93–102.

Fisher, J.E. (1977). 'Playing favorites in large organizations'. *Business Horizons* 20(3): 68–74.

Fleming, P. and S. Zyglidopoulos (2008). 'The escalation of deception in organizations'. *Journal of Business Ethics* 81(4): 837–50.

Foucault, M. (1972). *The Archaeology of Knowledge and the Discourse on Language.* New York, Pantheon Books.

Fredrickson, B.L. and T.-A. Roberts (1997). 'Objectification theory: Toward understanding women's lived experiences and mental health risks'. *Psychology of Women Quarterly* 21(2): 173–206.

French, L. (2014). 'Drastic Dave' takes on Tesco. *European CEO.* London, Tower Business Media. Freud, S. (1990). *Case Histories II.* New York, Penguin Random House.

Frey, D.E. (1998). 'Individualist economic values and self-interest: The problem of the Puritan ethic'. *Academy of Management* 17(14): 1573–80.

Friedman, M. (1963). *Capitalism and Freedom*. Chicago, IL, The University of Chicago Press.

Fry, M., ed. (1992). *Adam Smith's Legacy: His Place in the Development of Modern Economics*. London, Routledge.

Gabarro, J.J. (2007). 'When a new manager takes charge'. *Harvard Business Review* 85(1): 104–17.

Gallagher, D.R. (2004). 'Top management turnover: An analysis of active Australian investment managers'. *Australian Journal of Management* 29(2): 243–74.

Gangestad, S. and M. Snyder (2000). 'Self-monitoring: Appraisal and reappraisal'. *Psychological Bulletin* 126(4): 530–55.

Ganguly-Scrase, R. (2003). The Search for change: Karl Marx. *Sociology: Australian Connections*, ed. R. Jureidini and M. Poole. Crows Nest, NSW, Allen & Unwin.

Gaur, A., S. Sundaresh and S. Tripati (2004). 'An ancient harbour at Dwarka: Study based on the recent underwater explorations'. *Current Science* 86(9): 1256–60.

George, R.J. (1987). 'Teaching business ethics: Is there a gap between rhetoric and reality?'. *Journal of Business Ethics* 6(7): 513–19.

Ghoshal, S. (2005). 'Bad management theories are destroying good management practices'. *Academy of Management Learning and Education* 4(1): 75–91.

Giddens, A. (1973). *The Class Structure of the Advanced Societies*. London, Hutchinson & Co.

Gilmore, D.C. and G.R. Ferris (1989). 'The effects of applicant impression management tactics on interviewer judgments'. *Journal of Management* 15(4): 557–64.

Gioia, D.A. (1992). 'Pinto fires and personal ethics: A script analysis of missed opportunities'. *Journal of Business Ethics* 11(5/6): 379–89.

Goffman, E. (1959). *The Presentation of Self in Everyday Life*. New York, Anchor Books, Doubleday.

—— (1962). *Asylums: Essays on the Social Situation of Mental Patients and Other Inmates*. Chicago, IL, Aldine.

—— (1967). *Interaction Ritual: Essays on Face-to-Face Behavior*. New York, Pantheon Books.

—— (1974). *Frame Analysis: An Essay on the Organization of Experience*. Boston, MA, University Press of New England.

Goleman, D. (1995). *Emotional Intelligence: Why It Can Matter More than IQ*. New York, Bantam Books.

Gonthier, G. and K. Morrisey (2002). *Rude Awakenings: Overcoming the Civility Crisis in the Workplace*. Chicago, IL, Dearborn Trade.

Grameen Foundation (2015). 'What We Do – Financial Services'. Retrieved 23 February 2015, from http://www.grameenfoundation.org/what-we-do/financial-services/.

Groshen, E.L. and D.R. Williams (1992). 'White and blue-collar jobs in the recent recession and recovery: Who's singing the blues?' *Economic Review – Federal Reserve Bank of Cleveland* 28(4): 2–13.

Hage, J., R. Hanneman and E.T. Gargan (1989). *State Responsiveness and State Activism: An Examination of the Social Forces and State Strategies that Explain the Rise in Social Expenditures in Britain, France, Germany, and Italy, 1870–1968*. London, Unwin Hyman.

Haltigan, J. and T. Vaillancourt (2014). 'Joint trajectories of bullying and peer victimization across elementary and middle school and associations with symptoms of psychopathology'. *American Psychological Association* 50(11): 2426–2436.

Harris, S.E., ed. (1960). *The New Economics: Keynes' Influence on Theory and Public Policy*. London, Dennis Dobson.

Health and Safety Authority Ireland (2001). *Report of the Task Force on the Prevention of Workplace Bullying: Dignity at Work – The Challenge of Workplace Bullying*. Dublin, Stationery Office.

Hoel, H., B. Faragher and C.L. Cooper (2004). 'Bullying is detrimental to health, but all bullying behaviours are not necessarily equally damaging'. *British Journal of Guidance & Counselling* 32(3): 367–87.

Hoel, H., D. Zapf and C.L. Cooper (2002). 'Workplace bullying and stress'. *Research in Occupational Stress and Well Being* 2: 293–333.

Hogan, R. and J. Hogan (2001). 'Assessing leadership: A view from the dark side'. *International Journal of Selection and Assessment* 9(1–2): 40–51.

HSE (2012). Preventing workplace harassment and violence. *Joint Guidance Implementing a European Social Partner Agreement*. London, HSE UK.

Huehn, M.P. (2008). 'Unenlighteded economism: The antecedents of bad corporate governance and ethical decline'. *Journal of Business Ethics* 81(4): 823–36.

Husted, B.W. (1998). 'The ethical limits of trust in business relations'. *Business Ethics Quarterly* 8(2).

Ilies, R., F.P. Morgeson and J.D. Nahrgang (2005). 'Authentic leadership and eudaemonic well-being: Understanding leader–follower outcomes'. *The Leadership Quarterly* 16(3): 373–94.

Ip, G. (2008). World news: OECD speaks up on subprime's heavy toll. *Wall Street Journal*, A.11.

Johns, B.L., W.C. Dunlop and W.J. Sheehan (1989). *Small Business in Australia*. Sydney, Allen & Unwin.

Jones, E.E. and T.S. Pittman (1982). Toward a general theory of strategic self-presentation. *Psychological Perspectives on the Self*, ed. J. Suls. Hillsdale, NJ, Lawrence Erlbaum Associates, 231–62.

Jones, M.A. (1983). *The Australian Welfare State: The Growth, Crisis and Change*. Sydney, Allen & Unwin.

Jung, C.G. (1971). *Psychological Types*. London, Routledge & Kegan Paul.

Kanungo, R.N. (2001). 'Ethical values of transactional and transformational leaders'. *Canadian Journal of Administrative Sciences* 18(4): 257–65.

Karpin, D. (1995). *Enterprising Nation: Renewing Australia's Managers to Meet the Challenges of the Asia-Pacific Century*. Canberra, Australian Government Publishing Service.

Kerlin, M. (1998). 'The end of history, specters of Marx and business ethics'. *Journal of Business Ethics* 17(15): 1717–26.

Kernis, M.H. (2003). 'Optimal self-esteem and authenticity: Separating fantasy from reality'. *Psychological Inquiry* 14(1): 83–9.

—— (2003). 'Toward a conceptualization of optimal self-esteem'. *Psychological Inquiry* 14(1): 1–27.

Keynes, J.M. (2007). *General Theory of Employment, Interest and Money*. New Delhi, Atlantic Publishers & Distributors.

Khatri, N. and E.W.K. Tsang (2003). 'Antecedents and consequences of cronyism in organizations'. *Journal of Business Ethics* 43(4): 289–303.

Kilduff, M. and D.V. Day (1994). 'Do chameleons get ahead? The effects of self-monitoring on managerial careers'. *Academy of Management* 37(4): 14–37.

Kivimaki, M., M. Virtanen, M. Vartia, M. Elovainio, J. Vahtera and L. Keltikangas-Jarvinen (2003). 'Workplace bullying and the risk of cardiovascular disease and depression'. *British Medical Journal* 60(10): 779–84.

Kollock, P. (1994). 'The emergence of exchange structures: An experimental study of uncertainty, commitment, and trust'. *The American Journal of Sociology* 100(2): 313–45.

Konovsky, M.A. and F. Jaster (1989). '"Blaming the victim" and other ways business men and women account for questionable behaviour'. *Journal of Business Ethics* 8(5): 391–8.

Kuhn, R. (1995). 'Capitalism's collapse: Henryk Grossmann's Marxism'. *Science and Society* 59(2): 174–91.

Kurlansky, M. (2007). *Nonviolence: The History of a Dangerous Idea.* London, Vintage.

Lawler, E.J. and S.R. Thye (1999). 'Bringing emotions into social exchange theory'. *Annual Review of Sociology* 25: 217–44.

Leary, M.R. and R.M. Kowalski (1990). 'Impression management: A literature review and two-component model'. *Psychological Bulletin* 107(1): 34–47.

Lee, D. (2002). 'Gendered workplace bullying in the restructured UK Civil Service'. *Personnel Review* 31(1–2): 205–48.

Lee, D. and H. Newby (1983). Sociology and the growth of industrial society. *The Problem of Sociology: An Introduction to the Discipline.* London, Unwin Hyman, 26–39.

Lester, E., D. Scholfield and P. Chapman (2014). 'Self and Peer Assessment and Dominance during Group Work Using Online Visual Tools'. *Seminar.net* 6(1). http://www.seminar.net/volume-6-issue-1-2010/136-self-and-peer-assessment-and-dominance-during-group-work-using-online-visual-tools.

Lewis, S.E. (2006). 'Recognition of workplace bullying: A qualitative study of women targets in the public sector'. *Journal of Community and Applied Social Psychology* 16: 119–35.

Little, A. (1998). *Post-Industrial Socialism: Towards a New Politics of Welfare.* London and New York, Routledge.

Livingstone Smith, D. (2007). *Why We Lie: The Evolutionary Roots of Deception and the Unconscious Mind.* New York, St Martin's Griffin.

Locke, E.A. and J. Woiceshyn (1995). 'Why businessmen should be honest: The argument from rational egoism'. *Journal of Organizational Behavior* 16(5): 405–14.

Love, T. and C. Higgins (2007). 'Do we know enough about corporate philanthropy?' *The Journal of Corporate Citizenship* 27: 18–22.

Machiavelli, N. (1992). *The Prince.* Boston, MA, W.W. Norton.

Mackinnon, C. (2006). *Are Women Human?* Cambridge, MA, Harvard University Press.

Manz, C.C. and Henry P. Sims (1987). 'Leading workers to lead themselves: The external leadership of self-Managing work teams'. *Administrative Science Quarterly* 32(1): 106–30.

Marx, K. (1976). Co-operation. *Capital: A Critique of Political Economy*. London, Harmondsworth, 439–54.

McCarthy, D., S.M. Puffer, R.C. May, D.E. Ledgerwood and W.H. Stewart (2008). 'Overcoming resistance to change in Russian organizations: The legacy of transactional leadership'. *Organizational Dynamics* 37(3): 221–35.

McLean, P. (2007). *The Art of the Network: Strategic Interaction and Patronage in Renaissance Florence*. Durham, NC, Duke University Press.

Mathias, P. (1979). *The Transformation of England*. London, Methuen.

Mead, G.H. (1963). *Mind, Self and Society from the Stand-Point of a Social Behaviorist*. Chicago, IL, University of Chicago.

Miliband, R. (1973). *The State in Capitalist Society*. London, Quartet Books.

Ministry of Justice (2014). 'Definition of Violence'. Retrieved 24 March 2014, from http://www.justice.govt.nz/publications/global-publications/s/safer-communities-action-plan-to-reduce-community-violence-sexual-violence/definition-of-violence/.

Mintzberg, H. (2004). *Managers not MBAs: A Hard Look at the Soft Practice of Managing and Management Development*. San Francisco, CA, Berrett-Koehler.

Moore, G. (2008). 'Re-imagining the morality of management: A modern virtue ethics approach'. *Business Ethics Quarterly* 18(4): 483–511.

Morrison, K.L. (2006). *Marx, Durkheim, Weber: Formations of Modern Social Thought*. Thousand Oaks, CA, Sage.

Morse, G. (2004). 'Executive psychopaths'. *Harvard Business Review* 82(10): 20–22.

Naish, J. (2008). *Enough*. London, Hodder and Stoughton.

Newbert, S.L. (2003). 'Realizing the spirit and impact of Adam Smith's capitalism through entrepreneurship'. *Journal of Business Ethics* 46(3): 251–61.

Nick. (2006). 'Indian Professor Brings Bali and India Together'. Retrieved 15 March 2015, from http://www.baliblog.com/travel-tips/bali-daily/indian-professor-brings-bali-and-india-together.html.

OSHA (2002). 'Workplace Violence Fact Sheet'. *Fact Sheets*. Retrieved 27 February 2015, https://www.osha.gov/OshDoc/data_General_Facts/factsheet-workplace-violence.pdf.

Pauls, C.A. and N.W. Crost (2005). 'Cognitive ability and self-reported efficacy of self-presentation predict faking on personality measures'. *Journal of Individual Differences* 26(4): 194–206.

Peter, L.J. and R. Hull (1969). *The Peter Principle: Why Things Always Go Wrong*. New York, William Morrow and Company.

Peters, T.J. and Robert H. Waterman Jr., (1982). *In Search of Excellence: Lessons from America's Best-Run Companies*. New York, Warner Books.

Podsakoff, P.M., S.B. MacKenzie, R.H. Moorman and R. Fetter (1990). 'Transformational leader behaviors and their effects on followers' trust in leader, satisfaction, and organizational citizenship behaviors'. *The Leadership Quarterly* 1(2): 107–42.

Ponting, C. (2000). *World History: A New Perspective*. London, Chatto and Windus.

Prama, G. (2014). Long Journey of Making the Unconscious Conscious.

Prendergast, C. and R.H. Topel (1996). 'Favoritism in organizations'. *Journal of Political Economy* 104(5): 958–78.

Price, T.L. (2003). 'The ethics of authentic transformational leadership'. *Leadership Quarterly* 14(1): 67- 82.

Prieto, J.H. (2004). 'Bernard Mandeville's heir: Adam Smith or Jean Jacques Rousseau on the possibility of economic analysis'. *European Journal of the History of Economic Thought* 11(1): 1–32.

Quine, L. (1999). 'Workplace bullying in NHS community trust: Staff questionnaire survey'. *British Medical Journal* 318: 228–32.

Quinn, R.E. (1988). *Beyond Rational Management.* San Francisco, Jossey-Bass Publishers.

Rand, A. (1957). *Atlas Shrugged.* New York, Random House.

—— (1967). *Capitalism: The Unknown Ideal.* New York, New American Library.

Read, L. (2013). 'BBC criticised over workplace bullying after death of Russell Joslin'. *Coventry Telegraph.* March 27th, Coventry, Trinity Mirror Midlands.

Romney, M.B., W.S. Albrecht and D.J. Cherrington (1980a). 'Auditors and the detection of fraud'. *Journal of Accountancy* 149(5): 63–9.

—— (1980b). 'Red-flagging the white collar criminal: Potential fraud situations have common characteristics, according to a survey of published cases, which can be used as early warning signals to prevent actual acts'. *Management Accounting* 61(9): 51–6.

Rowbottom, S. (1975). *Hidden from History.* London, Pluto Press.

Samuels, H. (2003). 'Sexual harassment in the workplace: A feminist analysis of recent developments in the UK'. *Women's Studies International Forum* 26(5): 467–82.

Sartre, J.P. (1991). *Critique of Dialectical Reason.* London, Verso.

Shain, F. (2000). 'Managing to lead: Women managers in the further education sector'. *Journal of Further and Higher Education* 24(2): 218–30.

Sheridan, T.A. (2005). Voicing women managers' unemployment experience in Australia. *The Hidden Toll.* Perth, WA, Women Chiefs of Enterprises International, 1–100.

—— (2014). *Managerial Fraud: Executive Impression Management, Beyond Red Flags.* Farnham, Gower.

Shore, T.H., W.H. Bommer and L.M. Shore (2008). 'An integrative model of managerial perceptions of employee commitment: Antecedents and influences on employee treatment'. *Journal of Organizational Behaviour* 29(5): 635–55.

Shover, N. and F.T. Cullen (2008). 'Studying and teaching white collar crime: Populist and patrician perspectives'. *Journal of Criminal Justice Education* 19(2): 155–74.

Simmel, G. (1904). 'The sociology of conflict'. *The American Journal of Sociology* 9(4): 490–525.

Slater, D. (1995). Trajectories of development theory: Capitalism, socialism and beyond. *Geographies of Global Change*, ed. R.J. Johnston, P.J. Taylor and M. Watts. Oxford, Blackwell.

Smith, E.A. (2001). 'The role of tacit and explicit knowledge in the workplace'. *Journal of Knowledge Management* 5(4): 311–21.

Smith, J. (2015). 'Leviticus'. Retrieved 17 March 2015, from http://biblehub.com/summary/leviticus/1.htm.

Smith, T. (2003). 'The metaphysical case for honesty'. *Journal of Value Inquiry* 37(4): 517–31.

Snyder, M. (1974). 'Self-monitoring of expressive behaviour'. *Journal of Personality and Social Psychology* 30(4): 526–37.

Takala, T. and J. Urpilainen (1999). 'Managerial work and lying: A conceptual framework and an explorative case study'. *Journal of Business Ethics* 20(3): 181–95.

Tamayo, A. and F. Raymond (1977). 'Self-concept of psychopaths'. *Journal of Psychology* 97(1): 71–8.

The W Edwards Deming Institute. (2015). 'Edwards Deming the Man'. Retrieved 3 March 2015, 2015, from https://www.deming.org/theman/overview/.

'Thomas Hobbes' (2015). *Stanford Encyclopedia of Philosophy*. Retrieved 10 June 2015, from http://plato.stanford.edu/entries/hobbes/.

Thompson, E.P. (1968). *The Making of the English Working Class*. Harmondsworth, Penguin Books.

Titmuss, R.M. (1976). *Essays on the Welfare State*. London, Allen & Unwin.

Tracinski, R.W. (2015). 'The Moral Basis of Capitalism'. Retrieved 15 March 2015, from http://www.capitalismcenter.org/Philosophy/Essays/The_Moral_Basis_of_Capitalism.htm./

Tracy, S.J. and P. Lutgen-Sandvik (2006). 'Nightmare, demons, and slaves: Exploring the painful metaphors of workplace bullying'. *Management Communication Quarterly* 20(2): 148–85.

Tucker, S., N. Turner, J. Barling, E.M. Reid and C. Elving (2006). 'Apologies and transformational leadership'. *Journal of Business Ethics* 63(2): 195–207.

Turner, N., J. Barling, O. Epitropaki, V. Butcher and C. Milner (2002). 'Transformational leadership and moral reasoning'. *Journal of Applied Psychology* 87(2): 304–11.

Tyler, J.M., R.S. Feldman and A. Reichert (2006). 'The price of deceptive behavior: Disliking and lying to people who lie to us'. *Journal of Experimental Social Psychology* 42(1): 69–77.

Weber, J. (2010). 'Assessing the "tone at the top": The moral reasoning of CEOs in the automobile industry'. *Journal of Business Ethics* 92(2): 167–82.

Wenger, M.G. (1994). 'Idealism redux: The class-historical truth of postmodernism'. *Critical Sociology* 20(1): 53–78.

Wetzel Jr, W.E. (1987). 'The informal venture capital market: Aspects of scale and market efficiency'. *Journal of Business Venturing* 2(4): 299–314.

Weymes, E. (2004). 'Management theory: Balancing individual freedom with organisational needs'. *The Journal of Corporate Citizenship* Winter 2004(16): 85–99.

Whitener, E.M., S.E. Brodt, M.A. Korsgaard and J.M. Werner (1998). 'Managers as initiators of trust: An exchange relationship framework for understanding managerial trustworthy behavior'. *Academy of Management Review* 23(3): 513–30.

Wilson, P. (1995). *The Little Book of Calm*. London, Penguin Books.

Wood, D. (2006). 'Sub-prime time'. *Risk Management* 19(2): 36–6.

Woodman, P. and P. Cook (2005). Bullying at work: The experience of managers. London, Chartered Management Institute.

Workplace Bullying Institute (2014). 'Estimating the Costs of Workplace Bullying'. Retrieved 14 May 2014, 2014, from http://www.workplacebullying.org/2014/04/24/costs/.

World Health Organization (2015). 'Violence Prevention, Approach and Definition'. Retrieved 17 March 2015, from http://www.who.int/violenceprevention/approach/definition/en/.

Worsley, P. (1982). *Marx and Marxism*. Chichester, Ellis Horwood.

Yukl, G. (1992). 'Consequences of influence tactics used with subordinates, peers, and the boss'. *Journal of Applied Psychology* 77(4): 525–35.

Zimmerli, W.C. and M.S. Asslander (2007). Business ethics as applied ethics. *Corporate Ethics and Corporate Governance*, ed. W.C. Zimmerli, K. Richter and M. Holzinger. Berlin and New York, Springer, 37–54.

Index